They abducted him. They sexually assaulted him. They pummeled him with iron bars. They crushed his skull with a cement block. They flicked cigarettes on him and left him to die. The only thing they had in common was their age... **FOURTEEN**

"*Forty years ago, at 835 Hill Street in Bill O'Connell's hometown, something transpired that was terrible beyond words. But O'Connell—haunted by what happened that day—has given it words: thoughtful, precise, passionate words that seek to honor a stolen life, and to answer the question of how and why such a thing could have taken place. He brings humanity and dignity to a day that appeared to have neither, and to the darkest of corners brings light.*"

—Bob Greene, author of two *New York Times* bestsellers

"*Meticulously reported, written with great passion and delivered in intensely personal fashion, Bill O'Connell's Fourteen is a chilling true crime tale filled with a cast of compelling characters whose lives changed forever one bloody day long ago.*"

—Rick Kogan, *Chicago Tribune* columnist

"*Bill O'Connell has done the impossible by combining the passion of a great story teller with the detachment of an equally capable reporter in a brilliantly executed though disturbing tale of life and death in the heartland.*"

—Mark Vancil, editor of three *New York Times* bestsellers

FOURTEEN

FOURTEEN

The Murder of David Stukel

Bill O'Connell

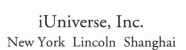

iUniverse, Inc.
New York Lincoln Shanghai

Fourteen
The Murder of David Stukel

iUniverse books may be ordered through booksellers or by contacting:

iUniverse
2021 Pine Lake Road, Suite 100
Lincoln, NE 68512
www.iuniverse.com
1-800-Authors (1-800-288-4677)

ISBN: 978-0-595-43995-9 (pbk)
ISBN: 978-0-595-69334-4 (cloth)

Printed in the United States of America

For Ray, Marilyn, Debbie, and Nancy

Acknowledgments

Cover Design
Rainer Schmidt

Editors
Mary Whitler Baskerville, Allen Daniel, Terry Godbey,
Greg Miller, Tim Pastore, Heidi Stevens, Jim Talarico

Historian
Joseph Giglietti Sr.

Photo Editor
Paul Iwanaga

Photo Credits
Chicago Tribune, Joliet Herald News

Author's Disclosure

Re-enactments in *Fourteen: The Murder of David Stukel*
have been meticulously constructed from Will County
Clerk of the Circuit Court records; Will County Sheriff's
Department documents; Prisoner Review Board transcripts;
Department of Corrections psychological evaluations;
Chicago Tribune and *Joliet Herald News* articles;
and interviews with at least one of the participants.

Prologue

The fronts of their headstones reflect the day's first strands of sunlight. David Stukel and Pat Pilon, two grades apart at East High School, share a hillside fifty feet apart at Mt. Olivet Cemetery, a rolling, tree-filled treasure of nature nestled between Route 30 and Hickory Creek on the East Side of Joliet, Illinois.

The deaths of David Stukel and Pat Pilon were the bookend tragedies of my high school years in the late 1960s.

While walking home from school, fourteen-year-old David Stukel was accosted and murdered by fourteen-year-old bullies Billy Rose Sprinkle and James Perruquet.

In an open letter to "The Youth of America," eighteen-year-old Pat Pilon described the horror of being hooked on heroin, then put a shotgun in his mouth and engaged the trigger.

When Pat Pilon's final words were picked up by the wire services and published in newspapers across America, his death garnered unprecedented attention for the suicide of a teenager.

The heinous sexual assault and murder of well-behaved, good-natured David Stukel elicited a banner headline in the local newspaper and a smattering of coverage deep inside the Chicago dailies. But nearly forty years after the murder of David Stukel, with ramifications that have grown exponentially and post-conviction twists that read like fiction, the case is ripe for scrutiny.

I explore the facts and implore the public servants associated with the case to help make sense of a senseless murder.

I pursue answers to the haunting questions surrounding the incomprehensible slaying of a five-foot, ninety-five-pound boy; track the homicide's impact on the Stukel, Sprinkle and Perruquet families; and dissect the backgrounds of the murderers, whose formative years were dominated by abuse and a lack of affection and direction.

The Stukels, clockwise from lower left: Marilyn,
Debbie, Nancy, and Ray.

At the outset of this extraordinary journey, I discover David Stukel's elderly parents are alive and full of life. For decades I had suspected that losing their son had shuttered the light from Ray and Marilyn Stukel's eyes. But I grossly underestimated this family. I failed to take into account the unparalleled power of the human spirit, especially when it burns in the souls of Ray and Marilyn and their equally strong-willed daughters, Debbie and Nancy.

With equal parts trepidation and anticipation, I call Ray and Marilyn Stukel and express my interest in writing about David's life and death.

"We're touched that someone else is thinking about David," Marilyn says. "We thought we were the only ones."

Contents

CHAPTER 1   In Our Element. 1

CHAPTER 2   Worlds Apart. 8

CHAPTER 3   Homeward Bound. 16

CHAPTER 4   Desperate Searches. 24

CHAPTER 5   Hoop Dreams 30

CHAPTER 6   On the Job 38

CHAPTER 7   "It Just Wasn't His Face". 50

CHAPTER 8   "Everything Ceases". 53

CHAPTER 9   David on Their Minds. 59

CHAPTER 10   Courting Justice 67

CHAPTER 11   Behind Closed Doors 75

CHAPTER 12   Where's the Love? 79

CHAPTER 13   A Glimpse into Their Worlds 88

CHAPTER 14   "Too Old for His Age" 93

CHAPTER 15   Working the System 100

CHAPTER 16   A Fantasy World 108

CHAPTER 17   The Bottom Line. 112

CHAPTER 18   If These Files Could Talk 119

CHAPTER 19   The Long Way Home 125

CHAPTER 20   Sending a Message 130

CHAPTER 21   "In the Middle of the Night" 136

CHAPTER 22   On Vacation 142

CHAPTER 23   Family First 149

CHAPTER 24   "A Gentler Spirit" 155

CHAPTER 25   Fueling the Rage 162

CHAPTER 26   One Victim after Another 169

CHAPTER 27   "Sleepin' Dog" 177

CHAPTER 28   Everything but the Truth 181

CHAPTER 29   "He Never Deserved to Die" 189

CHAPTER 30   A Split Decision 197

CHAPTER 31   In the Blood 204

CHAPTER 32   Lasting Impressions 211

CHAPTER 33   "We've Been Blessed" .222

1

In Our Element

We are tucked away in suburbia, swaying to Motown, and riding the crest of the British Invasion's wave. Our worlds revolve around sports, music, clothes, and girls. Bulky 8-tracks dent the marketplace, 45s fly off record-store shelves and onto our turntables, and the rumblings of garage bands resonate throughout our neighborhoods on never-ending summer afternoons.

We wear bell-bottoms and hip-huggers, Beatle boots and ultra-wide belts. Hem lines rise, waistlines fall, and psychedelia prevails. Mod is all the rage, and we are coming of age, navigating intricate paths to independence forty miles southwest of downtown Chicago in Joliet, Illinois, a crossroads-of-America town of 78,000 surrounded by corn and soy fields, framed by Interstates 80 and 55, and split down the middle by Route 66 and the Des Plaines River.

Though we are teenagers, we are not insulated from the atrocities in Southeast Asia, the finality of assassins' bullets, the bigotry in the Deep South, and the brutality just up the road at the Democratic National Convention. We absorb the grainy images on our black-and-white television sets; we hear the shocking bulletins on our transistor radios; and we scan the disturbing newspaper headlines. We are not immune to the turbulence that rocks our world near and far, but we are preoccupied with our passage from adolescence to adulthood inside the earthtone brick walls of East High, our sprawling, four-year-old sanctuary of a school on the gritty side of town.

Joliet circa 1968 is a city of chalices and calluses, with tabernacles and taverns seemingly on every other corner, and time clocks clicking without pause at steel mills, rail yards, and refineries.

Downtown Joliet's north-to-south-flowing Des Plaines is as much a sociological divide as it is a geographical one.

The money, commercialism, and four-year-old West High reside on the mostly affluent West Side, three miles west of the canal.

The history, clout, and sixty-seven-year-old limestone castle known as Central High are fixtures on the rugged outskirts of a thriving downtown, three-quarters of a mile east of the river.

And the crime, predominantly lower-to-middle classes, and East High define the landscape three miles southeast of the Des Plaines in the bosom of Joliet's blue-collar, multi-ethnic East Side.

Although 1968 is a turbulent time in the thick of the Vietnam War and at the height of the civil rights movement, it is a mostly tranquil existence at East High, where blacks and whites blend almost seamlessly. The same cannot be said of twin sister West High, where friction between the haves and have-nots fosters riots. The halls and walls of the two schools may be identical, but there are fewer racial barriers at East High, where most students greet diversity with open arms and open minds.

The soulful voice of the Rascals' Felix Cavaliere streams from our car radios with the nation's number one song, "People Got To Be Free." And at East High, amid the wide-open spaces of former farmland, with no neon signs in sight, we are free—particularly those of us having emerged from the constraints of parochial grade school. Fourteen-year-old David Raymond Stukel arrives from just such an environment—St. Mary Magdalene, where he attended Mass every morning and wore the school's required light-blue dress shirt, navy-blue pants, and navy-blue clip-on tie.

David graduates from a parochial school with 315 students spread over eight grades and enters a public school with an enrollment of 1,400. He leaves a tight-knit eighth-grade class of 37 and joins a massive freshman class of 446, the largest first-year class in East High's brief existence. He departs a modest parochial school's meager facilities for a stylish campus with well-manicured courtyards; boys' and girls' gymnasiums; a dance studio; a gymnastics center; a state-of-the-art auditorium; a sunken, glass-walled library; and auto, wood, and print shops.

David Stukel bursts onto the vibrant scene that is East High with unbridled enthusiasm and a sturdy three-ring blue binder on which he has emblazoned the names of past and present Kingsmen sports stars.

In '68, David is a new face, but he is not a newcomer to the East High athletic scene.

As an eleven-year-old in late-August 1965, wide-eyed David would walk the half-mile from his home on New Lenox Road to East High and intently watch football workouts, then struggle to cart a favorite player's helmet and shoulder pads to the locker room. Long before David sets foot in the school as a student, he attends East High basketball and football games with older sister Debbie and her boyfriend, Gregg Skrtich. And from the window of David's sports-themed bedroom in the family's modest home six hundred yards north of the East High football stadium, his heart pumps a little faster on Friday nights when the Kingsmen fight song thunders through the dark, crisp autumn sky.

In September 1968, it is not the "turn on, tune in, drop out" generation that walks the hallways of East High. The Summer of Love had come and gone without most of us noticing, and the drug counterculture, though present, does not run rampant. These are our halcyon days, a heady, magical time at a school that excels in drama, music, and academics, and whose football team is coming off a championship season.

Enthusiasm and anticipation course through our veins, and we are awash with optimism.

Anything and everything is possible.

I met David Stukel at Belmont Little League on Joliet's East Side in the spring of 1965. David and I fielded flyballs and groundballs, chattered "Hey batta, batta" till we were hoarse, then soothed our throats with ice-cold bottles of soft drinks, courtesy of beloved Manager Hank Gawenda, inside the under-lit, over-air conditioned East Side Athletic Club, just beyond the rickety, rust-colored right-field picket fence.

David and I were a year apart in grade school and belonged to Catholic parishes in separate East Side neighborhoods. We were more acquaintances than friends. We did not have exchange sleepovers. We did not take exploratory hikes into the woods. We did not have intimate discussions about girls and goals. But I know what kind of kid David was because I was that kind of kid—give or take an inch, a pound, and a venial sin or two.

Our worlds converged while proudly wearing the maroon-and-white uniforms of East Side A.C.

I was twelve. David was eleven. I was completing the sixth grade at St. Bernard's, two miles west of Belmont Little League; David was finishing fifth grade at St. Mary Magdalene, two and one-half miles southwest of the field.

David and I were small for our ages and had similar builds—somewhere in the ballpark of four feet eight, eighty pounds. We could run and catch, but we did not raise a pitcher's blood pressure by stepping in the batter's box.

The 1965 East Side A.C. Little League team, with David Stukel (bottom row, third from left) and Bill O'Connell (to David's left).

At our parochial schools, David and I stayed away from trouble and were much closer to being apple-polishers than bad apples. We rarely missed school. We turned in our assignments on time and avoided being whacked with rulers, which had more to do with parental pressure than parochial persuasion. While David and I chose not to become altar boys and thus dodged the arduous task of memorizing Latin phrases that we didn't understand, sports was a language we spoke fluently. Despite being small in stature, we were above-average baseball players, reliable wide receivers in flag football, and playmakers in basketball.

I started in center field for East Side A.C. in '65, and the next year David Stukel patrolled the same ground. During that lone season as David's teammate, my twenty-eight-ounce Louisville Slugger rarely ventured off my right shoulder, and I spent many an at-bat relying on the benevolence of the man in blue to reach first base. Returning to the dugout more often than not gave me plenty of time to look outside the white chalk lines and into the bright blue eyes of David Stukel, his maroon cap resting back on his head, its bill tilted upward, revealing a gapped-toothed smile as genuine as the cowhide on an official Little League baseball.

Whether sitting on the bench, doodling in the dugout dirt with the tips of his rubber-spiked shoes, or standing in the outfield with his head sometimes in the clouds, carefree David Stukel always wore a grin. Freckle-faced and with protruding ears, this innately good boy, who interjected words such as "gosh," "darn" and "golly" into conversations, was as happy catching frogs as he was snaring flyballs. He loved to play baseball, but play or sit, David's happy-go-lucky demeanor never changed.

I don't recall seeing David Stukel after the summer of '65. Two years later, a year before David would arrive at East High, I was recruited by a desperate drama teacher to portray a ten-year-old boy in the fall play. As a five-foot, one hundred-pound freshman with a voice that had yet to change, I was a natural for the role. And had there been a casting call for another child character the following autumn, David Raymond Stukel would have been a perfect fit. But life's script didn't call for David to play out his first year of high school—or even his second week. And my recollection of a Little League teammate with an infectious smile was eclipsed by an unspeakable act of violence at the old Fritz family farm—just a pop fly from East High.

John and Barbara Fritz emigrated from Belgium to America in 1890 and built a block-and-stucco, two-and-one-half-story home and accompanying barn on the wooded, five-acre lot at 835 Hill Street, where they tilled the soil from the turn of the century through World War I and into the Great Depression. They raised children, nurtured apple, pear, and cherry trees, and planted grapevines, rhubarb, tomatoes, and corn. They made an honest and hard-earned dawn-to-dusk living by filling their horse-drawn wagon with fresh yields and peddling them on the streets of downtown Joliet.

Old-timers tell the story of the driverless horse and buggy that on Saturday afternoons would wend its way from downtown Joliet to the Fritz farm. John would go to poker games, get overly lubricated, stumble into the buggy, give the horse a glancing blow with his whip, then pass out as the horse trotted along dirt roads three miles to Hill Street. Kids in the Fritz farm neighborhood, familiar with this Saturday routine, would chase down the wagon and climb aboard—until old man Fritz would awaken, pull out his whip, and send them scattering like roaches.

Despite losing his grip on Saturday afternoons, John Fritz maintained a firm grip on his farm. John and Barbara raised four children, lived off the land, and respected it. Son Bill, born at the homestead in 1895, and daughter Jennie, arriving two years later, remained on the farm, but two younger brothers escaped farm life and never looked back.

For forty years, the Fritz parents took care of their sturdy home, barn, and farmland. But after they passed away—John in 1937 and Barbara in 1940—son Bill took over the reins in his mid-forties and proceeded to run the homestead into the fertile northern Illinois ground.

Through the Roaring Twenties, the FDR years, and the baby boom, Bill Fritz kept money flowing into his pockets through a series of entrepreneurial projects—including running a bootlegging operation out of the family barn during Prohibition, an activity for which he spent time in a federal penitentiary.

Among his many talents, Bill was adept at raising pigs for profit, but he didn't have the patience to be a successful crop farmer. And after his parents died, Bill wasn't inclined to maintain the land or the house. Under his watch, the house and barn were in disrepair; the two acres of fruit trees died; the half-acre of grapevines dried up; and the planting and harvesting of crops ceased.

Bill Fritz was tall and lean and strong. His hair was dirty and uncombed. His body rarely came in contact with a bar of soap, and he had permanent tobacco stains on the sides of his mouth. An introvert, Bill didn't like his neighbors, but he loved horses, and he parlayed his earnings as a blacksmith into a stable of thirty workhorses. Bill landed a contract as a city garbage collector and used two-horse teams to pull wagons to restaurants and residences. And with Bill routinely bypassing the city dump and depositing the day's haul on the farm to fatten his pigs, the property overflowed with muck and junk.

Bill gambled away large chunks of his profits and didn't use what remained to keep the home in order, and sister Jennie didn't have the wherewithal to take care of herself, let alone the homestead. Jennie was a tobacco-chewing woman who looked like a man. She had a glass eye, rarely bathed and was banned from St. Mary Magdalene Church for urinating on a pew. She wore winter clothes in summer and spent her final years living in a tin coop that once housed chickens. She shared the land with the wild dogs that patrolled the property and the weather-beaten hogs that didn't make the one-way trip to the Chicago stockyards. Big-boned, gruff, and smoking a corncob pipe, Jennie unwittingly frightened neighborhood kids without uttering a word.

Bill Fritz exited the rubble and rubbish of the homestead in the early 1960s, leaving indigent sister Jennie to fend for herself amid the pigs and pigsty. All that remained were Jennie, her tin coop, and a dilapidated home that had been beaten down by the one-two punch of negligence and nature. Saplings and weeds engulfed the property. Fallen trees pierced the home, which was struck by lightning and mercifully burned to its shallow cement-block foundation. With no electricity or plumbing, Jennie relied on the kindness of neighbors for water. She had an oil lamp and a wood-burning stove, and lived all of her sixty-eight years at 835 Hill Street, passing away in November 1965—East High's second year of existence—inside her tin coop.

2

Worlds Apart

In the late afternoon of September 16, 1968, the worlds of three fourteen-year-old boys intersected at 835 Hill Street and were forever linked:

Billy Rose Sprinkle, fourteen years, eight months, twenty days.

James David Perruquet, fourteen years, four months, twenty-eight days.

David Raymond Stukel, fourteen years, three months, twenty-three days.

The three boys took radically different routes to that autumn day, when the five-foot-six, 140-pound Sprinkle and the five-foot-two, 110-pound Perruquet confronted five-foot, 95-pound David Stukel as he walked home from school after his first cross-country practice.

David Stukel

David Stukel lived just nine-tenths of a mile from Billy Rose Sprinkle and one and one-half miles from James Perruquet, two boys he did not know. Their ages and the proximity of their homes were all they had in common.

While David Stukel's quaint, picturesque world whispered Rockwellian, the bleak, hardscrabble worlds of Sprinkle and Perruquet shouted rock bottom.

These disparate existences became strikingly apparent to Sam Andreano, the Will County assistant public defender who in September 1968 examined evidence procured in Case No. W68C77:

The State of Illinois vs. James David Perruquet and Billy Rose Sprinkle for the murder of David Raymond Stukel.

"You know what has sort of stuck in my mind for what—thirty-five years or however long it has been—is going through the evidence," Andreano says. "The Stukel boy—he had a brand-new pair of underwear. Obviously, his parents bought him a new pair of underwear ... first week of school, et cetera. And the other boys—their underwear had holes. Their underwear was shitty and stained.

Billy Rose Sprinkle   *James Perruquet*

Their underwear was *way* too small and not fitting at all. And at that point, it hit me: It was just sort of, 'Here's where we are—look at his parents, and look at the other kids' parents.' All these years later I can still see the victim's underwear, those little, probably size ten Hanes shorts, all white as hell."

David Stukel, the second of Ray and Marilyn Stukel's three children, enjoyed an idyllic childhood with nurturing parents who provided stability, love, and guidance—role models who doled out discipline tempered with kindness. The Stukel family resided at 816 New Lenox Road in the Greenfield neighborhood, home to the Fritz farm and East High, smack-dab in the heart of middle class, where Ray and Marilyn instilled the same Midwestern values they inherited from their parents.

The Stukel children: David, Debbie and Nancy in 1962.

David, older sister Debbie, and kid sister Nancy were neatly dressed, respectful, and well-mannered, and the Stukels experienced a comfortable life in a cozy, wood-frame home. They had dinner as a family; they climbed into the station wagon and took vacations together; they played and prayed together. Life was good and clean and fun, and the Stukel children knew they were loved. The same cannot be said of the offspring of Grace and Edward Sprinkle Sr. and Hazel and Earnie Perruquet Sr., hardhearted parents whose children endured unthinkable existences in rough neighborhoods.

The Sprinkle and Perruquet parents each brought eight children into their unsavory worlds, and acted as if they wished they had not.

"We didn't have a normal upbringing, that's for sure," says Billy Rose Sprinkle's sister Lorraine, the fourth Sprinkle child, born after Ed Jr., Jim, and Johnny, and before Billy, Georgina ("Doll"), Steve, and Stanley.

"There was a lot of yelling and cussing and hitting, a lot of bullshit!" says Lorraine. "When you got out of line, you got your ass beat. My dad would tear into any of us. He gave me an ass-whoopin' when I was sixteen, and I deserved it. I stole a car, and my mother told my dad that if he didn't whip me, she would. She kept ragging on him to whip me, so he finally started beating my ass. My dad tried to make us walk the straight and narrow. The boys didn't, and he would beat their ass."

"My parents would tell you how rotten you were," says James Perruquet's sister Fern, the fifth Perruquet child, born after Earnie Jr., Stella, Joe, and James, and before Ila ("Tookie"), Larry, and Donnie.

"We didn't have parents who checked your homework, parents who cared if you even did your homework," Fern says. "I don't even think they ever looked at our report cards. And when the shit hit the fan at our house, you didn't want to be there. There was stuff going on where you feared for your life. One time my dad chased us with an ax. I believe to this day that if he would have gotten hold of one of us, they would be dead."

The rare moments when the Sprinkle and Perruquet children felt some semblance of love from their parents were offset by acts of negligence and violence. These low-income, uneducated parents rarely had enough money to pay the utility bills, but there was always cash for alcohol, which fueled the dark sides of both families.

David Stukel could not leave his yard without a parent's permission. Sprinkle and Perruquet, with their parents drunk, absent, or both, were free to run wild through East Side neighborhoods.

David rarely missed school. Sprinkle and Perruquet, who each had flunked a grade, regularly walked in one school door and out the other.

David and sister Nancy dreamed and schemed together, concocting practical jokes to pull on their grandparents. Perruquet and sister Fern played together and cowered together when a parent's rage surfaced.

David's book-smart sister Debbie loved her siblings but retreated to the solitude of her bedroom to reflect or read. Sprinkle's street-smart sister Lorraine loved her siblings and never retreated from a showdown, using her mouth and fists to protect her kin.

David's father, still donning the shirt and tie he wore to work as a project engineer at the Joliet Arsenal, would drive his son over to East High and toss batting practice, just to warm up the boy's swing before Little League games. Perruquet's father, with whichever tool was handy, would take swings at his son whenever he failed to properly complete a task.

David shied away from hunting with his dad because he couldn't stand to see a living creature die. Sprinkle enjoyed hunting with his dad or, better yet, taking his dad's rifle when he wasn't home and shooting whatever moved in nearby fields.

David spent hours building model cars, painstakingly gluing together each piece, sometimes with the help of his father. Perruquet and Sprinkle routinely inhaled glue fumes from paper bags—often when they were supposed to be in school.

While David Stukel was beginning his first season of Pony League baseball in the spring of 1967, Billy Rose Sprinkle and James Perruquet came face to face for the first time at Western Quarry, an unofficially named, enter-at-your-own-peril swimming hole frequented by hoodlums and hobos.

Western Quarry wasn't a safe haven for anyone, but braving this out-of-the way area to jump from its thirty-foot cliff into the murky water below was a rite of passage—even for adventuresome good kids such as David Stukel, who on more than one occasion dared to venture deep into the woods with friends Francis Ruettiger and Butch Markelz.

At Western Quarry, there were no parents, lifeguards, swim breaks or concession stands—only no-trespassing signs and discarded wine and beer bottles. In this most perfect of imperfect settings, the socially stunted James Perruquet, who aspired to be cool, tough, and feared, found the ideal role model in Billy Rose Sprinkle, who slicked back his hair, exuded James Dean-like coolness, hung out with twenty-year-old brother Johnny's rough crowd, had sex with girls, drank, smoked, stole, cussed, and picked fights.

Although the alliance between the swaggering yet insecure Sprinkle and the insecure and impressionable Perruquet lasted just sixteen months, they made the most of their time together. Unscrupulous and unsupervised, they were free to burglarize, vandalize, and terrorize. Their behavior did not go unnoticed by school officials, who regarded them as "disruptive and disrespectful," and they also caught the eye of local police officers, who classified them as "vandals and petty thieves."

Six weeks after meeting, Sprinkle and Perruquet, along with Perruquet's fifteen-year-old brother, Joe, went on a rampage and smashed several car windows with a hard-rubber club. Sprinkle, reportedly at his father's insistence, spent a night in jail, and Joe Perruquet, a repeat offender who took the rap for little brother James, was sent to a suburban Chicago juvenile detention center.

Six months later, arsonists set fire to Washington Junior High, where Sprinkle and Perruquet were classmates, and even though they were the prime suspects, no one was ever charged with the felony that nearly killed two firemen, caused $1.5 million in damage and closed Washington for two years.

In the seventh grade, the first half at Washington and, after the fire, the second half at Gompers Junior High, one mile west of Belmont Little League, Sprinkle skipped school sixty-five times, and Perruquet was absent on fifty-three occasions. Sprinkle flunked every one of his subjects but was given a "social" promotion. Perruquet's final seventh-grade marks included a B in art; a "satisfactory" in health/safety; D's in math, social science, physical education, music, industrial arts, and speech; F's in English and geography; and "unsatisfactory" in social habits and work/study. He, too, was given a "social" promotion.

With their minds fixed on breaking laws, not cracking open books, the sociopathic behavior of Sprinkle and Perruquet officially became rap-sheet fodder in May 1968. While eighth-grader David Stukel was in class at St. Mary Magdalene, seventh-graders Sprinkle and Perruquet ditched school, headed to the East High area, and broke into Edith Nolan's home, directly across Hill Street from the old Fritz farm.

Hill Street is a mere 400 yards of asphalt and not-so-broad dirt shoulders that connect New Lenox Road, the street on which David Stukel lived, to the back parking lot of East High. But when it comes to David Stukel's life and death, all roads lead there.

Although you would need a surveyor's eye to tell, Hill Street got its name from being slightly higher than the surrounding Greenfield neighborhood landscape. And from Assunta "Susan" DeAcetis' perch in her light-colored brick home, ten yards off Hill Street, she kept a watchful eye on her universe for six decades.

Bill and Susan DeAcetis emigrated from Italy to America in the early 1920s. They settled at 828 Hill Street, raised two children, and ran a small dairy farm next door to Edith Nolan's home and across the street and one lot north of the Fritz farm. Feisty Susan, often wearing waist-high boots, was the family workhorse, rising before dawn and staying busy until well after dark. When she wasn't feeding or milking cows, Susan was planting or weeding in one of her many vegetable gardens.

When Susan DeAcetis spoke, neighbors had difficulty understanding her hodgepodge of Italian and English. But over a four-month period in 1968, what Susan DeAcetis saw, did, and did not do had resounding effects on the lives of David Stukel, Billy Rose Sprinkle, and James Perruquet. In late May, from the vantage point of her home, sixty-seven-year-old Susan saw Sprinkle and Perruquet break into Edith Nolan's home. Susan spotted the boys in Edith's kitchen, drinking booze straight from the bottle and parading the firearms they had reaped while ransacking the home. A frantic Susan trekked 250 yards to the north, across rugged farmland to Mary and Victor Giglietti's home, and in her broken English, punctuated with spunk and spittle, she pleaded with the Gigliettis to call the police.

While David Stukel was in the final stages of leaving an indelible mark on St. Mary Magdalene Grade School, Billy Rose Sprinkle was carving his initials into Edith Nolan's banister. And in the light of day, when they were supposed to be in school, Sprinkle and Perruquet were found hiding in the kitchen closet when police arrived.

Two weeks after Sprinkle and Perruquet were arrested on burglary charges, David Stukel, with his proud parents and sisters in attendance, received his eighth-grade diploma. Four days later, Sprinkle and Perruquet, with their fathers begrudgingly by their sides, stood before Family Court Judge Angelo Pistilli and received juvenile sentences of six months' probation—appropriately labeled "Friendly Supervision."

Sprinkle, Perruquet, and their fathers signed twelve-point "Earn a Dismissal" contracts that, if successfully completed, would purge the burglary charges from their records. And in a precautionary move, the judge mandated that Sprinkle and Perruquet attend separate junior highs in the fall, with Sprinkle moving to Hufford on the West Side and Perruquet remaining at Gompers on the East Side.

In the most shocking link in a chain that led to murder, the very day that Billy Rose Sprinkle was placed on juvenile probation, he stayed out past his court-ordered curfew of 9 p.m. and was picked up by Will County officers for underage drinking—blatantly breaking two terms of the probation contract he signed twelve hours earlier. Even though Sprinkle was out past curfew, inebriated, and spent a night in the city jail, word of the probation violations, which surely would have kept him off the streets on September 16, 1968, never reached Will County Family Court Judge Pistilli.

It is the second week of the 1968 school year. James Perruquet is in class at Gompers in a rough East Side neighborhood. Billy Rose Sprinkle is roaming the halls of Hufford in an upper-middle-class West Side area.

Sprinkle, at the time living with sister Lorraine on the West Side, is fed up with his new school and leaves Hufford at noon, breaking "Friendly Supervision" term number six:

I will stay in school.

Sprinkle rides his bicycle six miles to the east on spacious, tree-lined West Side streets before crossing the Ruby Street bridge, the northernmost of downtown Joliet's five drawbridges that span the Des Plaines and accommodate heavy barge traffic bound for the Great Lakes or the Mississippi. Sprinkle pedals through depressed East Side neighborhoods, past the Elgin, Joliet & Eastern rail yard and up a steep hill to Gompers.

Sprinkle hooks up with Perruquet at 1 p.m., disregarding term number nine:

Do not associate with James Perruquet under any circumstances.

With Perruquet now tagging along, Sprinkle seeks an audience with the principal to discuss returning to Gompers, even though his assignment to Hufford was court-ordered. Sprinkle doesn't get past the secretary, then floats the idea that he and Perruquet run away to Kentucky, where Sprinkle's uncle lives. They leave on Sprinkle's bicycle with the intention of breaking term number five—*I will not leave the state without permission from my probation officer*—but they don't make it out of Joliet, let alone Illinois.

At 1:30, Sprinkle and Perruquet burglarize an apartment a mile east of downtown, stealing beer and a transistor radio, defying term number one:

I will obey the laws of the community.

They chain-smoke cigarettes and guzzle beer, breaking the seal on term number seven:

I will abstain from intoxicating beverages.

They buy glue and sniff it from a paper bag. They hang out near Central High, whistling at girls wearing dark-blue P.E. jumpers, and harassing passersby.

At 2:30, they set out on the two and one-half mile bike ride to the East High area.

At 3:30, Hill Street watchdog Susan DeAcetis notices the same two boys who burglarized neighbor Edith Nolan's home four months earlier sitting on the grass in front of the old Fritz farm.

DeAcetis paces, periodically peering out her front window to check on the two boys.

At 5:45, she sees a small boy walking alone on Hill Street. She witnesses a struggle, then sees the three boys disappear into the dense woods of the Fritz farm.

She sees—and does nothing.

She does not race to a neighbor's home as she had done in May.

She watches and waits.

Forty-five minutes later, Susan DeAcetis sees the two boys who had been hanging out on Hill Street emerge from the abandoned lot.

The third boy is nowhere in sight.

She sees—and does nothing.

At 6:30, Sprinkle and Perruquet leave the area on Sprinkle's bicycle. They head south across the East High campus and into the black neighborhood of Manningdale. They run into two boys taking a break from passing the local afternoon newspaper, and Sprinkle bounds from the bicycle and boasts to the boys about what he and Perruquet had just done.

At 6:45, they steal a mo-ped—burning term number eight:

I will not drive any type of motor vehicle.

They shed their plans to run away, and—hoping to retrieve the transistor radio they had left behind—return to the Fritz farm at nine o'clock—breaking term number four:

I will be home at night no later than 9 p.m.

From the back parking lot of East High, Billy Rose Sprinkle and James Perruquet gaze into the sea of flashing red lights of multiple county and city patrol cars parked along Hill Street. They retreat, riding the mo-ped back across the school practice fields.

They take back roads west for four miles and cross the city's southernmost drawbridge—McDonough Street—to Lorraine Sprinkle's home on Nicholson Street.

At ten o'clock, detectives knock on Susan DeAcetis' door. And despite her broken English, the officers do not need a translator when she utters one word:

"Sprinkle."

3

Homeward Bound

On the afternoon of the murder, I practiced on the same East High athletic fields as David Stukel—less than five football fields from 835 Hill Street. I was well aware of the abandoned lot that barely escaped the bulldozer's blade in the early 1960s, when construction of East High supplanted sixty acres of farmland, halting precisely at the property line of the Fritz farm. My father was East High's first basketball coach, so even before the school opened its doors in 1964, I had wandered its hallways, bounced on its trampolines, played basketball in its gymnasiums, and run across its expansive practice fields. I had explored every inch of East High, but I had only viewed the Fritz farm from a safe distance—never closer than a glance from inside a passing car.

In September 1968, although the dogs, hogs, and Jennie Fritz were part of the lore—not the landscape—I still had not found the courage to invade Jennie's former lair. But two days after David Stukel's last day at East High, I was drawn there.

I did not go alone.

I made the journey with fellow East High classmate Dan Haake, who had spent two seasons as David Stukel's Little League teammate.

Dan and I exited through the steel locker room door at the back entrance of the school. We walked north to Hill Street and its tree-branch archway.

We passed land where crops and fruit trees once thrived and the Fritz family barn once stood on the five-acre lot. When we finally turned toward the foreboding forest that encompasses the former farmhouse, we suddenly halted as if our legs had been encased in concrete. After a moment of silent contemplation, we maneuvered past a makeshift gate—a drooping cable bridging wooden posts, with a rusty no-trespassing sign dangling from a chain—and headed toward what was left of the Fritz homestead.

We walked across the remains of a winding limestone driveway covered by decades of vegetation. We navigated thick weeds that limited our visibility and rose two feet above our heads. We walked slowly, carefully as if in a minefield, unsure of what each step would bring. We passed old tires and discarded appliances, rusted-out barrels, junk, and litter. We sidestepped patches of mud and shattered glass.

In a small clearing between the home's foundation and the remains of the tin coop that once housed Jennie Fritz, we saw—scattered atop weeds that had been pressed to the earth—a handful of loose-leaf pages with David Stukel's handwritten notes on them—one with his name at the top. I picked it up, folded it, and slid it into my back pocket.

We had experienced the tragic losses of JFK, Martin Luther King Jr., and RFK, but for the first time in our young lives, death was more than an icon.

It had the name and face of someone we knew.

We could see it and touch it.

And we walked away—changed.

On his fifth and final day of high school, David Stukel sits in the air-conditioned comfort of his final-period social studies class, staring out the window of the first-level classroom and daydreaming about donning the Kingsmen green and gold for the first time as an East High athlete.

Billy Rose Sprinkle and James Perruquet, their pores oozing alcohol, seek shelter from the sun under a large mulberry tree fronting the old Fritz farm, one hundred yards north of East High's back parking lot.

The moment the final bell rings at 3:45 p.m., David races upstairs to his locker, just outside his homeroom that doubles as the chemistry lab. He places his blue binder and social studies book inside his locker, and grabs algebra and literature books, along with a spiral notebook that contains class notes and homework assignments. With his right hand pressed against books balancing on his right hip, and his left hand clutching the notebook, David hurries back downstairs and weaves through a sea of students. With his dark-brown hair neatly cropped, parted on the left with short bangs angling to the right, David speeds across shiny floors, past the young school's room-to-spare trophy cases, and into the boys' locker room, where he is issued a practice uniform, sweats, and running shoes.

Sprinkle, his light-brown hair well-oiled but tousled, and Perruquet, with sweaty strands of his dark-brown hair resting on his forehead, are high and hellbent on maintaining their buzzes. They walk one block west of Hill Street to Penfield Avenue, and commit their second burglary of the day, scoring a paring knife, cowboy boots, and whiskey to go along with the beer and radio they stole earlier.

They return to Hill Street.

David and two dozen East High cross-country runners stride across the athletic fields in the eighty-degree heat while a hundred or so football players' cleats pummel the sun-scorched earth as the screeching of a coach's whistle cuts through air thick with humidity.

Sprinkle, wearing blue jeans and a short-sleeve print shirt, flips the top of a cardboard pack of Marlboros. He hands one to Perruquet, who is wearing black trousers and a ratty short-sleeve dress shirt.

From the base of the mulberry tree, Sprinkle and Perruquet smoke, hoot, holler, crank up the volume on the stolen radio, hoist their bottles of Wild Turkey and Jim Beam, and taunt students as they stream by on buses, in cars, and on foot.

While Sprinkle and Perruquet draw attention to themselves, David Stukel inconspicuously participates in his first cross-country practice.

At 5:45, with the radio's batteries fading along with their highs, Perruquet turns to Sprinkle and says, "It's getting late, man. Maybe we should go home."

Then, strolling up Hill Street, a solitary East High student makes his way home.

On the morning of the murder, David Stukel rises at 7 a.m., washes his face, wets his hair, and quickly combs it. He puts on a new pair of briefs, beige pants, a T-shirt and a short-sleeve light-blue dress shirt. He slips on brown socks and brand-new brown shoes, buckles his brown belt, and sits down at the kitchen table for a bowl of cereal. David's mother puts his lunch money on the table, places an extra dime in his palm, and encourages him to call for a ride if the heavily predicted rain materializes.

The forecast calls for precipitation across northern Illinois, particularly late in the day and into the evening, with a high temperature in the upper seventies. At 7:30 a.m., David and sister Debbie squeeze into her boyfriend Gregg Skrtich's two-seat blue Rambler and head the half-mile to East High. The temperature is already sixty degrees and rising, seemingly by the minute.

At 5:30 p.m., nearly two hours after the final bell, the relative humidity reaches fifty percent, and the temperature soars to eighty degrees, but, surprisingly, the only showers at East High on this day would come in the locker room.

David Stukel, the freshly scrubbed and newly anointed Kingsman, has performed well in practice, so he celebrates the moment and exercises his newfound independence by electing to walk home from school for the first time in his life.

David and fellow freshman runner Fritz Bartels, a former classmate of David's at St. Mary Magdalene, leave the locker room together and make the short walk on the sidewalk, along the back parking, to Hill Street. They walk past practice fields and the vacant tennis courts before reaching Hill Street.

David, who looks as if he could be a seventh-grader, and Fritz, who is built more like a linebacker than a long-distance runner, plan to make the leisurely five-minute walk to New Lenox Road, where David would turn left and walk five blocks to his home, and Fritz would turn right and head one and one-half miles to his home near St. Mary Magdalene. But fate intervenes—in the form of a car leaving the parking lot.

Twenty-five yards up Hill Street, Fritz Bartels accepts a ride from a schoolmate who lives in his neighborhood.

David politely declines the short lift to New Lenox Road.

He waves goodbye and continues walking.

Seventy-five yards from school grounds, Hill Street is quiet, except for the faint sounds of eighteen-wheelers' engines whining on Interstate 80 and leaves rustling in the soothing twenty-miles-per-hour breeze.

There are no cars or students in sight when David Stukel enters the worlds of Billy Rose Sprinkle and James Perruquet.

In an unprovoked and unconscionable crime—unprecedented for the era and even for the East Side area—Sprinkle and Perruquet waylay a boy they do not know, a boy they later would say was stopped because he was dressed like someone who had money.

Once Sprinkle and Perruquet spot David, they spring from the ground to the pavement, backpedal in front of him, then stop, blocking his path.

"Hey, kid, you got a match?" asks Perruquet, flashing a smile and an unlit Marlboro.

David politely says no and starts to walk around Perruquet, but Sprinkle prevents him from moving forward by lightly pressing an open hand against the boy's chest.

"Wait a minute, kid. You want to buy a radio?" Sprinkle says in a non-threatening voice.

Again, David timidly dismisses the offer, sidesteps Sprinkle, and picks up his pace.

"Stop, you motherfucker!" shouts Sprinkle.

David's confident gait of just a few moments earlier becomes a desperate half-sprint. In a heartbeat, Perruquet throws the Marlboro to the pavement. Sprinkle tosses the transistor radio into the bushy grass beside the road, and they are on the same frequency as they rush after David, grab him from behind, shove him, and punch him.

With David facing Perruquet, Sprinkle bear-hugs the boy, and in one single, violent motion thrusts him into the air and toward the dirt shoulder on the Fritz farm side of the road. David gasps but holds onto his textbooks and spiral notebook, grasping them with both arms, tightly pressing them against Sprinkle's clasped hands.

Perruquet unfastens the cable fronting the farm, then struggles to corral David's flailing legs as Sprinkle drags the boy into the abandoned lot, carving a narrow path through the dense, towering weeds. Fifty feet from Hill Street, Sprinkle throws David to the earth. He lands ten feet from what's left of the farmhouse's foundation, most of which has disintegrated or is overrun with foliage.

In what must have felt as if it were happening in slow motion, David's world collapses in a flash as Sprinkle and Perruquet take less than twenty seconds to propel him from safety to seclusion.

"Give us your fuckin' money, or I'm gonna kick your ass!" says Sprinkle, grabbing David by the front of his shirt and, with one hand, picking him up.

"Yeah, give us your goddam money!" chimes Perruquet.

"I don't have any money," says David as Sprinkle and Perruquet rip the textbooks and notebook from his grasp, and toss them into the weeds.

Sprinkle again hollers: "Give us your fuckin' money!"

"I don't have any," repeats David while feverishly crawling on his hands and knees in a futile attempt to retrieve his books and notebook.

"You won't get your stuff back unless you give us your money!" says Sprinkle, kicking David's books farther into the weeds, then grabbing the boy by the back of his shirt and again lifting him to his feet.

"I don't have any money," David insists.

Sprinkle responds to the denial with a punch to the face that sends David back to the ground.

With David flat on his back, Sprinkle and Perruquet spot the boy's brand-new brown dress shoes.

"Take off your shoes!" orders Sprinkle.

"Yeah, take off your shoes, motherfucker!" says Perruquet.

David, whose small body had yet to grow into his size-ten feet, removes his shoes.

Too big for Perruquet and, surprisingly, even too large for Sprinkle, the shoes are cast aside.

"You'll get them back when we have your fuckin' money," Sprinkle says.

David rises and pulls out the front pockets of his dirt-smeared beige pants to show Sprinkle and Perruquet that he has no money, but Sprinkle is not convinced.

"Take your shirt off!" he demands. "And take your pants off too!"

Confounded by Sprinkle's demands, David doesn't respond fast enough to satisfy his assailants, so they shove him back and forth like a pinball.

"Hurry up, fucker!" screams Perruquet.

After David removes his pants and socks amid threats of a beating, Sprinkle and Perruquet rip his short-sleeve dress shirt and undershirt from his frail, pale body.

With David standing before them wearing only his briefs, Sprinkle and Perruquet rummage through his clothing and find no money—not even the dime his mother had given him to call home if it were raining.

In an attempt to make David divulge where the money is, Sprinkle and Perruquet rip pages from his books and notebook and toss them into the air.

"Here, you tear some out too!" orders Perruquet, thrusting a textbook into David's midsection and taking his breath away. David, unable to comprehend such a preposterous act as defacing a book, hedges and is punched by Perruquet. As David slowly removes pages from his algebra and literature books, hand-me-downs from sister Debbie, tears well up in his eyes.

When Sprinkle tires of belittling David, he screams, "Take your goddam underwear off!"

Fearing more punches, David complies, slowly sliding his bright-white underwear down his thin legs to the ground.

David stands naked, underwear around his ankles, knees bent, head lowered, hands covering his genitals.

What began as a mugging becomes molestation—behavior that had to be light-years beyond what David, a boy who had yet to kiss a girl, could fathom.

David is forced to perform oral sex. He is ordered to drop to his knees and place his arms over a rusted-out fifty-five-gallon oil drum, where he is savagely sodomized, his exposed chest repeatedly thrust against the sharp-edged cylinder.

When the raping of David Stukel is complete, Sprinkle shouts, "Get dressed!"

Traumatized and trembling, David rises from his knees, wipes his eyes with the backs of his hands, and, as he slowly attempts to fix his pants that are now inside out, Sprinkle hollers, "Put them on the way they was!"

When David doesn't obey fast enough, Perruquet slugs him in the chest and yells, "Hurry up, man!"

A sobbing David leaves his underwear, socks, and T-shirt on the ground. He feebly pulls on his pants—inside out. He slips on his shoes over his bare feet, and he puts on his torn short-sleeve dress shirt, not attempting to button it. He prays that he can head to the safety of his home, just five blocks away. But as the temperature drops slightly and the sun lowers, Sprinkle and Perruquet, seduced by the ultimate control they have over another human being, have no intention of letting David out of their grasp.

"I know I can kick his ass," boasts Sprinkle, smugly gesturing toward David. "Let's see if you can, James. You fight this cocksucker!"

Perruquet accepts the challenge, but David doesn't cooperate, keeping his arms at his side. Perruquet throws a punch that strikes David in the right side of the face, but David absorbs it without reeling.

"C'mon, James, don't be a pussy! This is how you throw a punch," says Sprinkle, before planting a roundhouse on David's jaw that sends him sprawling.

Sprinkle grabs David by his arms and props him up as if the boy were a tackling dummy, then instructs Perruquet: "Put your weight into it!"

Perruquet punches David in the face but again fails to level the boy.

Sprinkle throws a punch that sends David flopping into the weeds like a rag doll.

Sprinkle and Perruquet take a short-lived breather from beating David and amuse themselves by attempting to reduce their clean-cut victim to their street level.

"Cuss you motherfucker!" orders Sprinkle.

"We know you cuss, so fuckin' cuss for us!" says Perruquet.

David refuses to cuss and is punched, first by Sprinkle, then by Perruquet.

Perruquet stuffs a cigarette into David's mouth.

"Smoke it, motherfucker!" he shouts.

David spits out the cigarette, and he is rewarded with a Sprinkle cowboy boot to the stomach that leaves him doubled over on the ground and in a state of panic over whether he'll ever take another breath.

Sprinkle grabs David by the neck and pulls him to his feet. Then, using rusty iron bars plucked from junk piles, Sprinkle and Perruquet repeatedly strike David's face, chest, stomach, back, and legs.

"Let's see who can knock him further," says Sprinkle, knowing full well that his undersized accomplice is out of his league.

Laughing and egging each other on, Sprinkle and Perruquet take turns swinging their makeshift weapons into David's head and body, causing irreparable damage to his internal organs, breaking his nose, and busting out his front teeth.

After each blow, David would fall to the ground, only to have his relentless attackers lift him up and strike him again.

As David lay motionless, facedown amid the scrap metal and broken glass, the side of his face covered with blood, his tattered shirt twisted around his neck, his lips pressed against earth that reeks of pig manure, and the silence broken only by the gurgling of blood filling his lungs, Sprinkle and Perruquet take turns smashing the back of David's head with a broken concrete block, a remnant of the seventy-five-year-old farmhouse's foundation.

And in one final act of defiance, Sprinkle and Perruquet flick lit Marlboro cigarettes toward their victim.

One cigarette lands on the small of David Stukel's bare back and slowly singes his flesh as life leaves his body.

4

Desperate Searches

Lorraine Sprinkle was fifteen in 1964 when her family moved from one depressed East Side neighborhood to another at 602 Mills Road, a half-mile west of East High.

"We lived two blocks from Manningdale," Lorraine says of the black neighborhood across the street from East High. "That's why I had to quit school when I was sixteen—to kick the blacks' asses to get Billy and Doll [Georgina] and Steve and Stanley to and from school."

Lorraine recalls growing up poor and being considered "trash" because of her family's drawls, even though the children were born in Michigan.

"They all said we had Southern accents. When people said that I'd tell them, 'It's not a Southern accent, it's from hanging around all the blacks in Joliet!'" says Lorraine, laughing. "We were poor. You didn't have the things that you wanted; you had the things that you needed. We didn't have much, but we had each other."

Lorraine Sprinkle

Lorraine did most of the cooking and cleaning and caring for her four younger siblings. But in 1967 at eighteen, she cleaned her last toilet at the Sprinkle homestead.

"I was the second mother. My parents wouldn't let me date, and I was tired of cooking and cleaning, so I just said, 'Piss on it,' and I took off and got married."

Lorraine married Richard "Sonny" Nation and moved into the top apartment of a two-story house on Nicholson Street on the Near West Side, where brother Billy would come to live after being placed on "Friendly Supervision."

Lorraine Sprinkle has always felt a sensory connection to brother Billy, none more so than on the day of David Stukel's murder, when her intuition tells her to drive over to Hufford Junior High to check on Billy.

"It's some sort of bond. We know what the other is feeling—like the two of us is one," Lorraine says. "Even now, when he's in trouble or he's hurt, I can feel it. And that day I went over to his school around noon. I wasn't working, so I stopped by to check on him, and they said he's not there, that he took off. I said, 'What do you mean he took off?' And they said, 'He's gone.' I went home, but all day I felt that something was terribly wrong with Billy. The thoughts kept flooding my mind. My husband Sonny was at work. And when he came home, I was just feeling different, and Sonny could tell. He said, 'What's wrong?' and I said, 'Nothing.' Anyway, he lay on the couch, and I finally woke him up. I said, 'I can't take it no more, something's wrong with Billy! We have to go find him!' It was sometime after dinner, and we drove around and drove around, and couldn't find him."

While brother Billy is participating in David Stukel's murder, Lorraine is following her psychic trail throughout East Side neighborhoods.

"At one point, I told Sonny, 'He's in real bad trouble. He's hiding and he's scared, and I've got to find him.' We never could find him, so we came home after dark. I put my recliner by the screen door, and I sat and watched the street. And it was after midnight when I saw this car. I went right through the screen door—I didn't even open it. And the police had this boy in the back seat. I remember crying and screaming, 'Why are you taking Billy?' They told me, 'Get the fuck out of here!' Billy had been hiding underneath my house, and I didn't even know it. There was an apartment underneath us, and he was hiding under the pillars."

Life would never be the same for Lorraine Sprinkle.

"A few days after Billy's arrest, my grandmother died, and I went to Michigan for the funeral. When I came back, my landlord was in my apartment. He took everything that was mine and Sonny's and had it in lockup. He said he didn't want a murderer's sister living in his apartment."

Ray Stukel was raised during the Depression, so nothing gets wasted in his world.

"I don't think people these days have the temperament to live through a depression," Ray says. "Everybody was down and out, but they didn't steal from another person like they do now. We didn't have much, but if somebody would come to the door and was hungry, my mother would feed them."

With the Depression as the backdrop of his formative years, Ray learned to make do with whatever was available. He likes to boast that to this day he can walk into a junkyard, spot parts, and know immediately how they can fit together to form something, such as the small tractor he built out of scrap parts and an old, cast-iron Briggs & Stratton engine in the early 1960s so that he could give neighborhood kids rides through the fields.

In full scavenger mode on September 16, 1968, forty-two-year-old Ray Stukel has scrap wood on his mind. He gets a tip from brother-in-law George Meurer that a water tower ten miles east of Joliet is being razed and that the wood is free for the hauling. Ray makes after-dinner plans to take thirty-eight-year-old Marilyn, fourteen-year-old David, and eleven-year-old Nancy to the Meurer home, where he would drop them off so that they could visit with Barbara Meurer and her two children, while he and George load the wood atop Ray's Chevy station wagon.

Ray and Marilyn aren't sure what time to expect David because cross-country practice is his first after-school activity, but they figure he'll be home by five o'clock.

When David doesn't appear by 5:15, Ray drives the short distance to the back entrance of East High. He sees football players practicing and a few runners in the distance. He returns home to inform Marilyn that David's practice is probably not over. He tells her not to worry, but they agree that she should stay at home in case David calls for a ride.

Marilyn is preparing David's favorite meal—browned pork chops smothered with cream of mushroom soup, and green beans and mashed potatoes. Ray and Nancy sit down to dinner before jumping in the station wagon and heading east on New Lenox Road. They pass the north end of Hill Street at 5:50, just minutes after David's walk home abruptly ended.

Debbie Stukel and Gregg Skrtich, both sixteen, eat dinner, then head to the basement to play ping-pong. As Marilyn covers David's meal with foil and places it atop the warm oven, her concerns boil over.

Marilyn drives the family's '56 Chevy past the former Fritz farm, where strands of sunlight stream through the trees and weeds and onto David's battered, near-lifeless body. She pulls up by the school's glass back doors. She sees no one, then drives home, unable to contain her heightened anxiety as she enters the house.

"Gregg and I at first tried to make light of it when David hadn't come home," Debbie says. "But we both knew that something was wrong because it wasn't like David to not be where he was supposed to be."

Just before sunset, with an orange hue brushing across the western horizon, Marilyn, Debbie, and Gregg drive to the back of the school. There is no sign of anyone outside the school, so they pound on the doors outside the boys' gymnasium. A janitor makes a sweep of the locker rooms and reports that no one is in the building.

With the moon making an appearance in the eastern sky, Ray and Nancy arrive home with the load of wood, immediately followed by Marilyn, Debbie, and Gregg.

"As soon as we pulled in the driveway, I knew something was wrong," Nancy says. "The house was open, all the lights were on, and nobody was around. Then Mom and Gregg and Debbie pulled up behind us, and they said David hadn't come home and that he wasn't at school."

Ray and Marilyn desperately begin calling David's St. Mary Magdalene classmates now attending East High. When Ray connects with Fritz Bartels, he receives the ominous news that he had left David on Hill Street nearly two hours earlier.

A frantic Marilyn calls the Will County Sheriff's Department and is told that a missing persons report cannot be filed until midnight.

Ray calls the Joliet Police Department and receives the same response.

"They said, 'He's probably a runaway,'" Marilyn says. "And I said, 'No way is he a runaway!'"

"That really made me mad, that they would say that, not knowing anything about him. They would not go look for him, so I said, 'Hey, I know where he is all the time. He is not a runaway!'"

"The kid never would be a runaway," Ray sternly tells the officer to no avail.

Marilyn quickly regroups and steps into David's room, where moonlight illuminates his taut bedspread. She takes a deep breath, then takes charge, putting a search plan in motion. She tells Ray to get Gregg and meet neighbor Don Fenn at his farm, five hundred yards to the south. She calls Don, who enlists fourteen-year-old son Tom, and they begin checking the land west of Hill Street—including the abandoned Fritz farm.

"We just started walking out there, looking for David and calling his name over and over," recalls Ray. "It was no time before Tommy Fenn found him, and he called me over. I got down on my knees, and I put my hand on his back, and he was ice-cold. I knew he was gone. I had a bad feeling when we went to look for him. I was expecting the worst because it wasn't like David not to come home or call."

Fifteen minutes after Tom Fenn finds classmate and friend David Stukel's body, Ray Stukel finds himself answering questions from the back seat of a patrol car. According to the detectives at the scene, Ray Van Dyke and Dennis Jaskoviak, Ray

Stukel was never considered a suspect, but while reeling in grief minutes after seeing his son's body, he felt like one.

"They're throwing all kinds of questions at me, like they believed I had done it," says Ray, disgust in his voice.

Ray, with Gregg at his side and physically supporting him, returns home dazed and distraught.

"I remember Gregg saying that David was dead and telling me that when my dad saw David, it was as if it knocked all the life out of him," Debbie says.

"Gregg said he had to hold up my dad and that he could hardly walk himself."

Marilyn Stukel closes her eyes and is transported to the former family home on New Lenox Road. She sees David in the backyard wearing his father's U.S. Army Air Corps jacket, dog biscuit in hand, enticing Flipper, his liver-and-white pointer, to scale a sawhorse.

"I can see David trying to get Flipper to come to him," Marilyn says. "He's standing behind that sawhorse, saying 'C'mon, boy.'"

And in Marilyn's daydream, Flipper soars over the sawhorse and snares the biscuit from his master's hand.

David Stukel inherited his love of dogs from his father, who had two hunting dogs when his children were young.

"We had King and Flipper, and I was like the Pied Piper," Ray says. "All the kids in the neighborhood wanted to go along when I took the dogs out. David loved that. But he didn't want any part of shooting anything."

The evening of the murder, Ray walked through fields similar to the ones he patrolled with his hunting dogs—to look for his missing son. But before he departed, he quizzed a neighborhood authority—eleven-year-old Nancy—on the route David might have taken.

"We used to ride bikes up by the school, so my dad asked, 'If you were up by the school, which way would you come home?'" Nancy says. "I said, 'We would cut across the dirt track beside the old farm.'"

After Ray and Gregg left to meet Don and Tom Fenn, Marilyn and Nancy decided to conduct a search of their own.

"We had this idea that we'd take our dog Flip and go looking for David," Nancy says.

"We went up the back way toward the Fenns' house. We reached the end of the pavement and hit the dirt part, and the dog totally stopped, would not move. I grabbed his collar and tried to pull him, but the dog would not budge another inch in that direction, toward the field where we could look for David. It was as if Flip knew something was wrong."

Marilyn and Nancy returned home, put Flipper in the back seat of the '56 Chevy, and drove to Hill Street.

"As we pulled up near the Fritz farm, I remember hearing this awful crying … and it was my dad," says Nancy, her voice cracking and tears streaming down her face.

"He kept saying: 'My son is dead! My son is dead!' It just sticks in your mind forever. It never leaves."

5

Hoop Dreams

David Stukel loved to play basketball. But at five feet tall, with his shoes on, making the East High freshman team would be a tall order, so he devised a plan: Compete in cross-country, get in great condition, hustle his way onto the basketball team, then wait for his legs to sprout.

There wasn't supposed to be a cross-country season at East High in the fall of '68. A victim of budget cuts, the sport was eliminated the previous spring, but a summer-long paper drive resurrected the program.

When David Stukel reported to his first cross-country practice, he was greeted by Bruce Tompkins, a coach who was as interested in raising an athlete's self-esteem as he was in lowering his two-mile time. Nearly forty years after the murder, mention the name of any former East High distance runner, such as Tom Maher, an average runner who competed for two seasons in the late 1960s, and Tompkins doesn't break stride:

"Tall kid ... dark hair ... glasses ... lived over on South Chicago Street."

Maher, fifteen and a sophomore in '68, was one of the last students to see David Stukel alive.

"I think his locker was either next to mine or close by," Maher recalls. "What really brought him to my attention that day was how small he was. And how quiet he was. After practice we got dressed, and I was talking to him, and I recall that we left the locker room about the same time, and I vaguely remember seeing him walking down the sidewalk while I waited for a ride."

When Coach Tompkins hears the name David Stukel, his thoughts immediately return to the beginning of his fifth season as coach. No one could have prevented David Stukel's murder, but on that fateful day the freshman couldn't have been in better hands than those of Tompkins, a coach who after practice would set his stopwatch aside but would still be on the clock. Tompkins made it a practice to account for his athletes' whereabouts, often giving stranded runners rides home. And after literally watching David begin to walk home with Fritz Bartels, Tompkins had every reason to believe that the boy would return the next day.

"I got the call from the principal, probably about nine o'clock. The police told him the boy had been murdered," Tompkins says. "I was shocked that David had been murdered and that it happened so close to school. I was devastated and wondered how to deal with it."

East High's cross-country team elected not to compete in an invitational meet the day after David Stukel's murder and dedicated its season to him.

Fritz Bartels and David Stukel were friends at St. Mary Magdalene, but they rarely saw each other outside of school or during the summer months, except for one season as Little League teammates in 1966. After David and Fritz exited grade school in the spring of '68, they played on opposing teams in Pony League, after which Bartels spent much of August training for the cross-country season. He wasn't aware of David's interest in the sport.

David Stukel and Fritz Bartels in 1966.

"I hadn't heard that David was coming out," Bartels says. "This was a large class, so I hardly saw him. I didn't know he planned to be a runner. He hadn't trained, and I remember it surprised me that he was there. After practice, I was going to walk home and he was walking home, so we walked out together. We were walking and talking, and he was all excited about cross-country. He was smiling, and I remember thinking that he really ran well without training."

Moments after David Stukel and Fritz Bartels left East's campus, Thomas Smith pulled into the back parking lot in his red, two-door '66 Chevy Impala to pick up fifteen-year-old daughter Susan, a sophomore trying out for cheerleading. Susan, also a St. Mary Magdalene graduate, climbed into the car, and as the Impala reached Hill Street, Thomas Smith said, "There are two boys from grade school; you want to see if they want a ride?"

"It was just after we came out of the parking lot, where the shack is to the left, that nasty-looking property," Susan says. "We were right about at that abandoned lot when we asked both boys if they wanted a ride. Fritz says, 'Yes!' But David says, 'No thanks. All I need to do is cut across the field.' And my dad says, 'Are you sure?' and Dave says, 'Yes, I'm positive.'"

Of the 1,400 students at East High in September '68, a small percentage were graduates of tiny St. Mary Magdalene, so the odds were slim that the last students to see David Stukel alive, Fritz Bartels and Susan Smith, and the student who discovers his body, Tom Fenn, would be St. Mary Magdalene graduates.

Bartels, retired from Caterpillar and studying to be a minister, recalls his final moments with David.

"I had to get in the back seat of the Smiths' car, and it was a two-door. When I got in the car, my gym bag strap got caught on the front seat. As I was pulling on the strap, I remember looking back at David; I was glancing back out of the rear window at him and waving goodbye. And he was waving back. That's the last time I saw him alive."

While Fritz was unhooking his gym bag and the Impala was accelerating up Hill Street, Susan Smith recalls passing two boys who seemed eerily out of place.

"I remember there were two boys there with a bicycle," Smith says. "I am sure those were the two kids that murdered Dave. I hate to use this expression, but they were white-trashy."

In less than ten minutes, the Smiths dropped Fritz Bartels off at his home. Two hours later, Fritz was doing homework when Ray Stukel called.

"He wanted to know if I'd been with Dave and I said, 'Yeah,' and I told him about being picked up on Hill Street and David not taking a ride," Bartels says.

Later that night, long after Fritz had gone to bed, his father gave him the news that David had been murdered.

"My dad got the call from Ray Stukel, and I got up and didn't sleep the rest of the night," Bartels says. "I sat in a chair all night. I went to school the next day, and it was nightmarish. Other than those two calls from Mr. Stukel, I had no close contact with anyone regarding what happened. So I was picking stuff up through what kids were saying at school. And there wasn't any counseling at school. Teachers didn't talk to me. My folks barely talked to me about it. I can't remember anybody ever asking me how I felt. Nobody said, 'You can stay home.' Nobody said anything. I just went to school. And there wasn't anybody there to help."

Fritz Bartels experienced guilt over leaving David on Hill Street.

"I thought, 'Why him and not me?' I kept trying to figure that out and not for days but for years. I remember thinking, 'What would have happened if I had not gotten into the car and taken the ride home? Would he have been OK if the two of us were there together?' There's a good chance that he would have lived. I was a lot bigger than David, and would those kids have been willing to take a chance on jumping two kids? There will always be questions that I can't answer. I was glad to get the ride home. I was hungry and tired. But I just had to wonder, 'Why did this have to happen? What could I have done to change it? Would it have been both of us getting murdered instead of him?'"

Bartels also wonders if David had altered his route home just to keep him company.

"There was the paved path that runs west from the back parking lot to the football stadium that students from David's neighborhood would take. He was walking with me, so I don't know if he had deviated from that route because we were walking and talking."

Some men approaching their fortieth birthday purchase a roadster or run a marathon. Tom Fenn became a woman.

The decision may have come at mid-life, but this was no mid-life crisis, and it had nothing to do with finding David Stukel's body at fourteen.

For as long as Tom Fenn can remember, he has dealt with the conflict of having the spirit of a woman imprisoned within the flesh of a man.

Tom Fenn at 14.

"I started having those feelings when I was probably five," Fenn says. "But I was a boy living on a farm. Would I have loved to have worn a dress to first grade? Yes. But it wasn't something I could do."

At St. Mary Magdalene in the early 1960s, depression gradually engulfed Tom—the cumulative effect of the tempests swirling in his head and the constant teasing by classmates.

"In second grade, I was normal size, and then over the summer I discovered food," Fenn says. "I came back in third grade weighing a hundred pounds—with a size thirty-four waist. I was the last one to get picked for whatever game we played during recess."

By the seventh grade, Tom's excess weight had disappeared, along with the ridiculing. When he reached high school, Tom kept his weight in check by competing in wrestling, and he put a headlock on the gender war raging in his soul by transforming himself into one of the most popular students ever to walk East High's halls.

"I was able to put my feelings on the back burner because high school kept me occupied," says Fenn, who was elected homecoming king in 1971. "I liked being popular. It was more important to me than doing homework. And I thought as I got older that the feelings I had would go away."

Tom kept his secret through high school and joined the navy in 1976.

"I hoped it would make a man out of me," Fenn says.

The navy made him a machinist—not a man.

After his discharge from the service, Tom purchased his grandmother's home, 250 yards from his parents' farmhouse. He and his fiancé had a date with the altar in 1981, but he called it off four months before the wedding. Throughout the 1980s, depression had a stranglehold on Tom. Each night before going to bed, he would pray not to wake the next morning. He kept a plastic bag and a rubber band under his bed just in case he gained the courage to check out.

In 1990, Tom Fenn hit bottom.

"It was my birthday. I'm thirty-six years old, and I was working as a cook and dishwasher because I'm a transsexual and I could hide there. My whole life came down to me standing there with my hands in soap and water. It was, 'Do something! Become a woman or kill myself!'"

Four years later, in November 1994, Tom realized his dream of becoming a woman, and was finally able to remove the plastic bag and rubber band from under his bed.

When Sara Jayne Fenn peers out the window above her kitchen sink, she sees the East High football stadium where Tom Fenn was crowned homecoming king.

When she looks to the southwest, she sees her childhood home.

And when she looks to the southeast, she sees the former Fritz farm.

Tom Fenn's first and last memories of David Stukel involve the beginning of a school year. The first is from kindergarten, September 1959: Five-year-old David is wearing a yellow raincoat, matching hat, and black boots. The last is from high school, September 1968: Fourteen-year-old David is wearing his pants inside out, and his torn shirt is wrapped around his neck. His skull is smashed, and blood is everywhere.

The friendship between the Fenn and Stukel families goes back some seventy years, when Don Fenn and Ray Stukel roamed the same Greenfield neighborhood that their sons would explore a generation later.

Tom and David, whose mothers were pregnant at the same time in 1954, were born six days apart—Tom on May 18, David on the 24th. Tom and David attended kindergarten a couple of blocks south of the Fenn farm, at Thompson School, then moved on to St. Mary Magdalene for eight years of rigidity before escaping to public high school.

A middle child with two sisters, David was raised in a middle-class home. A middle child with two sisters, Tom was raised on a farm. Being the only male child in the Stukel home meant quality time with Dad—playing. Being the only male child on the Fenn farm meant quantity time with Dad—working.

Ray, who worked a nine-to-five government job, doted on David in his free time. Don, who worked construction by day and the land by the faint light of dawn and dusk, recruited Tom to bale hay and pick corn.

"I knew David my whole life, and we played a lot and always got along great," Fenn says. "But it wasn't like we were best friends. We were more like cousins. He was more into sports, and I was a hillbilly farmer. I was always a little bit envious of David because David and Ray did a lot together. On Halloween one year, we were sitting watching television, and all of a sudden a jack-o-lantern that was lit up comes right up to the window. Well, it was Ray and David, and they were going around to houses together. I remember going over to David's house and seeing all his model cars and airplanes. Ray had painted the little pilot in there, and they had built it together. I never held it against David, but I was jealous of him."

In the early 1950s, Don and Sue Fenn moved into their farmhouse and began working the five-acre tract of land that borders the Fritz farm to the east. Then, in the 1960s, the Fenns rented the five-acre lot directly north of the Fritz farm, where they began training harness-racing horses on a dirt track.

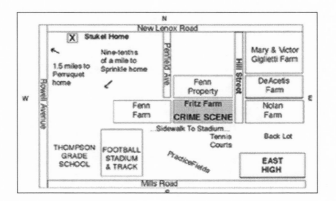

With the Fenn farm acreage butting up to the Fritz farm on its west and north sides, no one had more of a window into the Fritz family's world than the Fenns. And no Fenn spent more time working those borders and wondering what life was like for Jennie Fritz than Tom Fenn. Tom might have been curious, but it wasn't until November 1965, after Jennie had died, that the eleven-year-old ventured past the perimeter of the Fritz property and became intimate with the terrain. Tom culled through layers of debris, muck, junk, metal, and glass, searching for anything of value, especially old-time milk cans that were coveted porch ornaments in the mid-1960s.

On the day of the murder, Tom Fenn walks home from school on the paved path that leads to the football stadium. He does his homework, has dinner, and sits down to watch TV. But the quiet evening comes to a halt when Ray Stukel shows up at his door.

"Ray and Gregg Skrtich were looking for David. And Ray was pretty shook up because it was going on eight o'clock and nobody had heard from David," Fenn says. "I'm not religious, and I don't know why or how, but I just knew exactly where David was. They said something about retracing his steps. It was a jungle out there by the Fritz property, and being late in the summer all the weeds were eight feet high. So me and Dad, we took the dog, Bullet, just a mutt. Dad had a '54 Chevy pickup, and we drove up in the field there, and I remember Dad pulling up to the weeds of the Fritz farm."

Before entering the lot, Fenn recalls describing the layout to his dad, Ray, and Gregg.

"I brought it up that there was an old foundation and that I knew the layout pretty well, so I'm elected to lead the way," Fenn says. "Ray was calling out David's name, and I mention to them that the foundation wasn't very deep and that maybe somebody pushed David and he hit his head because there were a lot of concrete blocks back there. So they said, 'Whereabouts is the foundation?' I pointed and said, 'It's right over here.' I could have walked twenty feet this way or twenty feet that way, but I walked right into David. I hollered, 'There he is!'

"The area that they beat David up in, the weeds were all pushed down, so there was a clearing, and I spotted him outside the foundation. And Ray—he just started crying, 'Oh, God! Oh, God! Oh, God! My son is dead!' Then he dropped to his knees next to David. He knelt over him and was sobbing."

Fenn doesn't recall feeling any emotion in the minutes after finding David.

"I didn't cry when I found David. It was like it wasn't real. Then the three of them left right away to call the police, and told me to stay with David. I don't know why I was elected to stay with David, but if they would have said, 'You stand on your head and wait for us,' I probably would have done it at that point. I was just standing there in the dark. David was facedown, and his shirt was ripped up around his neck, wrapped around him like a scarf, so his back was exposed. And I remember kneeling down and touching David's back, and it was ice-cold. Maybe I had to feel the cold body for it to be real. Maybe it wasn't enough that I just saw him. I had to touch him, just to be sure. Seeing him dead, it's something I'll never forget. The top and back of his head was split open and his brains were hanging out. There was a lot of blood on the ground. When we had the cattle, I've seen when they'd butcher them down by the barn, all that blood would accumulate. It was like that."

After Will County detective Ray Van Dyke arrives at the scene, followed by his boss, chief investigator Dennis Jaskoviak, and a parade of county and city patrol cars, Don Fenn retrieves his son.

"It seemed like an eternity waiting beside David's body, but it was probably only ten minutes," the younger Fenn says. "When Dad came back, I went and sat in the truck, which Dad had pulled around onto Hill Street. Then I got scared. I didn't know if this was somebody at school who did this. I was sitting there, and Bullet was with me. He's shook up, whimpering. He knew something was wrong. And I just remember the cop lights flashing, those red lights, on and off, flashing into the truck. At first there was one cop car, then probably twenty. It seemed like forever before Dad actually came back to the truck and we left. We had an old army cot, and that night my parents let me sleep on the cot in their bedroom. I didn't feel like I could show emotion. Boys just didn't do that back then. The next morning, for me it was back to school like nothing happened."

6

On the Job

By the time Ray Van Dyke broke into law enforcement, his twenties had encroached upon his thirties. At eighteen, Van Dyke went to work for the phone company, but it didn't take long for him to realize that working for Ma Bell wasn't his calling, so he took a job as a salesman at a clothing store in downtown Joliet, not far from the Will County Sheriff's Department. On his lunch breaks, Van Dyke would stride over to the Sheriff's Department and chat with detective John Shelley, an officer whom Van Dyke had known since he was a youngster in the St. Mary Magdalene neighborhood.

Ray Van Dyke

In 1964, Shelley, who two decades later would be elected to two terms as Will County Sheriff, persuaded Van Dyke to become an auxiliary cop. Two years later, Van Dyke became a patrolman. And in '67, Van Dyke, an unassuming, no-frills officer, was assigned to Will County's investigative division. Over the next three decades, the straightforward cop would climb to chief deputy, the department's highest non-elected position.

With the same drive with which he chased the bad guys for thirty-three years, Ray Van Dyke now birddogs a little white ball around the Harbor Hills Golf Course in Lady Lake, Fla., where he lives with his wife, Pat, and stays in shape by playing slow-pitch softball.

When Van Dyke talks about his career, he rations his words, getting maximum mileage out of the ones he chooses. Asked about his career accomplishments, he politely and succinctly states:

"I did my job."

On the day of David Stukel's murder, thirty-year-old Ray Van Dyke was working the afternoon shift when he got the police radio call shortly after 8 p.m. that a boy's body had been found in an abandoned lot next to East High.

"I got to the scene in an unmarked car just as a patrol car pulled up. There was a lot of junk back there. Woods and thick brush. It was a mess," says Van Dyke in a staccato, no-nonsense fashion.

"They had tortured the Stukel boy. Anal sex. Oral sex. Burnt him with cigarettes. Pages torn out of his schoolbooks. Hit him in the head with a concrete block. The scene shocked me, but I had only been on the investigative unit since February of 1967. It was all pretty new to me, and you hadn't seen much of that kind of crime in Joliet, and not that vicious. I regard it as one of the worst crimes I've ever dealt with. I've seen bloodier messes, but that scene was just gross. And when you've got a young kid like that and two other boys doing it—the Stukel boy was so small. The murderers weren't that big, but there were two of them and they were bullies by reputation alone."

Although Van Dyke managed to go about the business of working the crime scene, he found it difficult to keep his emotions intact.

"You're trained to do the job, but it's not easy. I had two sons by that time. They were little; the oldest was eight, and his name is David, too."

Praise comes from all precincts when the subject is Dennis Jaskoviak, who "fiddled around with law enforcement" for parts of five decades. Jaskoviak answered law enforcement's calling at age twenty-two, then proceeded to do everything from battling organized crime to serving as police chief of Crest Hill, a small community bordering Joliet's Northwest Side.

Dennis Jaskoviak

Jaskoviak had such an impeccable reputation as a leader that after he stepped down as Crest Hill's top cop in 1990, he was lured out of semi-retirement by Will County to run its criminal division for the second time.

An intense and polished lawman whose sense of fashion was a reflection of his dedication to professionalism, Jaskoviak was always most comfortable in the driver's seat. Even after officially retiring, for a couple of years he and wife Dolores toured the country in a recreational vehicle. The Jaskoviaks have retired the RV and are enjoying life in the retirement community of Sun City Center in Florida.

Nearly forty years after David Stukel's death, Jaskoviak, the county's lead investigator at the time of the murder, explains why he does not have automatic recall of the particulars of the case.

"During the thirty-seven years that I was in that business, I probably was involved in hundreds of homicide investigations," Jaskoviak says. "In the Will County Sheriff's office alone, I ran the criminal division at two different times.

And every homicide that Will County was involved in, I was involved in, and all those things meld together, so it's very difficult to pick something out thirty-five or so years ago and remember with any assurance to be accurate. But I do remember that the two young defendants were from semi-literate backgrounds and that they lived a world apart from what the Stukel boy lived."

When Jaskoviak reviews court documents, he recalls the case but is not fazed by its gruesome details.

Jaskoviak is not a callous man, but he was a cop who survived by quashing his emotions inside and outside the yellow tape.

A crime-scene investigator collected evidence the day after the murder.

"I don't know how to say this other than to say I've seen things that were as bad or much worse," Jaskoviak says. "What I saw at the Stukel crime scene didn't impress me, and that's not nice, you know, because even though you still have feelings and you have a soul, you see enough over time that it becomes part of what you're doing as your job and your responsibility to society, and emotions and the rest of it are off to the side somewhere."

At the crime scene, Ray Van Dyke is focused and deliberate, working with an evidence technician and a photographer, conferring with the coroner and tap-dancing with the media.

"There was no DNA in those days. The most we did was dust for finger-prints," Van Dyke says.

"We combed every inch of the area, but we didn't touch the body. Only the coroner does that."

At 9:30 p.m., the officers turn their attention to finding witnesses. With no homes, only farmland butting up to the Fritz farm, and only three homes across the street, a massive net does not need to be cast.

"I started interviewing neighbors to see if anybody saw anything, and lo and behold, somebody saw something," says Van Dyke, referring to Susan DeAcetis, the neighbor who witnessed Sprinkle and Perruquet jumping David Stukel on Hill Street but did not alert police.

"She described those two to me. I think she knew the Sprinkle kid, maybe both of them. We started looking at the suspects' houses. We talked to both families, and I guarantee you we didn't get any help from either family."

It takes just three hours for officers to round up Sprinkle and Perruquet—at 12:30 a.m. below Lorraine Sprinkle's Near West Side apartment.

The suspects are transported in separate squad cars to the second floor of the three-story Will County Sheriff Department's administrative offices, where an elegant room with mahogany paneling serves as the interrogation division. Elected sheriffs once lived in these stylish quarters, but by '68 the house was home to the investigation unit.

At 1:30 a.m., Sprinkle is the first to be ushered into an interrogation room. He is joined by his father, Ed, and older sister Lorraine.

Sprinkle tells Dennis Jaskoviak that he spent a portion of the afternoon in the vicinity of East High, but he repeatedly denies any knowledge of the murder, even when confronted with eyewitness Susan DeAcetis' account of his participation in the altercation on Hill Street.

Perruquet, with father Earnie Sr. by his side, admits to nothing, claiming that he had not even been in the area.

"Their attitudes were kind of so-so," Van Dyke says. "It didn't seem to bother them. They weren't intimidated."

During Sprinkle's second interview in which he continues to claim that he has no knowledge of the murder, Van Dyke leaves the interrogation room and makes an announcement within earshot of Perruquet and his father:

"We're getting the tape recorder. Sprinkle's confessing to everything."

The savvy Sprinkle had not confessed, far from it.

But when Perruquet is questioned for the second time, he implicates himself and Sprinkle.

"Perruquet talked freely enough to tie in everything with whatever physical evidence there was," Jaskoviak says. "With that confession, there wasn't a whole lot of extra work that had to be done to satisfy the rules as far as an indictment is concerned."

Jaskoviak recalls that Sprinkle never flinched, sticking to his denials throughout the long night of grilling.

"I think you could sum up Sprinkle's demeanor in one word: detached. He was more streetwise, probably because his family had a criminal history. I think if you look it up, you'll find a majority of them were involved in anti-social activities."

Van Dyke says he was not at all surprised that it was Perruquet who broke down.

"Sprinkle came from a family of thieves, so he was used to the system. And I would bet you a thousand dollars that his father told him, 'Don't say nothin'.' His father was an arrogant, ornery son-of-gun who knew how to play the game. Perruquet described everything almost matter-of-factly. He certainly wasn't upset, and he wasn't bothered by the recorder—not one bit. He told us what they did. No denials."

Asked to speculate on a motive and, specifically, if he would classify the murder as a thrill-killing, Van Dyke says, "Yep. I think they were having a good time. Why did they do it? Because they were mean little assholes—that's all they were, to be completely honest. But you've got to remember the families they came from, too."

Nine hours after the murder, Dennis Jaskoviak and Ray Van Dyke listen as James Perruquet confesses. The interview lasts just twenty minutes, but it is a chilling account of the nightmarish final forty-five minutes of David Stukel's life.

James Perruquet sits at the nondescript wooden table with father Earnie's work-worn hands resting on his boy's right forearm.

Jaskoviak sits across the table from the Perruquets. Van Dyke sits in a chair against the wall, facing the suspect.

Jaskoviak pushes the record button on the sheriff's department's bulky tape recorder and addresses Perruquet:

This is a recording of an interview conducted on September 17, 1968, starting at 4:10 a.m.

What is your first name, Mr. Perruquet?

"James."

James, are you aware that this interview and statement is being recorded on tape, and are you willing to give us a statement knowing that it is on tape?

"Yes."

Now, today is the seventeenth of September, a Tuesday, and it is rather early in the morning, and I want you to think back to yesterday, which was September 16, 1968, a Monday. Did anything unusual occur during that day?

"Yup. Me and Billy Sprinkle, we was over there by East High School, and some boy come walking down the road. We stopped him and asked him if he wanted to buy a radio. He took off walking, and we stopped him again and asked him again if he wanted to buy a radio. We told him to come on back this way, and we was walking that away, and Billy hit him and then I hit him."

What do you mean by hitting him, James?

"With our fists."

Where did you hit him?

"In the stomach."

Where did Billy hit him, if at all?

"Chest."

And then what?

"Then we took him over by the cable, and we took him back around behind the cable and then we started to ..."

Can you describe this area for me?

"There was a bunch of old ice boxes, barrels, a bunch of iron bars, a blade, a bunch of weeds."

All right. The boy, you stopped him; you asked him if he wanted to buy a radio. Where did this radio come from?

"From an apartment over on Cass Street. Billy picked it up when we walked in."

And did you go into anybody else's house yesterday without permission?

"Yes, over there by East High, where we got the boots."

What else?

"And a knife."

What kind of boots were they?

"Cowboy boots."

What color?

"Brown."

Who was wearing those after you obtained them?

"I was."

Who was wearing them when you found this boy walking down the road.

"Billy was."

You say you obtained a knife. What kind of knife was this—can you describe it?

"Black handle, about a three-inches-long blade."

Would this be like a paring knife that a lady would have in the kitchen?

"Yeah."

Who had this knife in their possession?

"Billy had it, then when we got up there with the boy, I got it from Billy."

All right. So you stopped the boy on the street and asked him if he wanted to buy a radio?

"Yes."

Now, describe the radio—what color was it?

"It was brown; it had three knobs and a black button on the side."

OK, James. Now, the boy kept on walking and then, you say, you and Billy grabbed him and punched him around a little bit. Then where did you go?

"Into the weeds."

What happened when you got in the weeds?

"Billy told him to take off his clothes."

What did the boy do? Did he tell you 'no'?

"He took off his clothes; he didn't say nothing."

What did he take off?

"He took off his pants and his underwear and his shoes."

Did he have any socks or a shirt on?

"He took off his socks, and me and Billy tore off his shirts."

Shirts—he had more than one shirt on?

"He had a T-shirt and a plain old shirt."

You're saying he was standing there naked?

"Yes."

What happened then?

"Billy made him give me a blow job."

Now let's not get ahead of ourselves, James. What happened after his clothes were off? Did you threaten him or did he try to run away or what?

"No."

What happened?

"Billy told him to lay on the barrel, and Billy was doing it to him in the rear."

What do you mean by doing it to him in the rear?

"Uh ..."

Sticking his penis in his back end?

"Yes."

Then what?

"Then Billy told him to give him a blow job."

Will you tell me what you mean by a blow job?

"Suck ... the blow ... I don't know how you say it."

You mean when you stick your penis in his mouth?

"Yes."

All right. You say Billy had an unnatural act with him over a barrel?

"Yes."

And then you say this boy committed an unnatural act with you and his mouth?

"Yes."

Then what happened?

"And then Billy told him to give him a blow job, and then I got him in the back ... rear end."

What was this boy doing all that time? Did he try to run away or resist?

"No."

Why don't you think he tried to resist or run away?

"He was scared."

Why was he scared?

"Because we threatened to beat him up."

Did you hit him before this happened?

"No ... yes."

When?

"When we was out on the road."

All right, the boy was naked; then what happened?

"Billy told him to put his pants on."

What did he do?

"Put them on backwards."

Inside out or backwards?

"Inside out."

Then what?

"Billy started hitting him and working him over."

How was he hitting him and working him over?

"He was hitting him in the face, on his left-hand side, below the eye, by his nose with his fist."

And then what?

"Billy told me to hit him a couple times, so I hit him below his right eye."

Did he bleed?

"No."

Did anybody kick him?
"Yes."
In the face or where?
"In the face and in the stomach."
Who did this?
"Billy and me."
Both of you kicked him in both places, in the face and in the stomach?
"Yes."
Did he bleed?
"He started bleeding in the nose."
Then what happened?
"And then ... then ... I ... me and Billy picked up an iron bar and hit him across the head."

Now, let's not get ahead of ourselves, James. Both of you can't pick up the same thing. Who picked up what and what happened?

"I picked up one iron bar, and Billy picked up another one. And then Billy told me to hit him in the head, and I hit him in the head; and then Billy hit him in the head."

What did the boy do?
"Nothing but said 'ouch.'"
Now, let's think a little bit, James. Did he fall down, did he scream or what?
"He didn't scream. He fell."
Did he bleed about where you hit him?
"No."
He didn't bleed when you hit him with the iron bars?
"No, not yet."
All right, James. Where did you hit him the first time with the iron bar?
"In the back of the head."
Where in the back of the head?
"About three or four inches from his neck."
How many times did you hit him with that iron bar?
"I hit him once in the head, in the shoulder, in the back, on the ankle, and in the arm."

And then what happened?
"And then I ... I picked up a block and hit him in the head ... back of the head."

What do you mean by a block, James?
"A sand block."

You mean like a concrete block?

"Yes."

A whole block or a portion of a block or what?

"A half."

And what did you do with the block?

"Hit him in the head."

Where in the head?

"About three inches from his neck."

Did you hit him anyplace in the front of the head?

"With the iron bar, I did."

Did you hit him with the block anyplace else in the head?

"Yes, in the back of the head."

Did you see anybody else hit him with this block?

"No."

Did anyone hit him around the mouth or in the forehead or his eyes with a bar or with a block?

"Billy hit him in the head with the bar. I hit him in the face with my fist a couple of times."

Did you hit him in the face with the bar or the concrete block?

"I hit him in the face with the bar."

Now, you mentioned before this black-handled paring type knife. What happened to this knife?

"It broke on his back."

How did this happen?

"I was acting like I was going to stab him—and I bent the knife, and it was bended a little and I tried to straight it and it broke."

You mean you had this knife against his back and it bent?

"Yes."

All right. Who hit him in the mouth with an iron bar and knocked his teeth out? Did you?

"I didn't hit him in the mouth; I hit him above the nose."

Did you see anybody else hit him around the mouth with a bar?

"I think it was Billy because I wasn't looking all the time."

What were you doing?

"Looking for the block."

Why were you looking for the concrete block?

"To throw it away."

What happened to this block?

"I don't know. I couldn't find it."

Didn't you pick it up and throw it away in the weeds?

"After I hit him in the head, I threw it somewhere, but I don't know where I threw it at."

What was this boy that you hit with the bar and concrete block, what was he doing when this was all over?

"Laying there making a funny noise."

What kind of noise?

"Like a gurgling."

What did you do then?

"Left—leave—kicked him in the side and then left."

What made you kick him in the side?

"See if he was still alive."

What did you find after you kicked him in the side?

"He moved—jumped like."

Then what did you do?

"Went over to Lorraine's house."

Who is Lorraine, and where does she live?

"Lorraine is Billy's sister, and she lives over on Nicholson."

And did you go see Lorraine?

"No."

What did you do?

"Went down near her basement and went to sleep."

Then what happened?

"Then the cops came."

Did you know that this boy would come by the path that he took on his way home?

"No."

Did you know this boy?

"No."

Ever see him before?

"No."

Did you know if Billy knew this boy?

"Uh-uh."

Do you know what this boy's name was?

"David something. I don't know."

How did you know that?

"I seen it in his book."

What about his books; what happened to those books?

"Tore them up, me and him."

You and who?

"David."

Do you mean you and Billy tore up his books?

"No, me and David tore them up."

Why was David tearing up his own books?

"I handed it to him and asked him if he wanted to tear his books up, and he said 'yes.'"

Now, which way did you propose this to this boy, James? I'm sure you didn't say, 'You want to tear up your books?' and he started tearing them up. What did you say to him?

"I said, 'Tear this book up or I'll whomp you.'"

Dennis Jaskoviak turns to Earnie Perruquet, Sr.

"Mr. Perruquet, is there anything you would like to ask?"

James Perruquet's weary father does not respond or even make eye contact with Jaskoviak.

James, if these questions were asked of you at a different time, would your answers be the same?

"Yes."

Can you tell me why?

"Because you got them on tape."

I don't think you understood my question. Why would your answers be the same? Is what you're telling me the truth?

"Yes."

So that if you answered these questions at a different time, would your answers be the same?

"Yes."

Why would they be the same?

"Because it is the truth."

At 4:30 a.m., Jaskoviak stops the recorder, and James Perruquet innocently asks the veteran interrogator, "Can I go home now?"

"No, young man," Jaskoviak says.

"The judge will see you in the morning."

7

"It Just Wasn't His Face"

Three days after his son's murder, Ray Stukel viewed David's body at Blackburn Funeral Home on Joliet's Near West Side.

"I had to go there to see if we wanted the casket closed," Rays says. "They had him all fixed up. He looked like he was sleeping, so I said, 'Leave it open.'"

Blackburn Funeral Home could not accommodate the extreme volume of mourners who were lined up out the front door and around the block.

"You never saw so many people in your life," says Barbara Meurer, Ray and Marilyn's sister-in-law. "There were even strangers, people who heard about the murder and just wanted to express how sorry they felt for them."

Although Ray and Marilyn believed that their son looked as if he was at peace, many who attended the viewing, including daughter Debbie, could hardly recognize David.

"When I first saw him, it just wasn't his face, and that was awful to see," Debbie says. "I just know that he was beaten bad because they didn't know if they were going to have an open casket. And when they did, it just wasn't my brother. It's him but it's not him. His face was so swollen, and I just kind of stayed in the background. It was like it wasn't really happening. And the horrible things that you kept thinking, over and over, 'What was he *thinking*? What was going through his head at the time they were beating him? Did he feel much pain?' I still think about that today: 'What was he *thinking*?'"

Nancy Stukel recalls very little about the wake.

"I just remember a lot of people," she says. "I don't think I understood death at first. It's more as the days unfold and you realize that you're not going to see him anymore that it hits you."

Francis Ruettiger, David's St. Mary Magdalene classmate and best friend, remembers the complexity of dealing with death for the first time.

"Oh, God, all the kids that went to school with him were sitting around sobbing, and his mom and dad had blank stares on their faces. I went up to the casket and just stood there looking to see if he was going to sit up because I just couldn't believe that he was actually gone. It was just so weird to see your best friend laying there. You'd never experienced death before."

David's St. Mary Magdalene classmate Butch Markelz recalls seeing the tortured expressions on the faces of Ray and Marilyn Stukel.

"You hear stories about the loss of a child, how devastating it is, and I think you could always see it on his parents' faces, even years later. When I'd see them after that, they looked like they never got over it. Ray was always a happy guy, and when that happened, I never saw the same person again."

Dick Mandella, a class behind David at St. Mary Magdalene, lived three houses away from the Stukels. He recalls talking about the brutality of the murder with classmates before the wake.

"I remember hearing at school that they were going to have an open casket just to show what he had gone through, and you could see where they broke his nose in I don't know in how many places. And at that age, you were petrified about what to say to his family."

Fritz Bartels says he was overwhelmed at the wake.

"I remember watching, just watching Dave's mom and dad, trying to figure out how they could possibly handle this. Then Dave's dad came up to me and asked about cross-country practice. He asked, 'Was he happy?' And I remember telling him that Dave was happy and that I thought he had enjoyed practice and had run well, and that he was having a reasonably good time, however much of a good time you can have at cross-country practice. And I remember thinking, 'What can I do to help?' But when you're that young, there's not much you can do or say."

Marilyn and Ray Stukel were in a daze.

"Everything seemed like it was far away ... out of my grasp," Marilyn says. "I was there, but I wasn't there."

"It was like viewing it all from a distance," Ray says.

The Stukels may have felt disoriented at the wake, but Ray vividly recalls an unpleasant incident that morning.

"The Sprinkles sent flowers," says Ray, with disgust in his voice.

"I told Jim Blackburn, 'We don't want those flowers anywhere near David's casket!'"

At David Stukel's funeral mass, Ray and Marilyn were overwhelmed by how St. Mary Magdalene celebrated their son's life.

"The Catholic Church has a season where all the statues are draped in purplish-black colors," Marilyn says.

"In the church, everything's covered—all dark," Ray says. "And all the vestments are purple. But the day of the funeral, they uncovered all the statues, and the vestments were a pinkish-red color for martyrs. It was the Mass for martyrs!"

"And the bishop was there!" Marilyn says.

"It was the bishop's idea, and I remember one of St. Mary Magdalene's sisters coming up to me," says Ray, letting out a heavy sigh, then pausing to catch his breath before breaking into tears.

"We've made it this far, old boy," says Marilyn, patting Ray on the back. "Maybe it's good you get it out. C'mon, Ray, let it go!"

Ray pulls a handkerchief from his pants pocket, dabs his blue eyes, takes a deep breath, and sits back in his chair.

Marilyn deftly changes the subject to her son's carefree personality, but within a couple of minutes Ray directs the conversation back to his son's funeral.

"What I wanted to say is that one of the sisters came up to me and says, 'St. Mary Magdalene Church has its first saint!' And I don't doubt it. If David's not a saint, then I don't know who else is going to be!"

After the service, the funeral procession made its way north to Mt. Olivet Cemetery, less than two miles southwest of Belmont Little League. The pallbearers, including Francis Ruettiger, Butch Markelz, and Tom Fenn, removed David's casket from the hearse.

"I remember carrying his casket all the way to the grave site, and the whole time I'm crying," Francis says. "I couldn't stop crying."

Ray and Marilyn recall the dreary weather in the days leading up to their son being laid to rest.

"It was supposed to rain the day David died, and it didn't. He never would have walked home if it had rained," Ray laments. "The forecast called for rain that day, especially late in the day and into the evening. It never rained, but the rest of the week was one of the grayest weeks ever. It rained every day till the day of the funeral. And then, the sun broke through and shone right down on David's grave!"

"Just like a beam of light coming down on his grave," Marilyn says. "I went to the cemetery the day after the funeral. I just needed to be there. It was a beautiful, bright Saturday morning ... no school ... and I thought, 'David would be out riding his bicycle today; he'd be having fun just like he always did.' But there he was ..."

8

"Everything Ceases"

A medical examiner is the deceased's link to the living, and an autopsy report is the ultimate body language, allowing those no longer with us to reveal the details of their demise. The night of David Stukel's murder, his body was taken to the East Side's Silver Cross Hospital, two miles west of Belmont Little League, where he was given last rites by St. Mary Magdalene Pastor Vincent Lavery. The next morning, David's body was transported to St. Joseph Hospital on the West Side, where pathologist Dr. John Keith performed just the county's seventh forensic autopsy three-quarters of the way through the year.

"As surgical pathologists, the autopsy work that we did was ninety-nine percent on individuals who died in the hospital," says Keith, who retired in 1993. "The outside forensic cases were a small part of the practice, and we didn't have training in forensic pathology, so we weren't comfortable doing it. But homicides were rare and spaced out between us. I probably performed only fifteen to twenty forensic autopsies before they turned them over to the forensic experts in the mid-1970s, so I still have a clear picture in my mind: young boy, attacked, cement block dropped on his head. The poor kid's skull was so terribly crushed. What were these kids thinking?"

Nearly four decades after Dr. Keith performed the autopsy, he examines a copy of the report and translates his findings into layman's terms.

"The cause of death was fractures of the frontal area of the head combined with the trauma with the back of the head that caused significant brain-swelling—or areas of bleeding around the brain—which caused cardio-respiratory arrest. There's a respiratory center in the brain that controls the breathing, and the heartbeat is controlled from the brain as well, and when those things are interfered with by brain-swelling, everything ceases."

Dr. Keith likens David's head injuries to those sustained in a head-on traffic accident in which a seat belt is not worn.

"To compare with the head injuries in this case, it would had to have been an accident in which the individual was thrown up against the windshield. You can have head injuries like this in an accident, but you don't have this degree of bruising and internal injuries. In this case, there were severe injuries, and not just to the head."

Dr. Keith's report states that sections of David's liver and right kidney were bludgeoned—signs that he was struck with blunt objects.

"It's almost impossible to determine at what point he became unconscious," Dr. Keith says. "But one would think that he became unconscious when they hit him with the concrete block."

Death, taxes, and running for coroner are certainties in Patrick K. O'Neil's family. In the 1930s, O'Neil's grandfather, Joe, opened a funeral home in Joliet. Patrick's father, Pat, now runs the family funeral home seven miles northeast of Joliet, where son Patrick worked before becoming Will County's coroner in 1992 at age twenty-six.

"Grandpa ran for coroner and lost in 1932," Patrick K. O'Neil says. "FDR was running for president, and [Henry] Horner was running for governor, so Grandpa's slogan was: 'Roosevelt, Horner, O'Neil for Coroner!' And Dad ran for the office and lost three times—first against Willard Blood. He gave him a good race, but I don't think anyone was going to beat a coroner with the last name of Blood! And when I decided to run, Dad thought I was nuts because I was so young."

The O'Neils are nothing if not persistent, and now that they have one of their own in the coroner's office, they won't let go. O'Neil, in his fourth term as Will County coroner, was just three when David Stukel was murdered. But when presented with the autopsy report, he dissects it as if he had been in the room assisting Dr. Keith.

"This kid was bludgeoned to death with some type of blunt object to the head," O'Neil says. "Maybe a tire iron, a tree branch, a baseball bat, or a brick. This kid's entire body was battered. There are a lot of lengthy words that refer to bleeding, bruising, and blunt trauma. These lacerations—the gaping wounds on the skin—aren't from a sharp object that would just automatically break open the skin. It takes great force to do this. Sometimes with a boxer, after several rounds of getting severely beaten, you might see a small laceration, after a long fight, but in this case, we're talking about large lacerations sustained over the course of a few minutes. And his eyes were swollen and that would indicate he still had a heartbeat. No one would ever probably be able to say in what order the injuries were received. One could only hope that he sustained the head injuries first and was unconscious for the rest of the beating."

While acknowledging the heinousness of the crime, O'Neil says he regularly sees cases with similar injuries.

"They are sad cases, but they aren't uncommon today. It's sad when you're dealing with youngsters. But nowadays, we handle cases like this quite often. A case like this would not shock me. It looks like an experimental killing. They wanted to see what it would feel like to kill another human being. This is almost overkill. You tend to see an overkill type situation with sexual offenders."

Conspicuous by its absence from Dr. Keith's autopsy report is the mention of a sexual assault. With a murder confession, that information was not critical, but Dr. Keith does not recall being informed of the crime's sexual nature.

"I certainly would not have been thinking about a sexual assault on a fourteen-year-old boy by fourteen-year-old boys. But with a confession, I think that back in those days the idea was, 'Hey, Doc, just give us the cause of death.'"

One long-standing rumor associated with the Stukel murder is that the assailants tortured their victim by burning his back with cigarettes.

"I did not see cigarette burns on the body, and there's no mention of it in my report," Dr. Keith says.

Court documents support Dr. Keith's findings, stating: "At the small of the victim's back one Marlboro cigarette butt was found and at that location on his back there were some ashes and some discoloration of skin."

But former detective Ray Van Dyke, the first officer at the scene, is certain that David Stukel was repeatedly burned with cigarettes. "I'd bet my life there was more than one burn mark on his back," Van Dyke says.

The case's most sensational rumor—that David Stukel's penis was cut off by his assailants—is untrue. But after the murder, that tale—or some variation of it—developed a life of its own, spreading fast and wide like the area's goldenrod population. The rumor permeated all walks of life—from David's relatives to his closest friends to his classmates and teammates to strangers to the murderers' siblings. In fact, the only people who are impervious to the rumor are David's parents and sisters.

"I would have noticed if that was absent," Dr. Keith says in a no-frills tone. "I'm sure it was present."

Fritz Bartels has long believed the rumor.

"I still have images of underwear stuffed in his mouth, cigarette burns, his penis being cut off. Stuffing underwear in his mouth seemed to make sense because they were probably trying to keep him from yelling."

Sara Jayne Fenn has grown weary of dispelling the tale.

"I was there. There was no penis in his mouth. Someone brought it up recently, and I thought, 'I ain't even gonna say anything because that's what everybody thinks, that's the urban legend, so what's the use?'"

Former detective Dennis Jaskoviak is familiar with rumors that sprout from particularly violent crimes.

"Every time you have a situation that's grisly, something that is disgusting, especially when there are other kids that are talking about it, and certainly kids do talk about it in school and after school, and somebody starts a little rumor and then somebody else builds on it, and after a period of time it becomes fact."

On the day of David Stukel's murder, William "Brad" Pinnick was a seventh-grader attending Gompers Junior High. The chance meeting that Pinnick had with Billy Rose Sprinkle and James Perruquet after they left the crime scene was an encounter Pinnick would never forget and Sprinkle would live to regret.

Brad Pinnick was taking a break from passing the local afternoon newspaper with friend Donnie Simmons in the black neighborhood across the street from East High when Sprinkle and Perruquet approached them.

Brad Pinnick at 13.

Asked four decades later if he remembers the meeting, Pinnick says:

"Yeah, they gave me the boots! They told me they had killed a boy, and they gave me a pair of boots."

In interviews with Pinnick and his mother, Gladys, at their modest home north of Joliet, they recount the events of September 16, 1968:

Brad, who said they had just killed a boy?

"Sprinkle. He was talking, bragging."

What was Perruquet doing?

"Laughing. He didn't say a word. Sprinkle did all the talking."

Why do you think Sprinkle gave you the boots?

"I don't know—he crazy. I took them home to my mother. I told her what they had told me, and she thought I was lying and made me go to bed."

Brad, what was your reaction when Sprinkle said he had just killed a boy?

"I was scared as hell! I knew they was telling the truth."

Why did you believe him?

"Because he handed me them bloody boots."

There was blood on the boots?

"Yes!"

Brad, Sprinkle was wearing the boots during the murder. He must have taken them off afterward.

"I think they was the boy's boots."

Brad, the victim wasn't wearing cowboy boots. He was wearing dress shoes.

"All this time I thought they were the boy's boots."

How were Sprinkle and Perruquet acting?

"Like they was on top of the world. They was on a rush or a high or something—like they got high off killing the boy."

Tell me about their physical appearances.

"Sweaty, dirty. They was real dirty. Hair all messed up. Looked like they'd been in a fight."

What's your most vivid memory of the encounter?

"Them boots ... brown, pointed-toe cowboy boots, blood on the toes and on the sides of the boots. Dark brown, stitches up the side."

You knew Billy Sprinkle from the neighborhood. What kind of kid was Billy?

"He wanted to be known all the time like he's the toughest man on the block."

Did you know Perruquet?

"I just know he was Billy's little flunky."

Were you afraid of Billy Sprinkle?

"No. I've got six brothers."

Gladys, what are your memories of the day of the murder?

"It was a bowling night. I'm getting ready to go, and this one comes in with boots. I said, 'You're not taking anything from Billy Sprinkle' because I knew he wasn't so cool. And he was asking me to go with him by the school, because Billy had told them where the body was. I said, 'Billy's just lying; I'm late for bowling.' So I went, and when I got there I found out someone had been killed behind the school! I immediately called the police and told them that we had those boots. And they came and got the boots. Then I think you went down there and made a statement, didn't you?"

"Yes," Brad says.

"They said he probably wouldn't have to testify," Gladys says. "They knew the Sprinkles were rowdy people. And they said if we had any problems with the

Sprinkle brothers, because they were all bad people, too, that they would give us protection or whatever, but we didn't have a problem."

Gladys, did you personally know any of the Sprinkles?

"No, the kids just knew them. They lived three or four blocks down the street. They had a reputation, and I just thought Billy was lying. I was shocked when I found out about the murder because I was thinking about how the father found him. I worked with his father at the Joliet Arsenal, and if I would have gone over there with Brad, I could have spared him the agony of finding his boy."

Brad, can you recall everything that happened that day from the time you got home from school?

"I was passing papers. They came up and said they took a slab or something, and Sprinkle done smashed his head, like this," says Brad, showing how Sprinkle re-enacted hoisting the concrete block over his head and thrusting it downward. "Then they both started laughing. Did they smash his head with a cement block?"

Yes, Brad, they did. What exactly did Sprinkle say to you when he and Perruquet approached you.

"He said, 'Hey, we just killed a boy, smashed his head and cut off his penis and stuck it in his mouth,' and then they gave me the pair of bloody boots."

Excuse me, Brad, Sprinkle said that—that he cut off the boy's penis?

"Yeah, Billy Sprinkle."

Brad, are you positive that Sprinkle boasted about cutting off the boy's penis?

"Right, that's what he told me. Did they?"

They did not. Did you tell anyone what Sprinkle said—about cutting off the boy's penis and sticking it in his mouth?

"Oh, yeah, I told my mom. I told everybody. All this time, I thought that's what happened."

Brad, is it possible that Sprinkle didn't say that about the penis, that you heard the rumor later from someone else, and now it's all mixed together in your memory?

"No, that's not possible. Billy Sprinkle said it."

9

David on Their Minds

Ray is the booming baritone. Marilyn is the lilting soprano. Ray Stukel is always in the mood for a debate, which sometimes causes rifts in the ranks, but there's no debating who is the sweeter half of this union.

Ray is a man of many facets. There is white-collar Ray, who for twenty-six years worked at the Joliet Arsenal. There is blue-collar Ray, who can wire a house. And there is artistic Ray, who can capture the essence of the great outdoors with bold brush strokes. Ray has the hands of a pipe fitter and the heart of a poet. He is multi-talented, but he is not complicated. You don't have to guess what's on his mind because he'll tell you, and when Ray thinks he's right, he doesn't back down, which explains the two bobblehead beagles on the dashboard of his spotless '96 Buick Century.

"They respond *'Yes'* to everything I say," Ray says.

Marilyn Stukel has an angelic smile, short-cropped white hair, and soft blue eyes. She loves to read and sink her hands into the soil. She is a homebody whose craft work can be spotted throughout her home.

Marilyn is the embodiment of the 1950s housewife who raises a family and runs the home. She is a sensitive, gentle woman who has a simple philosophy: Be nice to people.

"I talk to people," Marilyn says. "There's always someone coming up to me and talking in stores. There are some people just walking around, and they're lonesome and just want someone to stop and talk to them, so I do."

In the fall of 1948, Ray Stukel, twenty-two, and Marilyn Meurer, eighteen, formally met at Montgomery Ward, where Marilyn was a bookkeeper.

"On Monday nights, the stores stayed open till nine, so my friends and I would go downtown and roam the streets," Ray says. "And we just happened to go into Montgomery Wards that night, and I started talking to her."

The office where Marilyn kept the books at Montgomery Ward was in the basement, hidden away from customer foot traffic, nestled at the base of a stairwell. Anyone other than a man on a mission would have had an impossible time locating her. Still, Ray claims that the meeting was accidental, even though the former first baseman played baseball with her brother and had spotted her in the stands at local league games.

"OK, I suppose I did go in specifically to see her," Ray finally concedes.

Three years later, in May 1951, Ray and Marilyn married. The next year, Debbie was born, followed by David in '54 and Nancy in '57.

Ray and Marilyn Stukel in 1951.

When asked to recite the date of their wedding anniversary, Ray responds in his finest debate voice:

"May … 12 … 1951!"

"Good boy!" Marilyn says.

When quizzed if they remember when and where Ray proposed, they respond as one:

"No!"

"Did you say yes, dear?" Ray sheepishly asks.

"I said maybe!"

"*Maybe*, Marilyn? Fifty-some years later, and it's still maybe!"

"You know, Ray, David told me that he was gonna marry me when he grew up."

"I'd marry you too, dear, when I grow up."

"Well, Ray, we're still waiting for that to happen, aren't we?"

David Raymond Stukel entered the world at eight pounds, four ounces, on May 24, 1954. He was a good baby and a good, cordial young boy who most days was kind to his sisters.

Telling Ray and Marilyn what a pleasure it was to have known their choirboy of a son is like preaching to the choir. Their responses to one comment—"Tell me about David"—leave no doubt about how much the time their son graced their lives means to them.

"Even as a baby, he had a really good temperament," Marilyn says.

"He was a good sleeper almost from the time we brought him home," Ray says. "And as a youngster, David was never a problem. If you asked him to do something, he just smiled and did it. And he never asked for money, did he?"

"No, Ray, he was fine with what he had. David was a good boy, and he was a jokester. When we'd take a picture, he was always finding something to put on his head just before the picture was taken. There he'd be in the photo with a stuffed animal or something on his head."

"Something he used to do—he'd make me feel pain just by looking at him—he could walk on his toes!" Ray says. "He'd be barefoot and be walking on the knuckles of his toes. He'd laugh, and I'd cringe."

"Right up on his toes like a ballerina," Marilyn says.

"If he was with kids that started to swear, he would walk away from them," Ray says.

"He did? How do you know that, Ray?" Marilyn asks.

"After he was gone, some of his buddies told me that David just walked away from swearing," Ray says.

"When Nancy came along, David and her got along beautifully," Marilyn says. "They played with their toy cars. He loved putting together model cars. I've still got a bunch of the cars he didn't finish."

"Our grandsons and granddaughter have played with those cars," Ray says.

"And now our great grandsons, too," Marilyn says.

"In school, David never had any conduct problems," Ray says.

"Oh, Ray, David had the devil in him! He and Francis Ruettiger, they were troublemakers at noontime at school," says Marilyn, citing the day that David, best friend Francis, and a few other classmates lifted a female teacher's sports car and placed it in a different parking spot.

"He'd grasp things real quick," Ray says.

"David was intelligent. He was a thinker," Marilyn says. "I enjoyed talking to him. He was a good listener."

"In sports, he was out there to have fun, but he was competitive," Ray says. "He didn't need a lot of coaxing to play sports. He had some natural ability. He wasn't real tall, but he was quick."

"And he was going to get taller," Marilyn says.

"He had pretty good size feet," Ray says.

"We had just bought him new shoes from Penny's just before he got killed," Marilyn says. "He was wearing the dressy brown shoes that day."

"He was just starting to get his growth spurt," Ray says. "I'm five-ten and a half, and I'll bet he would have been at least that—maybe six feet."

After the murder of their son and brother, Ray, Marilyn, Debbie, and Nancy Stukel relied upon a phenomenal magnitude of fortitude to deal with their devastating loss. During the long days that magnified David's absence, Marilyn wanted people to talk about her son, but few were comfortable even speaking his name.

"Family and friends were afraid to talk about David. I'd say, 'David was a person! He was here!' I needed to talk about David."

For several months after David's death, most days Marilyn could not reel in her emotions.

"Right after David died, we painted my mom's two-story house. All the kids were there, all my nieces and nephews. We were in the back. And I walked to the front of the house and started crying. I thought, 'Hey, David should be here today.' It was a beautiful fall day, 'He should be here, too!' And I remember going to the doctor's office for a checkup, and he asked me, 'How are you doing?' And I said, 'Well, I'm breathing.' That's how I felt back then—that I was just breathing, not much more."

If we are measured by how well we handle adversity, then Ray and Marilyn Stukel are extraordinary people. Still, there were times when Ray thought, "This isn't really happening. I'm going to go home, and he's going to be there."

"It's the way he went, and so suddenly. That was a shocker," Marilyn says.

"You couldn't believe that it happened to us," Ray says.

"But I never thought about giving up," Marilyn says.

"I got depressed, but dying is part of living," Ray says. "You don't dwell on it. You start thinking good thoughts, and you do something!"

"Yes, dying is part of living, Ray, but not everybody dies that young—that way. What was really hard was when I was taking the girls to East High, and I'd think, 'I'm passing that spot where it happened to him.' I cried every day. Ray never knew that. I didn't want him to know. I'd drop them off and come home crying. Then I'd scrub the floor and be crying. But I'd stay busy."

"That's the thing, you keep busy. There's one of my hobbies," says Ray, pointing to one of several paintings jockeying for wall space throughout the ranch-style home they moved into seventeen years after their son's murder—three miles east of their former home—in New Lenox, just outside Joliet.

"Ray's going to paint us out of the house!" Marilyn says. "I did a lot of crafts after David died. It helped me, but grieving was a slow process. We took a lot of color slides of the kids before David died. It took a couple of years before I could look at them. It was tough seeing him so full of life. Around the house, I couldn't look at a picture of him, so I took them all down. And I didn't disturb his room for about a year. Finally, I put his trophies in a box and gave his clothes away."

Ray Stukel helped coach a youth baseball team in 1964 that included son David (middle row, left).

After seeing his son's body the night of the murder, Ray Stukel returned home and embraced Marilyn before slipping out the back door to be by himself. "I followed Ray because I didn't want him to be alone," Marilyn says. "I told him, 'We've got to be strong for our daughters.'"

In the 1950s and '60s, Ray Stukel was a typical post-World War II father who followed the pink-and-blue blueprint for raising girls and boys. He painted a large baseball crossed by two Louisville Sluggers on the ceiling of David's bedroom, and he drew a large gem on the ceiling of the bedroom Debbie and Nancy shared. Welcome to the pre-Title IX world of team sports in which boys played, girls watched, and tennis balls were white. Despite the times, life for Debbie and Nancy was hardly all cupcakes and curtsies. They climbed trees and skinned their knees. They played in pickup baseball games and preferred the White Sox to bobby socks.

Ray loved his children equally, but he connected with David in the special way that fathers and sons often bond.

"We never felt slighted," Debbie says. "They didn't have girls' sports like they do now. Dad took David hunting and always spent time with him playing basketball or baseball. And he even helped coach David's basketball and baseball teams, but Nancy and I didn't think anything of it. That's just the way it was back then."

A few months after the murder, Ray Stukel had an epiphany: The tragedy of losing his son opened his eyes to the many splendors of his daughters.

"You'd be surprised what I saw in those two girls after David was gone," Ray says. "I had focused a lot of attention on David, but I found my girls liked to fish! They liked to play golf! I had a lot of fun with them just doing things I would have done with the boy. All of a sudden I opened my eyes to how special they really were."

When their brother died, Debbie was a sixteen-year-old high school junior, and Nancy was eleven and in sixth grade. Debbie, now in her mid-fifties, is five feet eight, assertive, and independent. Nancy, in her late forties, is five feet four, sensitive, and introverted. Debbie lives in Morris, twenty-five miles west of her parents. Nancy is literally the girl next door to her parents. Debbie got married at twenty-one and had two children in her early twenties. Nancy married at thirty-seven and had two children in her late thirties and early forties. While Nancy was raising toddlers, Debbie was spoiling grand-toddlers.

It wasn't until Debbie and Nancy had children that they fully understood the strength their parents had to muster to carry on after David's death.

"As a parent, now you know how devastating it had to be," Debbie says. "My parents showed tremendous courage. David's death makes you question your faith. Why does this happen to good people? Before that, my parents would get down on their knees every night and pray. Then that happened—it just tore them apart."

"It had to be overwhelming for my parents," Nancy says. "It was hard to think about David without thinking, 'Why isn't he here?' I wondered, 'How could a loving God let something like this happen?'"

Debbie has dealt with two tragedies in her life—the murder of her brother and the death of her husband—twenty-nine years apart.

After David died, Debbie leaned on husband Gregg. After Gregg died, she immersed herself in her work and caring for her two sons.

"After David, I would think, 'I'm going to wake up, and it's a bad dream,' and after Gregg, I would always expect him to come walking in the door," Debbie says. "Until David's first practice at East High, the three of us had always packed into Gregg's little blue Rambler and gone to and from school. David rode to school with us that morning. If he just would have called, we could have picked him up. After David died, Gregg changed for a while. We all changed for a while."

In the 1960s, Nancy shared a bedroom with Debbie, but it was David with whom she shared her heart.

"I looked up to him, and he was good to me," Nancy says. "He always let me tag along, which was a pretty good thing for a big brother to do with a little sister."

In the days and months following David's death, Nancy was drawn to her brother's room.

"I would go into David's room and just look around, see his things. It was a strange feeling because he wasn't there," Nancy says. "It was a long time before I moved into his room, but after a while I felt comfort being there, being closer to him. I think he's always been with me. I don't think he ever leaves me. I do feel that. And I don't know if that's his spirit or memories or what you'd attribute that to, but he's just kind of part of me."

Nancy, who was comforted by the fact David always would choose her in neighborhood pickup games, relishes memories of David's sense of humor.

"David was kindhearted and loving, but he had a bit of mischief in him. My dad's parents lived in the same neighborhood as us, and Grandpa used to come over I don't know how many times a day, and if we were watching TV, he'd just come right in and turn the TV to whatever he wanted to watch, so one day David stood behind the door and Grandpa was trying to push it open, and my brother was standing there holding it shut. We kept hearing Grandpa yell, 'The door's stuck. I can't get it open.' We just stood there laughing."

Debbie was often the recipient of David's antics.

"I had this frilly-type skirt, and one time he put on my skirt and was dancing around the house. It was hilarious. But I was mad. I said, 'Get that off!' and chased him around the house, which I had to do a few times over the years, and he'd just laugh because he knew he could outrun me."

Nancy could always count on David being her eyes and ears during the Christmas season.

"My brother always knew what every present was under the tree. He would shake them, and he could tell by the shape. My mom and dad would let us open one present on Christmas Eve, and if there was one thing that I really wanted, like a certain doll or something, my brother would let me know: 'Now this is the one you want to open.'"

David and Nancy Stukel in 1966.

In high school, Nancy displayed incredible stick-to-itiveness after David's death. She entered East High in the fall of '71, which would have been David's senior year, and she did not miss one day of school, for four years traveling in a vehicle—never on foot—past the spot where David died.

Asked if she ever considered seeing a psychologist to help deal with the loss of David, Nancy replies: "No, it's nothing a good cry every once in a while doesn't help. And then you pick yourself up and you go on. I had to be determined to keep going after David died. The kid that I was then—that eleven-year-old child—that was another lifetime. And that was it. I was a kid up until that time. Then, after he died, you're no longer a kid."

10

Courting Justice

After James Perruquet's early-morning confession, he and Billy Rose Sprinkle spent what little was left of the night in makeshift holding cells, awaking to the clamor of adult inmates stirring at the Joliet City Jail. It was their first of what would be thousands of mornings behind bars. Sprinkle and Perruquet hid behind bravado. They relished the attention and did not begin to comprehend the seriousness of their crimes. But they would go to bed that night with less swagger and more understanding of the travails that awaited them.

At the 6 p.m. arraignment, Sprinkle and Perruquet were indicted for deviate sexual assault and murder. State's attorney George Sangmeister and his assistant, Martin Rudman, filed a motion requesting that further action on the indictment be suspended until they can file a petition with family court to have the case transferred to the criminal division.

At eight o'clock, Family Court Judge Angelo Pistilli granted the delay.

At nine, Judge Pistilli addressed the same two boys whom he had placed on "Friendly Supervision" four months earlier.

Public defender Thomas Vinson and assistant Sam Andreano were appointed to represent the boys, and Vinson asked to have the recording of the confession played for him before cross-examining coroner Willard Blood and investigator Dennis Jaskoviak. The court took a ninety-minute recess while Vinson and Andreano listened to the graphic confession by Perruquet and the statements of denial by Sprinkle.

At 11:30, Judge Pistilli ordered the murder suspects confined to the city jail.

Ten days later, prosecutors Sangmeister and Rudman filed the petition in family court seeking the transfer of the case to the criminal division, citing the heinous nature of the crime. Having listened to Perruquet's shockingly graphic confession nine days earlier, public defenders Vinson and Andreano did not object to the move.

The next day, Judge Pistilli allowed the transfer.

"It was a rather vicious crime," recalls Sangmeister.

"It's a difficult decision. These kids have their whole futures ahead of them. But this case was heinous enough, and it appeared that these two could repeat. They had tempers, that type of demeanor. I thought, 'If there ever was a case for prosecution as adults, this was it.'"

The days, weeks, and months after David Stukel's murder were unbearable for his family. And, compounding the Stukels' grief, they were receiving taunting phone calls most every night.

"They used to call and ask for David," Marilyn says. "It was a young kid, a boy. It was almost a Southern voice, a drawl: *Is Daaaavid theeeere? Is Daaaavid theeeere?* I got tired of it. I didn't want to hear it anymore, so I called the police and they took care of it."

"We thought it might have been one of the families of the boys who killed David," Ray says. "After we called the police, the calls stopped."

For Marilyn, the worst moment of the post-homicide ordeal occurred at a courthouse hearing, when she saw her son's murderers for the first time.

"I was in the courtroom when they brought those two boys in. I wanted to see what they looked like and hear what they had to say. Boy, I was gung-ho. I wanted to hear everything that happened, why it happened. Well, I'm hearing details, and I'm looking at these two boys and it was horrible, so I left and never went back. When the lawyers started saying what the boys did to David, I lost it. I couldn't stay."

Before another hearing, Ray had a chance meeting with Sprinkle and Perru-quet outside the courthouse.

"The deputy was bringing them in, and they were laughing and smiling like they had done something great. Good thing I didn't have a gun on me, I think I'd have shot them both. It's just the way I felt that day. They were acting like big shots. It was all a joke to them. They were having a good time. This was a thrill-killing. I heard they had already killed cats and dogs, and they just wanted to see what it was like to kill somebody."

At the time of David Stukel's murder, Democrat George Sangmeister was fin-ishing up his term as state's attorney. In January, Republican Louis Bertani was in charge, having unseated Sangmeister in the November election. Will County's top attorney had changed, but the one constant in both regimes was assistant Martin Rudman.

Prosecutor Martin Rudman

"The most significant aspect of the Stukel case was getting it transferred from the juvenile court," says Rudman, who was state's attorney from 1972 to '76 and served as an associate judge from 1986 to '99.

"If left in juvenile court, they would have walked at twenty-one," says Rudman, who has no difficulty recalling the case, one of several cases he handled from both sides of the bench.

"No question it was bad. It was among the worst in how you die. And it is true that it always tugs more at your heart when it's a child, because when a child dies, they don't get a shot at life."

Rudman explains why he believes that public defender Vinson, who died in 1987, did not attempt to quash the transfer of the case to the criminal division.

"You could never get a set of facts worse than this, so if you didn't transfer in this situation, you'd never transfer."

Rudman also defends Family Court Judge Pistilli, who died 1994, for his decision not to block the transfer.

"Judge Pistilli on more than one occasion had declined to transfer to the adult division, so this wasn't a gimme, where you'd always get a transfer. But in the Stukel case, it was just so bad. This case is just as gross as it gets, so that's why he transferred it."

Six months after receiving probations on the pre-murder burglary charge, Billy Rose Sprinkle and James Perruquet were scheduled to appear before Judge Pistilli in family court to receive their "Earn a Dismissal" certificates. Instead, they were shackled defendants charged as adults with murder and deviate sexual assault, and appearing in criminal court before Judge Michael Orenic, who denied their public defenders' request to suppress statements made the night of the murder.

Judge Orenic, a widower and father of nine children who served for twenty-six years as a circuit court judge in Will County, will tell you that he chose law school because he couldn't find an architecture program that met his needs.

"When architecture didn't work out, my dad says, 'Why don't you go to law school?' I hadn't the slightest idea what law was all about. When I became a lawyer in 1950, I'd never been in a courthouse, a courtroom, or even a lawyer's office!"

Orenic will insist that the reason he ran for judge was because he was having trouble supporting his wife and expanding family in the early '60s.

"I wasn't getting wealthy, and the judges had a hell of a good pension plan!"

Orenic will scoff at those who say he was too lenient.

"You don't use a slide rule to decide the disposition of a case. You use common sense. I did not kick the crap out of a guy just because he was a criminal. I always wanted to do what was the right thing. And even if I had to bend the law a little bit to get there, I would do what is right. I did the job the best I could, then I took my robe off and went home."

Actually, Mike Orenic walked home. Each weekday morning, Orenic would traverse the Jefferson Street drawbridge to the downtown courthouse, hold court, then make the one-mile trek back to the family's Near West Side home.

"We only had one car, and my wife needed it to get the kids from here to there and back," Orenic says.

In the mid-'60s, Orenic responded to wife Kate's displeasure with his crew cut by letting his hair grow.

"She got tired of the crew cut, so I just stopped getting haircuts!" Orenic says.

One Saturday, the longish-haired Orenic—donning handyman's attire and appearing more crooked than courtly behind the wheel of his beat-up Volkswagen bus—was mistaken for a burglary suspect.

"The description was that the guy looked raggedy and was driving a junky car," Orenic says. "Six squad cars surrounded my bus! I put my hands above the steering wheel so they could see I wasn't armed. When they saw me, it was, 'Oh! It's you Judge!'"

Three weeks after the murder, Billy Rose Sprinkle and James David Perruquet faced Judge Orenic and pled "Not Guilty" to the charges of murder and deviate sexual assault. Orenic accepted public defender Vinson's motion for separate trials, and the first trial date—for Perruquet—was set for January 6, 1969.

State's attorney Sangmeister objected to the date and recommended November 25.

"We are ready to go to trial at any time … tomorrow if necessary," Sangmeister said.

Public defender Vinson argued that he cannot be ready for trial before January.

Orenic allowed the January court date to stand.

Will County was prepared to prosecute the defendants in separate trials. Every piece, including jury selections, was in place for justice to run its course, but in a shocking twist, on January 6, 1969, Sprinkle and Perruquet changed their pleas from "Not Guilty" to "Guilty."

"All of a sudden, there was no trial," Marilyn Stukel says. "That was the end of it. I was surprised by that. I don't know what their thinking was, but the lawyers never asked us what we thought."

"I heard nothing about a plea bargain," Ray Stukel says. "All I know is that they decided to have the judge sentence them, not to have a jury trial. They said they were going to talk to us during the process. They said they were going to let us know everything that was going on. I don't know if we could have approved it or not, but we were never given an option. We would have just liked to have heard our options, but we weren't included."

"Everything was behind the scenes," Marilyn says. "And I guess we weren't too sharp."

"What else could we have done—sit down on the steps of the courthouse and ask 'em every day what was going on?" Ray says.

The Stukels now agree that sitting through one trial, let alone two, would have been intolerable.

"Maybe it's best there wasn't a trial," Ray says. "At least the little bums saved the taxpayers some money by confessing. I was just hoping that while they were in prison somebody would put the shiv to both of them. Your armed robbers and offenders like that, they frown on sexual assaults."

On January 6, 1969, James Perruquet and Billy Rose Sprinkle stand before Judge Michael Orenic at the brand-new Will County Courthouse, a four-story mass of concrete and tinted windows. The state is represented by Louis Bertani and Martin Rudman. Perruquet and Sprinkle sit at the defense table with Thomas Vinson and Sam Andreano.

Judge Michael Orenic

When Judge Orenic addresses Perruquet and Sprinkle, he speaks in a stern, fatherly tone. The co-defendants respond politely, if not assuredly, to each query:

Now, Mr. Perruquet and Mr. Sprinkle, you are entitled to a trial by a jury to determine the question of your guilt or innocence. Do you understand that if I accept your plea of guilty, there won't be a jury trial; there won't be any question of guilt or innocence? Mr. Perruquet, do you understand there won't be a trial?

"Yes, sir," says Perruquet.

Mr. Sprinkle, do you understand?

"Yes, sir," says Sprinkle.

Now, you have a right to be represented by lawyers of your choosing or by the public defender. I have appointed Mr. Vinson and Mr. Andreano to represent you gentlemen. Are you satisfied with those appointments?

"Yes, sir," says Perruquet.

"Yes, sir," says Sprinkle.

Knowing your right to be tried by a jury to determine the question of your guilt or innocence, do you, Mr. Perruquet, still desire to withdraw your plea of not guilty, and to enter the plea of guilty to the charges of murder and deviate sexual assault?

"Yes, sir."

And you, Mr. Sprinkle, do you still desire to withdraw your plea of not guilty, and to enter the plea of guilty to the charges of murder and deviate sexual assault?

"Yes, sir."

Mr. Perruquet, has anybody made promises to induce you to withdraw your plea of not guilty to guilty?

Before Perruquet can answer, Rudman addresses the judge:

"Your Honor, the state has represented to Mr. Vinson and Mr. Andreano that if both Mr. Perruquet and Mr. Sprinkle entered pleas of guilty for the offense of murder, we would recommend a sentence of not less than seventy-five nor more than ninety years, and for the offense of deviate sexual assault, the state would recommend a sentence of not less than thirteen nor more than fourteen years, and that the sentences be served concurrently."

Vinson interjects, "That is correct, your Honor, and I will indicate to the court that we have conferred in-depth with each of the defendants and with their parents."

All right. Mr. Perruquet. You heard the state's attorney recommendation, and you heard the statement of Mr. Vinson. Are these statements correct?

"Yes, sir."

How about you, Mr. Sprinkle—are their statements made about recommendations correct?

"Yes, sir."

You understand that the recommendations that have been made are not necessarily binding on the Judge. The Judge does not have to follow them. You understand that, Mr. Perruquet?

"Yes," says Perruquet, his voice lacking conviction.

Well? Do you understand?

"Not too clearly," says Perruquet.

Well, you have been told that, haven't you?

"Yes, sir."

You have been told that too, haven't you, Mr. Sprinkle?

"Yes, sir."

Has anybody threatened you in any way to force you to plead guilty, Mr. Perruquet?

"No, sir."

Mr. Sprinkle?

"No, sir."

Mr. Perruquet, are you pleading guilty because you really are guilty?

"Yes, sir."

Mr. Sprinkle, are you pleading guilty because you really are guilty?

"Yes, sir."

All right, Mr. Vinson. Have the defendants step up here for sentencing.

The young co-defendants rise and approach the bench wearing white dress shirts, open at the neck, and dark trousers. Their hair is neatly combed, their heads bowed.

Their mothers weep.

Stoic Ray Stukel and teary-eyed Marilyn Stukel sit in the first row behind Bertani and Rudman.

In the hushed courtroom, Judge Orenic peers above his black-rimmed reading glasses and down at Sprinkle and Perruquet. With a hint of disgust in his voice, Orenic delivers a sobering dose of reality to the co-defendants:

Mr. Perruquet and Mr. Sprinkle, I am going to follow the recommendation of the state's attorney with respect to the sentence to be imposed. And I will just tell you one thing now, and I think you are both old enough to understand what I am saying. In fact, I am sure you are. The only thing that keeps you boys out of the electric chair is your age. If you were older, you would be sentenced to death—that I can assure you because of the viciousness of your crime. But because of your age, I am going to follow the recommendation of the state's attorney.

After Judge Orenic closes the proceedings, Ray and Marilyn Stukel walk out of the courtroom and into the hallway, where Lorraine Sprinkle, Billy's older sister, approaches them.

"She says, 'I hope you're satisfied!'" recalls Ray. "She hopes I'm satisfied? My son is dead! I'll never see him again in this life, and she hopes I'm satisfied? I thought, 'Satisfied? Give me my son back, then I'll be satisfied.' She's blaming us for her poor little brother having to go to jail. Like it was our fault."

"We did not respond to her," Marilyn says. "We just walked away. We were shocked, but you've got to remember who you're dealing with. They don't understand what they did to this family."

11

Behind Closed Doors

Billy Rose Sprinkle was a slick kid who learned from his father and older brothers that less is best when talking to the authorities, so while James Perruquet confessed, Sprinkle said little of significance to detectives in the early-morning hours after the murder. In his taped statements, Sprinkle denied any wrongdoing. But less than five minutes after leaving the crime scene, he boasted to the two boys across the street from East High that he and Perruquet had committed a murder.

"Not confessing doesn't mean anything because Sprinkle made statements to third parties," former prosecutor Martin Rudman says. "That's the way he gets convicted. How does he explain the comments to the two boys? You know, you have arguments when you make confessions, 'Well, they browbeat me. They coerced me.' What arguments do you have if your mouth is opening up to two kids on the street?"

"Two mouths talking," says former investigator Dennis Jaskoviak. "Bragging to the two boys convicts Sprinkle. A confession wasn't necessary."

There wasn't the possibility of Sprinkle and Perruquet being tried together, says Rudman.

"There's a problem of constitutionality. If you try two people together, and this one confessed and this one didn't, this one's confession is hurting the one that didn't, and he's saying, 'Why am I being tried with a guy who confessed? That's hearsay. I should be tried by myself.' That was the idea of severance."

Former public defender Sam Andreano says Perruquet's statements still could have hurt Sprinkle.

"They would never have allowed Perruquet's confession to be used against Sprinkle. Now, if Perruquet wanted to come and take the stand at Sprinkle's trial, they would have allowed it."

In the 1970s and 1980s, if you were working in the field of law in Will County and Martin Rudman threw a party in your honor, it was a sign that you had arrived or—more to the point—you had arrived decades ago, enjoyed an illustrious career, and had reached a milestone. In the early 1970s, one such occasion was the party to commemorate Thomas Vinson's twenty-five years of service as public defender.

"We had a cake with the words of what one client had said to a judge in front of Tom," Rudman says. "The cake was in the shape of a book; the left-hand page read: I don't want the Public Defender. And the right-hand page read: I want a Real Lawyer."

Public defenders aren't often appreciated or praised, but Tom Vinson didn't enter the law field thirsting for accolades.

"Tom Vinson was a very seasoned lawyer," Rudman says. "He was like an owl sitting on a branch. You had no clue from the expression on his face where he was coming from."

Vinson, who served as an associate judge in Will County after stepping down as public defender, lived his life to the letter of the law.

"He was dedicated to the law," Rudman says.

Public Defender
Tom Vinson

Dedicated to law in life and, apparently, in death.

Before passing away in September 1987, Thomas Vinson requested that his ashes be placed in front of the courthouse.

"Yes, it is my understanding that his ashes are buried at the courthouse," Rudman says. "As you face the building, it's in the grass to the right, on the west side. There was no formality to it. It was just done."

On the afternoon of Friday, January 3, 1969, three days before justice was to begin being played out in a Will County courtroom, Thomas Vinson was negotiating with the co-defendants and their families. Vinson met with Sprinkle and Perruquet, conferring with them separately and together. He also had conferences with their parents, Ed and Grace Sprinkle and Earnie and Hazel Perruquet, separately, jointly, and with their sons. Family members, including sixteen-year-old Joseph Perruquet and nineteen-year-old Lorraine Sprinkle, shuffled in and out of rooms. For three hours, Vinson encouraged the co-defendants to rescind their "Not Guilty" pleas and accept an agreement that would keep them from facing jury trials.

Shortly before 5 p.m., the boys and their parents, weary from the intense conferences, agreed to the plea bargain.

Four decades after Sprinkle and Perruquet accepted the plea bargains, there are accusations that the co-defendants were coerced by Vinson into changing their pleas.

"I remember Thomas Vinson coming in there," Lorraine Sprinkle says. "He says to Billy, 'Boy, if you don't plead guilty you're going to get the electric chair!' And Billy looked at me, and he was crying. He says, 'Well, then what should I do?' It was me, Mom and Dad, and Billy. Billy said it again, 'What should I do?' I didn't know nothing, and my parents just figured that was the best way to go because Vinson told them so. He said, 'If these boys don't plead guilty, they're going to get the electric chair!'"

Today, Billy Rose Sprinkle refuses to talk about the alleged death-penalty threats, any aspect of the case or his life. But his accomplice is an open book.

Through an exchange of letters over several months, James Perruquet answers all questions presented to him regarding the murder of David Stukel, and, in one correspondence, offers a version of the plea-bargain sequence that is strikingly similar to Lorraine Sprinkle's account:

We got totally tricked by Thomas Vinson. Billy and I was sitting beside each other, my mom and dad, Billy's mom and dad and Lorraine, and my brother Joe. Tom Vinson looked in and said there's nothing I can do for these boys. If you want to save their lives, they gotta plead guilty. If they don't plead guilty, they're going to find them guilty and give them the electric chair. My brother Joe said No, that's bull! Vinson turned to my mom and told my mom if you don't get him out of here, there ain't nothing I can do for James. Joe told us not to take the deal and Vinson ran Joe off. They took Billy and his family into the jury room, talked to them, came back and lay the law down on me, Mom, who had been crying, and Dad. Then they had us all back together. We all set there, my mom's crying, Billy's mom's crying. My dad had tears in his eyes. Billy's dad had tears in his eyes. And they told us again, If you guys don't plead guilty, you're going to die. We was like—what do you mean plead guilty? But we did. Vinson lied to both of us, had us both wondering what we gotta do to stay out of the electric chair. My mom and dad didn't know any better and Billy and me was both kinda dumbfounded.

Thomas Vinson is not alive to refute accusations that he force-fed death-penalty threats to the young defendants and their families, but former colleagues are quick to defend him.

"I don't recall the plea-bargain process because Mr. Vinson handled all that," says Sam Andreano, who succeeded Vinson as public defender in 1972 and served in that position for twenty years. "But knowing Mr. Vinson, he would never have said, 'Rest assured these boys are going to get the death penalty.' I don't know what he said, but he would not have said, 'Plead guilty or you're going to get the chair.'"

Martin Rudman wholeheartedly agrees that Vinson would not have used the death penalty to extract plea bargains from the young defendants.

"No way! I don't think that the death penalty was a realistic bargain because I can't conceive of any judge giving fourteen-year-olds the death penalty in those days or now. When people are bargaining, they are bargaining against what a judge is likely to do. As lawyers, we were not in the habit of making idle threats, and Tom Vinson knew exactly who he was in front of. When you're dealing with lawyers who are in court every day and who are operating in the same courts as you are and know the same judges as you do, you don't negotiate that way. We all knew Judge Orenic, and the odds of Orenic putting a fourteen-year-old to death was slightly less than snow in July."

Although Rudman doesn't believe the death penalty was used to gain the pleas, he has an idea of what might have induced deals.

"One of the things they were eligible for is consecutive sentences, and that would have been a basis for a plea bargain. The deviate sexual assault occurred first, then the homicide, and there is a possibility they could have had to serve the first sentence, then serve the second one—so making the sentences concurrent, that would have been a legitimate compromise to going to trial."

Rudman says Vinson would not have sought a plea bargain unless it was in the best interest of his clients.

"Tom Vinson was not a lay-down type person. If he thought he had a chance of getting a favorable result from a jury, he wasn't going to plead the guy. That was just the kind of guy he was, so he wasn't walking these people through the system."

12

Where's the Love?

When his children were young, rugged Ed Sprinkle didn't shy away from disciplining them, oftentimes with his fists. While Ed worked long days, wife Grace spent her days at home drinking beer.

In 1963, ten-year-old Billy Rose Sprinkle's role model, fifteen-year-old brother Johnny Ray, was sniffing glue, drinking whiskey, and skipping school, so Ed Sprinkle, in an attempt to scare some sense into the boy, reportedly arranged for him to spend some time in an Illinois Youth Commission facility.

Ed Sprinkle and his fourth child, daughter Lorraine.

"Dad figured jail was the best place for Johnny," says Lorraine Sprinkle, a year younger than Johnny. "With my dad, when you got out of line, you got your ass beat. If he told you to get out there and move this pile of rocks from one spot to another and then put them back, you better do what he says. He was a tough one, but he was a good one."

After Johnny was released from a suburban Chicago juvenile facility, he continued his reckless ways for more than twenty-five years and died of pneumonia at forty-two.

"Johnny loved his beer," says Warren Barker, who married Lorraine in 1984. "Johnny loved to fish and he drank beer. I remember when we lived in the trailer by Lorraine's dad's house—I'd be sitting there eating my breakfast at seven o'clock in the morning at a picnic table, and I'd hear, *'Poooosh,'* and I'd say, 'Johnny's up.'"

Long before Johnny passed away, he passed down his rebellious tendencies to brother Billy, born five and one-half years after Johnny. Billy began sniffing glue at ten, drinking and smoking at eleven, and having sex at twelve. And Billy passed down his penchant for sniffing glue to younger brother Steve.

"I was a little guy, maybe six when Billy had me sniff that glue," says Steve, three years younger than Billy.

Steve dropped out of East High at sixteen and began painting with twenty-five-year-old brother Johnny.

"Alcohol's been a problem my whole life," Steve says. "Beer was around so much when I was growing up, and I liked it. My dad never drank that much. My mom would drink beer all day long. She used to have it in a glass, and me and Stanley, we was little kids, seven or eight, and we used to go behind her rocking chair and sneak a drink or two. We thought we were cool. Next thing you know, we're starting to grow up and drinking all the time. When I quit school, I would paint with Johnny, and he'd drink two beers on the way to work and two beers on the way home. He'd always be sneaking beer to me, and before you know it, I was a hooked alcoholic. Johnny was a bad drinker. He drank himself to death. They say pneumonia is what killed him, but with all the alcohol he drank, he didn't have any strength to fight the pneumonia."

When Lorraine Sprinkle assesses the lives of family members, it is an examination steeped in alcohol.

"My mom would drink beer and say she was drinking coffee or tea. I never saw her *drunk* drunk. And I don't ever remember seeing my dad drunk but maybe twice. Johnny, he was a heavy drinker. And when I had my restaurant and cocktail lounge up north in Gurnee, I was drinking a quart of booze a day. I used to do my share of drugs, too, but I quit it cold turkey, just like the alcohol, more than twenty years ago."

Asked how she was able to overcome substance abuse when her siblings could not, Lorraine responds, "When you see a person going down a toilet, you don't want to be the next load of shit going down behind them."

Lorraine, who has not lived in the Joliet area for a quarter-century, is raising her daughter and son only an hour south of Joliet's East Side but a world removed from her violent childhood. Despite leaving that life behind, Lorraine hasn't dodged misfortune in recent years. Her left lung has shut down, and her right lung is operating at one-third capacity, the result of forty years of smoking. Her husband has been laid off, and worst of all, her daughter was molested before she turned sixteen by the father of one of the teen's friends.

"I'll tell you, God she's a strong little shit," Lorraine says. "That girl got on that witness stand, and she wasn't afraid. She never cracked. She just told it like it was. That son-of-a-bitch, he'll die in prison. Let me tell you something, I was raped when I was young and I can still smell that son-of-a-bitch's breath! I know what that girl is going through in her heart and in her mind. And she'll never, ever be the same."

Asked if she had been raped by someone she knows, Lorraine says:

"Yeah."

Did the person get sent away?

"Un-uh."

Why not?

"Because my mom wouldn't listen to me."

She didn't believe you?

"Nope."

Was it somebody you were dating?

"No, it was a brother."

Which brother?

"An older brother."

How old were you?

"I was very, very young, like eleven."

You told your mom but not your dad?

"I knew if I told my dad, my dad would kill my brother, and my dad would go to prison."

Did this happen once?

"No, no. That's why when I was old enough to have sex, that's where the drinking and drugs began because I couldn't have a relationship unless I was under the influence."

How many times were you raped?

"Quite a few times."

And your mom didn't believe you?

"Nope."

Did you go to your mom more than once?

"A couple of times. One time she slapped me and told me, 'I don't want to hear that trash. Not true!'"

How could you have been molested without someone noticing?

"The first time, we were coming home from the laundromat, and it was dark … in an alley."

Did he threaten you to not tell?

"Yeah."

Did he beat you?

"No, he covered my face with a pillow."

Cora Sprinkle, the wife of Jim Sprinkle, Ed and Grace's second child, was born in a refugee camp in Albania just months before her family crossed the border into Greece. Six years later the family immigrated to America. Growing up in an Albanian family in northern Illinois, Cora didn't have a traditional Midwestern upbringing.

"I wasn't even allowed to go to high school," Cora says. "I had three more months to go. I would have finished eighth grade when I quit school to go to work full time."

In March 1967, union painters Ed Sprinkle and sons Ross, Jim, and Johnny frequented the restaurant where Cora worked as a waitress. Nine months later, seventeen-year-old Cora eloped with twenty-three-year-old Jim.

"My parents believed in arranged marriages," Cora says. "They didn't believe in mixed marriages. If you're Albanian and you're a Muslim, you marry an Albanian Muslim. They would have never accepted Jim, and that's why I eloped."

While Cora was dating Jim without her parents' knowledge, she rarely set foot inside the Sprinkle home. But after she moved to the Sprinkle homestead for the first six months of her marriage, she was devastated by what she saw and heard.

"The Sprinkles reminded me of the outlaw Jessie James or Bonnie and Clyde," Cora says. "They were like a total shock, and my world collapsed."

Cora quickly realized that the person at the core of this terribly dysfunctional family was Grace Sprinkle.

"It was a heartless, cold home. There was evil present, and I think Billy and all those kids would have been good kids if it hadn't been for the mother. She was not a good person. She really didn't stop them from doing anything. I think she reared the kids wrong. She let them do whatever they wanted. There was a lot of cussing, swearing, you name it—it was there. I had never heard anybody call, especially family members, 'You mother fucker!' I think the dad was basically a good guy, but he wasn't always around. I never saw the dad drink. But the mother was home 24/7, and she drank. Granted, it was only beer, but enough beer to where she was mean, vulgar. One thing about Grace, she was a bad mother, but her kids could do no wrong. She did protect her chicks, even if they were wrong, but I didn't see any love in that house, not from her."

Cora says Grace didn't make any attempts to welcome her into the family.

"Jim's mother was verbally and emotionally abusive to me, and I just took it all. I'll give you an example of how cruel she was. My mother-in-law's washer broke once. It was just before Christmas, and I talked to Jim and I said, 'You know, I'd like to buy her a washer.' So we bought her a washer, and she said to me, 'That fucking thing isn't for me, is it?' I go, 'Well, yes. This way you don't have to wash by hand.' She says, 'I don't give a fuck! That's a house gift, not a Christmas present!' My heart just broke."

Cora says the Sprinkles shared a deep bond.

"The Sprinkles looked out for each other but not necessarily in a good way. If somebody was lying about something and they didn't want you to know, they would stick together on the lie. Like I had found out things about my husband that I didn't know, like he had been in prison [for burglary in the early 1960s] and they'd try to keep their story together on that. It was a close family but maybe close in the wrong ways sometimes."

Cora witnessed the destructive role alcohol played in the Sprinkle family.

"They are a strange kind of family, and I wish I would have never met them. They're just bad, so bad, and they constantly drank. Maybe there isn't anything wrong with drinking if you can drink one drink or two. But with the Sprinkles, it was to get drunk. After I saw what they do, I never wanted to be a drinker. I wish every distillery would blow up. That's how strongly I feel about alcohol."

James Perruquet and childhood friend Judi Jelley were born one month apart in southern Illinois, with James growing up in Herrin and Judi living seven miles up the road in Royalton. Judi and James and their families socialized, but most times it was alcohol—not their combined thirteen children—on the guest list.

Judi Jelley was just four years old when her father left the family and landed in Joliet, 260 miles to the north. Eight years later, Earnie and Hazel Perruquet decided to move their family to Joliet to be closer to fourteen-year-old son Joseph, who was caught stealing a car and sent to the same Chicago-area juvenile facility where Johnny Sprinkle had done time.

When Judi Jelley heard about the Perruquet family's decision to move to Joliet, the twelve-year-old seized the opportunity to get a fresh start with her father.

"I told my mom that I wanted to go, and she said, 'OK. Bye.' And that was it," Judi says.

When Judi Jelley speaks of the bleakness in James Perruquet's home life in Joliet, it is expressed in a sing-song fashion that could be the chorus of a country song:

His mama was a drunk.
His daddy was a drunk.
His brothers was drunks.

Although Judi says that violence was a staple in the Perruquet household, she spent as much time with the Perruquets as her strict father would allow.

"It was a mean, wild bunch. Those kids got more and harder whippings than anyone. Sometimes, all of them would be screaming and throwing stuff. I'm sure it wasn't a great life with all the fighting and whippings, but having a father like mine who was an emotional clump of wood and who'd soon as break his leg as tell you he loved you, to me that was worse than getting a whipping."

Like Cora Sprinkle, Judi Jelley blames the family matriarch for the unstable home life.

"Their mother was the mean one. She'd get drunk and beat her old man," Judi says. "I never seen him raise his hand to her, but she'd get drunk and she'd get on him bad. There was a bar right down by the corner, not half a block away from their house. I remember we'd go in the bar to ask their mom for money, and she'd give them money just to get rid of them.

"That was a wild house. I remember one time, and I don't know how serious they were, but I heard them say, 'Let's kill Dad. We'll push him down the stairs!'"

Amid the chaos of the Perruquet home, a strong bond blossomed between Judi and James.

"My brothers and sisters were older, so I saw more of James than my own family," Judi says. "He was like a brother. I practically lived at their house. James was a good kid. He was sweet and funny."

Judi's kinship with James led to an introduction to Billy Rose Sprinkle.

"I had a crush on Billy," Judi says. "Billy was a tough kid. We were all tough kids. I had this friend, Mary Kay. One day, when James wasn't there, Billy made me and Mary Kay fight. Billy threatened to whip our ass if we didn't. We were in an old, empty garage, and he said, 'Ain't nobody leaving here unless you fight.' I didn't want to hurt Mary Kay, but I was five-foot-eight. People sometimes mistook me for a teacher. We were both crying, and I hit Mary Kay and hurt her. I thought what he did was awful cruel. I stopped seeing Billy after that. That was the beginning of my thinking, 'What's wrong with him?'"

When the Perruquet family moved from Herrin to Joliet in 1966, they settled into a two-story home in a run-down area not far from Western Quarry. Earnie Sr. took a job as a laborer at the Joliet Arsenal, the same government organization that signed Ray Stukel's paychecks. Hazel, who didn't work in southern Illinois, took a job at a nursing home.

"My mom went to work, and she was drinking more," says James' younger sister Fern. "We didn't have that much supervision—except at nighttime when we were supposed to be in bed. Even then, we would sneak out. We could slip out a window onto the roof, then we'd step down to the bathroom roof on the lower level and jump off. When we moved to Joliet, our family life just went to hell. My parents tried to keep a tight rein on us. They bought us a season pass for the Joliet Beach Club over on Rowell Avenue, but I don't think we went there one time. We went across the street to the quarry instead. But they never even knew that.

Fern Perruquet at 13.

They never knew we found a dead man floating in the water at the quarry."

The best years for the Perruquet children came in southern Illinois.

"It wasn't a rose garden there either, but it was better," Fern says. "I think it's because we got out more, and we had things to do. We'd go on picnics and to the drive-in. As a family, we did more things together. We all hung out together, and then when we went to Joliet everybody kind of seemed to go crazy and everybody went their own way."

When it came to domestic violence, the Sprinkles had nothing on the Perruquets. As a twelve-year-old, James—after helping a firefighter put out a blaze—dreamed of becoming a fireman. But having ruined his winter coat in the process of being a "hero," James was severely whipped by a father who didn't see the beauty in a young boy's bravery.

Beatings in the Perruquet home were commonplace.

"I remember my dad one time hitting James in the head with a hammer," says Fern of her father who died in 1999 and whose mother has dementia and lives in southern Illinois. "James was working on the roof, and he did something wrong, so my dad whacked him with his hammer and knocked James clear off the roof! Other times, he'd hit James with boards or anything that was in arm's reach. I've got a dent in the back of my head where my mom hit me with a telephone. My parents were drunk every day. It wasn't a very happy childhood. We didn't get spankings with the belt or just a slap. We got hit with key chains and extension cords."

When asked if the abuse inside the Perruquet home extended beyond emotional and physical abuse, Fern pauses, then responds:

"Yeah."

Sexual abuse?

"Yeah, there was."

Was James sexually abused?

"I don't know. I couldn't tell you that."

Were females in your family sexually abused by male members of your family?

"These are hard questions that you're asking me."

I understand, Fern, and I'm sorry, but were you sexually abused as a child?

"Yes."

By a brother?

"Yes."

By James?

"No."

How old were you when this happened?

"Real young."

At what age?

"I'd say from ten on it never happened again."

Did it happen more than once?

"Yeah ... one of my brothers, he apologized to me."

Brothers? You were abused by more than one brother?

"Yes."

But not James?

"Right, not James. I don't hate my brothers. I just feel that if we had had more structural parenting while growing up, that stuff wouldn't have happened. I don't blame my parents either. I don't know. I really don't blame anybody. I've overcome it. I've got my own life now, and I don't ever think about it. It happens to a lot of people, and you can let it get you down and destroy your life or you can move on."

The day that James Perruquet participated in the murder of David Stukel, sister Fern was thirteen and in seventh grade at Gompers Junior High.

"I just couldn't believe he did it," says Fern, who rode the bus to school with James that morning. "I mean, I know he did it, but it was a total shock. I never asked James about the murder. I guess maybe I didn't want to know everything. James was a good kid up until that happened, a quiet kid."

Fern's life took a dramatic turn after the murder.

"It was rough when we had to go back to school. We took a lot of verbal abuse, even from teachers. They kind of classified you as a troublemaker. If people know you're from a family where somebody did something like that, they just treat you different. I quit school after the eighth grade. I would have gone to East High, and I didn't want to go to East 'cause that's where the boy they killed was from."

The conversation that Fern had with her mother at fifteen is strikingly similar to the one Judi Jelley had with her mother when she left home at twelve.

"I started running away when I was twelve," Fern says. "And I always told my younger sister, Tookie [Ila], 'If they let me go, I'm not ever coming back.' I had a kid at fifteen, and I told my mom, 'I'm leaving,' and she gave me my coat and said, 'Leave.' That was it. I couldn't handle the mental and physical abuse there anymore. It was an awful place to be. Now Tookie, she had to stay until she was seventeen, and she got the worst of it 'cause Mom's drinking got even worse."

Asked if her mom loved her and her siblings, Fern thinks about the query for several seconds, then says, "Did my mom love us? I don't think my mom even *liked* us."

13

A Glimpse into Their Worlds

Reminders that their son and brother was a murder victim are never far from the Stukel family. David is on their minds every holiday and at every family gathering. But there have been times when the reminders have hit too close to home.

In January 1975, Debbie Stukel and husband Gregg Skrtich, who married three years after graduating from East High, moved out of an apartment and—with two-month-old son Brad—settled into a new home on Kinder Drive in a new subdivision in Elwood, a tiny farming community south of Joliet.

Debbie gave birth to her second son, Kevin, three years later, and she took care of the home and the family while Gregg worked long days at ComEd, the regional power company.

Living just five miles south of East High but away from the East Side's rising crime rate, Debbie was immersed in a simple, good life with a loving husband who doted on his boys.

"I was raising children. I was happy, and at some point, I was able to get over that paranoid thinking of 'Oh my gosh, we don't want something terrible to happen to our children like it did to my brother,'" Debbie says. "But it was still, 'You go, but you go with friends.' It's hard because it's always there, even now, after all these years."

In the mid-1980s, Debbie's heart halted for a moment when she heard the name "Perruquet" in the neighborhood and realized that her brother's murder had followed her from the abandoned lot behind East High, across thousands of acres of farmland and miles of blacktop to 17641 Kinder Drive.

In 1973, Charlie Brown moved into a home at the corner of Kinder Drive and Ridge Road, just three houses down and across the street from where Debbie and her family would settle two years later. And in 1978, Charlie Brown, forty-six, welcomed twenty-three-year-old Fern Perruquet and her two children, Cecelia Perruquet, eight, and Dawn Mathis, five, into his home.

Charlie and Fern may have hooked up in '78, but their connection dated to the mid-1960s, when Charlie lived a few blocks from the Perruquets on Joliet's East Side. Charlie's daughter Sherry married Earnie Perruquet Jr. in 1968, and Fern, attending the same grade school as Charlie's daughter Cindy, was a constant guest in the Brown home.

Less than a year after Fern moved in with Charlie, she gave birth to his namesake daughter, Charlie. Fern and Charlie married in 1979, the same year son David Brown was born.

"The Browns lived just up the street," Debbie says. "We passed that house a lot. There were four children, two around Brad and Kevin's ages living there, and they all had different last names. One of the daughters had the last name 'Perruquet,' and obviously I recognized it when I heard it, but I never knew, for sure, if they were related. I thought it might be the same family, but I just didn't want to know. I didn't want to ask around about it. I didn't want my curiosity being told to them. It wouldn't have changed things, and it might have stirred something up. I didn't feel like I was in any danger. I felt sorry for their kids. If it was really cold out, most kids would sit with their moms in a heated car and wait for the school bus. But with their kids, no one ever did that. They didn't have warm coats. They didn't have gloves."

In the early 1980s, two of James Perruquet's nieces—Dawn Mathis and Charlie Brown—and David Stukel's nephews—Brad and Kevin Skrtich—were classmates at tiny Elwood School.

"As a kid growing up, you thought the Brown home was kind of a broken-type home," recalls Brad. "It seemed like the kids were never well taken care of. They were dirty or didn't have the greatest hygiene. They were decent kids. They would play with us. They never caused any problems, but you could tell just by looking at the outside of their house that they lived in a different world."

Although Debbie was aware of the possible connection between her children's classmates and one of her brother's murderers, she did not discuss that possibility with her boys.

"There was no reason to bring it up," Debbie says. "There was no purpose of saying anything to Brad and Kevin. They were schoolmates. Brad had one of the girls [Dawn] in his class, and Kevin had another one of the girls [Charlie] in his class. Brad and Kevin knew they had an uncle, and they knew in very brief terms what happened to him and that you have to watch out for bad people. There wasn't any need to go into any detail or bring it up when they were children."

While Brad and Kevin were growing up, details of David's death were not discussed.

"Kevin and I never asked questions," Brad says. "Grandma really didn't want to talk about it. Grandpa really didn't want to talk about it. We never knew growing up exactly what happened."

Kevin, who was in second grade in 1985 when the family left the Elwood subdivision and moved to Morris, twenty-five miles to the west, says the subject of David's murder was off limits.

"I remember playing with toys that had David's name on them," says Kevin, who inherited some of David's belongings, including his electric guitar. "I remember asking: 'Who is David?' Mom didn't talk much about David, and I never asked Dad about him. What happened to David just wasn't talked about much in the family."

Debbie says that when she was a teenager her parents sheltered her and Nancy from the murder.

"They just didn't talk about it. To this day, I don't bring up the subject with my dad because he has a tendency to get emotional. He still has a lot of anger, and I can't blame him for that. My parents kept everything about the case from us. We just would catch bits and pieces when they didn't know we were listening. And the newspapers just disappeared from our house during that time."

While her deceased brother's name was rarely spoken in Debbie and Gregg's household, James Perruquet was a frequent topic of conversation down the street at sister Fern's house. In what appears to have been a family project, Fern's ten-year-old daughter, Cecelia, and the family's seventeen-year-old, live-in, twin baby-sitters, Kristen and Karen Loftis, wrote letters to the state seeking Perruquet's release. The Loftis twins later admitted that they had never met James Perruquet at the time their letters were written:

> Uncle James has been in prison for almost eleven years for ~~just~~ committing murder. If you had some one in prison that you love and really care about you would probably let them go so please let him out. He needs us and we need him. I don't mean to critize so much but let him have a second chance. People that kill someone gets away with it for temporary insanty and keeps on killing and keeps on getting away with it. Why do you give these people chances after chances. Why cant you give James a second chance. If you ask me I think the court system is screwy. James committed murder he's sorry.

He was just a teenager how long are you going to keep him until he's in a wheelchair. Maybe you can put him on Parole "Please pretty Please!

—Kristen Loftis

I think James should get out of prison because I love him and miss him very much. I would like him to come home. He did wrong and he knows it and he could do no more wrong I know because he served his time in prison long enough. He will never get in trouble again he promise me and he never breaks his promise to me. I think you made a wrong decission in making him stay in prison. If you are not going to let him out let him know so he don't get his hope's up. I had law in politics this year in high school and we had a laywer in talking to us and he told us the Judge always gives you three chances but he only had 1 before he went to prison I know murder is a serious crime but you read in the newspaper about dope dealers, robbers get out on bond or get away with it nothing happens to them but six months on probation. I want him to be free again and our family will make sure he doesn't get into trouble.

—Karen Loftis

I'm writing about James D. Perruquet he is my uncle and I rely love him vere much and I hate wating especially wen it comes to him he is my faveret uncle and I'm in 4Th graed and I dont went to grow up having him in prison all of my lief so plese let him out of presn. I wese he wes here. 10 years is to long to be in prison and I'd like him to come home to the famile I apprecate if you put him on parole.

—Cecelia Perruquet

Living near the Browns for seven years in the 1980s gave Debbie Stukel insight into what the Perruquet and Sprinkle worlds must have been like in the 1960s.

"All you had to do was look at those children in Mr. Brown's house to know something was wrong," Debbie says.

Told that Billy Rose Sprinkle and James Perruquet had alcoholic parents who verbally and physically abused them, Debbie replies, "The parents are as guilty as the kids. You don't want to sound uppity, but this is a lower, trashy type of people. And unfortunately it just goes from generation to generation. They just didn't have that good example from their parents. My parents were strict. They were loving. They had rules. We couldn't leave the yard whenever we wanted to."

"We are what we are because of our parents," Marilyn Stukel says. "We were fortunate enough to be raised in decent homes. Then when we got married, we passed it on to our kids. But these kids, unfortunately, weren't raised like that, and I blame the parents. From what I heard, there wasn't any supervision, there wasn't any parenting. There was always fighting in the home. These boys had been in so much trouble, and the parents didn't try to do anything to straighten them out."

"Their home environment was terrible, so they're going to be terrible kids," Ray Stukel says. "But they should know right from wrong, even if they don't get it from their parents. There should be the power of reasoning. Maybe all they got from their home life is their 'I don't give a damn' attitude."

Or, as one retired grade school administrator, who was a guidance counselor at Washington School when Sprinkle and Perruquet were in seventh grade, puts it: "Whenever I had a kid in junior high who was off the wall, I mean off-the-wall bad, I'd go to the kindergarten teacher. And I'd find that by the time they got to kindergarten they were already screwed up—the die had already been cast. Either they'd been bounced from baby-sitter to baby-sitter or they had been abused. If General Motors had to make Cadillacs out of junk dropped at their door ..."

14

"Too Old for His Age"

After David Stukel's murder, Will County detective John Shelley, the man who guided Ray Van Dyke into law enforcement, was constantly reminded of the viciousness of the crime.

John Shelley moved up the ranks from Will County patrolman to sheriff.

"We kept the cement block in the evidence room. It was bloodied, broken, a good-size piece of concrete—eight inches high, more than a half-foot long," Shelley says. "I'd see it every time I'd go back there. You couldn't miss it."

At the time of the murder, Shelley did not collect evidence or participate in the arrests or interrogations of Sprinkle and Perruquet, but his fingerprints were all over the case. Shelley gained rare access to Sprinkle and Perruquet when he was given the assignment of transporting the co-defendants to and from meetings with their public defenders.

"I remember public defender Tom Vinson was getting touchy about the case," says Shelley, who rose from patrolman to investigator to chief investigator to lieutenant to sheriff, retiring in 1986 after serving two terms as the county's top cop.

"Vinson didn't want the boys talking to anybody, so I had to make sure they were kept isolated. They were cocky, kind of brazen. They didn't show any remorse. I don't feel they comprehended what they had done. They acted like kids, laughing and joking. I never heard them talking about the case. I think it was the furthest thing from their minds."

During his thirty-six-year career as a lawman, easygoing John Shelley made friends wherever he ventured. He was a good conversationalist and a better listener. And he was an excellent cop, a good old boy who found leads when others could not. When he ran for sheriff in 1978, Shelley conducted a grass-roots campaign on a shoestring budget. Sans spit-and-polish politics, Shelley won back-to-back Will County elections because people knew him and trusted him. Quick with a hello and handshake, Shelley had been campaigning for the job for three decades without knowing it.

After joining the Will County force in 1950, Shelley developed a network of informants, men on the fringe of society who thought of him more as a friend than a cop.

"John had all kinds of people that he had done favors for, people who owed him, so when you had a bad thing happen in the county and you didn't have any leads, he could develop leads," says former prosecutor Martin Rudman. "He had one of those smooth personalities that people felt like he was their uncle, and they wanted to talk to him. He could read people their rights now till doomsday. Didn't matter. They were still going to talk to him."

One such person who confided in Shelley and resided squarely on the outskirts of law-abiding society was Ed Sprinkle, whose family lived one-half mile from East High.

The Sprinkles occupied a two-home, one-acre lot bordered by an Elgin, Joliet & Eastern Railway spur to the south and Milwaukee Road Line tracks to the west. The two-story, seven-room main home was rundown. The furniture was old and battered. There was no television set. Every time the sump pump ran, the lights dimmed. Blankets nailed above windows served as curtains. Graffiti was scrawled on the children's bedroom walls. The house trembled when freight trains rumbled by. Junk and garbage littered the backyard.

"There was a lot of violence in the main home," Shelley says. "The parents would get into arguments, and once in a while there was a little knocking around. Sometimes it was kids against kids or kids against parents. Ed supported the family as best he could. I never saw him drunk, and he was strict, but he was always working. The mother was eccentric, and you could always tell that she had been drinking. The dad tried to run the show, but the kids ran the show, and they didn't get much supervision from the mother."

Ed Sprinkle may have been an absentee parent with abusive tendencies, but he was a dependable informant.

"He'd give me a call and say, 'Hey, I've got something for you.' He would tell me different things going on around town," Shelley says. "He would call and say, 'Somebody's selling ammunition' or 'Somebody's doing drugs.' And he was pretty reliable with his information."

While Ed Sprinkle was operating as a snitch for the county, sons Ross, Jim, Johnny, and Billy reportedly were committing crimes in their own neighborhood.

Ed Sprinkle Sr. was a hard-working union painte

In 1969, just months after Billy Rose Sprinkle's plea bargain, the family-owned Mancuso Cheese Co. moved next door to the Sprinkle homestead.

"The Sprinkles were bad news," says Dominic Mancuso, whose company's loading dock faced the front porch of the Sprinkle's main home. "It was a ramshackle house, and they were a bunch of animals. The mother was rough. The kids were alcoholics. There was violence all the time. One time, the kids were beating the hell out of the mother on the front porch. The Sprinkles used to come around after hours and throw beer cans all over the driveway. We couldn't put up with that. We were running a food-production plant, and we were getting rats and mice from their messes."

Mancuso eventually persuaded the Sprinkles to stop littering his company's driveway, but he says preventing them from breaking into his business was a different matter.

"They broke into our building a few times, and they'd steal all the batteries out of the trucks parked outside," Mancuso says. "The Sprinkles were breaking into every place around here."

Bill Kurkamp owned Blacktop Paving, just west of the Sprinkle homestead, and son Bruce, a 1970 East High graduate, says the Sprinkles were a recurring headache.

"They were just unrelenting thieves. They constantly broke into our building and stole us blind. Because of the Sprinkles, we had one of the first high-powered alarm systems in Will County. Once, I had to leave my brand-new pickup truck overnight. I figured I'd get a tow truck the next day. When I came back, it was stripped, and I'm about ninety-nine percent sure that the Sprinkles were the ones who did it. I could look over and see new tires and wheels on their old pickup truck. There was another time when the alarm went off, and the sheriff's police came over here. This was in the winter, and the police found a bunch of stuff on the railroad tracks that run behind both properties. They were hauling things over to their house on the tracks, and when the police came, they ran for it and got away. There were footprints in the snow leading to their house, but they left everything on the tracks, so they weren't arrested. But they had disabled our alarm system, and later that same night they came back and cleaned us out! We never could catch them in the act. And they were the weirdest, wildest, 'Deliverance'-type people you'd ever imagine, so you weren't going to approach them."

The Mancuso Cheese Company's loading area (upper left); the two-home Sprinkle homestead (right); and Mills Road (foreground).

One business owner, whose company has been in his family and the neighborhood for four decades, requested anonymity when talking about the Sprinkles, fearing retaliation.

"One time in the mid-1980s, the Sprinkles broke in to our business," the owner says. "We had a dog door in the back, and they'd send the little ones in through the dog door, then open the door, and they stole our lawn mower. It had snowed and you could see the tracks where they pushed it out. It was a larger mower and it had a flat tire, so it couldn't have been easy pushing it. And the tracks led right from our building to their driveway. We called the police, but the Sprinkles had already gotten rid of the lawn mower—probably put it in the back of their pickup truck and got it out of there. Without the lawn mower, the police couldn't do anything, even with the tracks leading right there. Just shows how brazen these people were.

"My dad and uncle ran the company for years. They were [from another country] and being burglarized was something foreign to them. They just couldn't understand why someone would do that. They were burglarized many times. They had small dogs that they left in the building. They would bark, but they weren't watchdogs.

"Their idea of security was to keep getting bigger and bigger dogs, thinking that would do the trick. They even tried to rig up a camera with a string. The only person they ever caught on camera was my dad!"

Because of the Sprinkles, the company installed a state-of-the-art alarm system complete with bullet-proof windows, sensors on the outside of the building and speakers that warn trespassers to "Step Away From The Building."

"Old man Sprinkle used to sit on the porch with a shotgun," the businessman says. "They were a nasty bunch."

From the moment Billy Rose Sprinkle was arrested, Ed Sprinkle claimed that his son was innocent.

"I think the dad knew that you never admit you're guilty," former Will County cop John Shelley says. "The dad wasn't the type who was going to admit that his boy did anything wrong, and he probably passed that on to his son. I think Ed wanted to prove that Perruquet did it. I think he truly believed that Billy was an innocent bystander."

Billy Rose Sprinkle has never been an innocent bystander.

"I had been around those boys quite a bit, and there was no doubt that Billy was the leader," Shelley says. "Billy was more outgoing. He had the more forceful personality."

Mike Giglietti, Larry Miller, Jim Vietoris, and Jim Snikeris—members of East High's class of 1973—got firsthand looks at Sprinkle and Perruquet at Washington School, where they spent the first semester of seventh grade before moving to Gompers after the fire at Washington.

"Billy had a pony and I had ponies, so we kind of chummed around," says Giglietti, who also lived in the East High neighborhood.

"Billy and I weren't friends, but we had the horses in common. I used to hunt along the railroad tracks over by his house, and I remember going over that way once with my BB gun. And Billy had always bragged about how he could go out hunting with his dad's shotgun. I come up on him that day and—boy!—he was hunting with a shotgun, but he wanted to see my BB gun. I let him see it, and he started shooting me in my legs with my BB gun. And I'm like, 'Hey, that really hurts,' and he's laughing and shooting. When I sit back now and think about the stuff he did then, you could have bet a million bucks that he was going to get into some kind of trouble. Like the way he treated his pony. It did something wrong once and he hobbled the pony's legs, beat it with a two-by-four. I saw him transform into an out-of-control person. I wish other people would have seen it. I always knew he was a bomb just waiting to go off."

Giglietti says that Sprinkle was a textbook bully.

"If your kid couldn't sleep at night, Billy Sprinkle was the reason why. Billy Sprinkle was your son's worst nightmare. He'd be shaking him down for money: 'Bring me fifty cents tomorrow, or I'm going to kick your ass.' He was wild and ornery. Billy wasn't afraid of anybody, a tough cookie."

Asked who would have been dominant between Sprinkle and Perruquet, Giglietti doesn't hesitate: "Billy, no doubt about it. Perruquet was the kind of kid who would hit you when your back was turned, then run. Billy was always bragging about what he could get Perruquet to do. If he ordered Perruquet to go into a store and steal a pair of sunglasses, he'd do it. I'm sure Billy could have manipulated Perruquet into doing anything. That kid idolized Billy."

Giglietti is one of the few people who had relationships with Sprinkle and David Stukel.

"Billy Sprinkle was a push-you-around, give-me-a-dollar kind of kid," Giglietti says. "Well, here comes David. He'd always lived a fairly sheltered life. I mean, David couldn't even go out of the yard without permission. His mom and dad wouldn't let him come up and play ball at our house, but we could come down there, one of those deals. He didn't have a clue how to deal with someone like Sprinkle."

Larry Miller lived a couple of blocks from the Sprinkles and spent a portion of his childhood trying to distance himself from them.

"I still got a scar on my mouth, right over my lip, from where I got kicked by Billy," Miller says. "A boy had gotten into it with Billy, and I said something to Billy about leaving him alone, so the next day Billy started saying what he was gonna do to me after school. When we got out of school, his sister and two little brothers had met Billy at the corner, and Lorraine had a chain. She was swinging it high and fast, and they double-teamed me. And his little brothers, Steve and Stanley, was throwing stuff at me. I slipped and fell. And as I was getting up, Billy had boots on and kicked me right over my top lip."

At five feet eleven, 170 pounds in 1967, Jim Vietoris wasn't concerned about being picked on by Billy Rose Sprinkle.

"Actually, we were halfway decent friends until he did that shit," Vietoris says.

Asked who would have been dominant between Sprinkle and Perruquet, Vietoris chuckles at what he perceives to be an absurd query, then, in a no-nonsense tone, states: "Bill Sprinkle. No doubt about that. He would have been calling the shots."

Asked how he can be so certain, Vietoris says, "Because I was there. Billy Sprinkle was a pretty tough kid for his age. Really, he was too old for his age—just a mean bastard. He wasn't a regular kid. He told me he used to knock off gas stations, and I'm pretty sure he did. One day he came to school, and he had a big wad of money, all big bills, tens, twenties, and fifties. Junior high kids don't run around with money like that in their pockets. Billy was just a different cat. One day, he wanted to get thrown out of class, but the teacher knew better and wouldn't throw him out, so he walked over to the window and threw his books out the window."

In the seventh grade, Erik James "Jim" Snikeris was small, standing a little over five feet and weighing 125 pounds, but he was tough enough to play cornerback on Washington's tackle football team, so he wasn't picked on by bullies.

Snikeris had just one class with Sprinkle, but Billy made a lasting impression on him.

"He was in wood shop, and he was always kind of a rabble-rousing troublemaker there," Snikeris says. "Billy Sprinkle did what he wanted to do when he wanted to do it. I think a lot of people were trying to get control of him, but nobody could. He wouldn't pay attention to anybody. I recall one time in the bathroom when he was talking about some black kids who said they were going to beat on him. So he pulled out a gun! And he said, 'If they do, I'm just going to shoot them!'"

15

Working the System

Before the sound of a striking gavel marked the close of the court proceedings in the David Stukel murder case in January 1969, Judge Michael Orenic gave Billy Rose Sprinkle and James Perruquet every opportunity to proclaim their innocence.

"My idea was this: I don't know whether or not you were coerced into a plea of guilty, so I'm going to ask you, 'Are you pleading guilty because you really are guilty? If you're not guilty, I'm the guy you should talk to. If you're innocent, if the plea was beaten out of you, now's the time to speak up.' It was basically, 'See that kindly old judge up there. He wants to know, and he's asking you, so now's the time to tell that old man, yeah, I got beat.' So when a guy says, 'I'm pleading guilty because I'm really guilty,' I believe him. He can bitch to the appellate court and the Supreme Court all he wants, but he told the trial judge, 'I'm pleading guilty because I really am guilty.'"

Sprinkle and Perruquet did "bitch" all the way to the U.S. Supreme Court, which refused to hear the case after an Illinois appellate court and the Illinois Supreme Court refuted the co-defendants' claim that they should not have been tried as adults and that their sentences were too harsh.

Just one year after the murder, Sprinkle, from his cell at the Sheridan Correctional Center, an Illinois Youth Commission institution seventy miles west of Joliet, began his quest for freedom by writing to Judge Orenic and declaring his innocence:

To Hon. Michael Orenic, Circuit Judge Will Co. Ill.

I guess it takes a lot of things and thinking to come to your self and wonder why I'm here for my small part in this when we were harassed and no one would listen to me. I was never given a chance by lawyers or any one else to prove I didn't hurt that poor Blessed boy, god is my witness and help me plese appoint me a lawyer and send some one to talk to me, I have no money to hire one.

Truly yores, God Bless.

Bill R. Sprinkle

Perruquet, also incarcerated at Sheridan, waited three years after the murder to reach out to Orenic. He accepted culpability for the murder but sought relief from the long sentence:

Dear Honorable Mr. Orenic.

My name is James David Perruquet. You sentenced me for Murder and Deviate Sexual Assault. I like to know what is going on with my appeal for I have not find out yet and I am getting very worry about what is happening to me, see I have been locked up for three long and lonely years and I try all I can to get out and be free again for I learned my way and it was the hard way. Mr. Orenic I got a long time to live and I hate to do it in prison so please try your best to help me know what is going on. I know what I did is very wrong for I see life a little better than before. Would you please send me a copy of what went on in court from Sept. 17, 1968 to Jan. 6, 1969, for I got to know the cell house lawyer and he said he would give me some help on this, and I also want the copy, so I can see what happen in court for I don't know any thing that went on or any thing I sign in court for Mr. Vinson. I don't know what my new lawyer is doing for me but what ever it is I hope it is better than that Mr. Vinson did, so ask him to come and have a talk with me an let me know what he have done for me.

Truly yours.

James Perruquet

There is no record of Judge Orenic responding to Sprinkle or Perruquet, but in 1971 the judge communicated with the Department of Corrections by signing the transfer orders that sent the seventeen-year-olds from the juvenile facility, where they could have stayed until age twenty-one, to the penitentiary.

Sprinkle, inmate C-15277, was sent to the maximum-security Pontiac Correctional Center, fifty miles southwest of Joliet.

Perruquet, inmate C-10300, was placed in the maximum-security Menard
Correctional Center, 315 miles southwest of Will County.

Three years after entering
the adult division of the
DOC, Sprinkle pursued an
executive clemency, writing
to Illinois Gov. Daniel
Walker and presenting, for
the first time on record, his
account of the crime, which
contradicted statements he
made to detectives the night
of the murder—that he was
near East High but had no
knowledge of the crime. It is
a scenario that places the
blame squarely on his accomplice's shoulders and portrays
David Stukel as a foul-
mouthed boy who willingly
agreed to fight Perruquet:

*This kid came down the
street and James Perruquet
went to ask him for a match. I
seen the boy go in his pocket
and James grabbed him. I ran
up and asked what the hell was happening. James said that he wanted to fight.*

*There was this field and James pulled him into it. James and the boy fought and
the boy thought I was going to help James whip him. David kept cussing at me and I
told him that I had no part in it, I swung on him and then him and me fought, I
kicked him in the face and in the side and back. James wanted to fight some more so I
said that I would go by the road and watch out. The boy said that if I didnt jump in
he would like to fight James to prove that he can whip him.*

*I went out to the road. I went back and James had the boy over a barrel and was
doing it to him in the behind. I knocked James away. Me and the boy was talking
when James hit him in the back of the head with a cement block. The boy fell and
James hit him in the back of the head again. I hit James in the mouth, He fell and I
jumped on top of him. I screamed at him and he said that no one would find him here*

in the woods. I told a black kid that day that there was a body in the field behind East High and that I thought he was dead. I was scared then and didnt know what to do or say to the police.

Two months later, Gov. Walker's office responded to Sprinkle's letter, stating that for his case to be presented at a public hearing, he would need to file a petition with the governor's office, and that copies of the petition would need to be served upon the judge, prosecutor, and all surviving members of the victim's family.

Sprinkle never filed the petition, putting to rest his bid to have his sentence commuted by the governor.

It took Sprinkle just nine months after sentencing to claim that he did not sexually assault and murder David Stukel. Perruquet waited thirteen years to alter his confession. In a letter to the state, Perruquet accepted responsibility for causing David Stukel's death, but he excluded himself from the sexual assault:

We'd been drinking beer and sniffing glue. Then David Stukel came by. We wanted to sell the radio. He said he had no money, so we got to pushing him around, until we got him in this lot. We destroyed his books and started on his clothes. Once we got to his shorts, Billy Sprinkle ask me to check if I had put the cable back up by the road. So I went to check, it took about 30 or 60 seconds, when I got back Billy was having sexual intercourse with him. At the time I liked Billy and never said any thing to him.

After Billy did the thing with David then we got to really pushing him around. We even tried to get him to fight back, and he would not. While David was kneeling we both hit him in the head and he fell, and then we left. I've tried to forget, but a person can't forget something like this. I know I must pay for what I did. I've always wanted to tell someone I was sorry, but I don't know who or how to do this.

After their arrests, Billy Rose Sprinkle and James Perruquet resided for twelve days in separate cells at the Joliet City Jail, isolated from the adult population. Because that facility was not equipped to handle juveniles, and construction of the new Will County Jail was incomplete, the co-defendants were transferred fifty-five miles southeast to Iroquois County, where they shared a cell for two months. Responding to questions in a letter regarding his days with Sprinkle in the Iroquois County Jail, Perruquet writes, in part, that Sprinkle helped him hone his fighting skills:

As a kid, I was always afraid to fight or stand up for myself. I was always afraid of getting hurt. I wasn't a fighter. I was more of a coward. I remember my older brothers, me and this other kid wanted to hang out with them. They said well, you two fight and the winner of the fight can hang out with us. We wouldn't fight. My brother said, OK, wrassle him, whoever pins the other first gets to hang with us. And while we were wrasslin' they took off and left us there on the ground. In county Billy was always teaching me how to fight. Even when we was with David Stukel Billy was showing me how it's done. And Billy punched me a lot in jail, showing me the ropes. I could only run in circles to get away from him, and I got stitches from hitting my head against the bars. When we was getting ready to go to prison, he was always telling me I had to be tougher. He claimed that he was only trying to help me.

While Sprinkle was teaching Perruquet how to throw a punch in jail, obstinate Ed Sprinkle was trying to KO Perruquet through the legal system. In a letter, Perruquet writes about the betrayal:

What I learned a few years later, his father and them was trying to put all the blame on me for what happened. From what I heard, he blamed everything on me. I did everything and Billy did nothin'. That it was all my fault, that I killed the kid and Billy set out by the road. That I had the sexual ... matter of fact, my sister Stella told me this at the time and I didn't believe her and I called her a liar. She said, Billy is blaming you for everything. I was naive. I was stupid. My family use to come to jail and tell me they heard that Ed Sprinkle was telling Billy to blame me. They said that in Billy's statement to the police he said he didn't do nothin'. I never listened to my own family. Plus I was in love with Doll [Georgina], Billy's sister. I wasn't about to let anyone mess that up. Kids stuff. Can you see how stupid I really was?

After sentencing, Sprinkle and Perruquet were transported to Sheridan, where they were placed in separate areas of the juvenile institution, and they remained apart while there. In a letter, Perruquet writes about his union with Sprinkle coming to an end:

I didn't know nobody in there when I got to Sheridan, other than Billy, but they kept us separated. I'd see Billy in passing or at a distance. Other than that, they kept us completely apart. He was in one building, I was in another. There was one time he was in seg and somebody brought word back to my cell house that Billy wants to see you, come to seg. They had little windows in the door and I knew if I busted that out they would send me to seg. And I busted it out and got sent to seg and he was already gone and I was stuck in seg for two weeks.

Perruquet had difficulty adjusting to life at Sheridan, but Sprinkle's pre-prison survival tutelage helped Perruquet stay out of the infirmary—if not the warden's office:

You always had to fight in juvenile. The fighting I did do got me through. You just couldn't back down. You had a choice of going down or you had a choice to stand up. I did what I had to do. If I had to fight, I'd fight if I couldn't talk my way out of it. Usually they push you to see if you will fight. If they see that you will fight, they won't mess with you.

Although Perruquet had his share of skirmishes at Sheridan, he was not considered a dangerous resident. That was not the case with Sprinkle, who was the subject of a damning personality assessment while at the facility:

"He is dangerous to himself, dangerous to other inmates, and dangerous to society. He presents a serious problem, as he has vowed that nothing will stop him in order to succeed in his escape. He has a demoralizing impact on other youths, and it is the consensus that he is basically unchangeable. He seems only to be concerned with the gratification of his needs. He attempts to deny and justify his crime but contradicts himself. He seems to have no remorse after having committed a repugnant crime. The prognosis for personality change is extremely poor. A longer period of incarceration seems absolutely necessary."

When Sprinkle graduated from juvenile jail to the penitentiary at seventeen, he underwent more psychological evaluations over several days at the Joliet Correctional Center's Reception & Diagnostics Services Unit. In the first of many harsh profiles, Sprinkle blamed his junior high teachers for his high rate of truancy:

"The inmate states he did not like his teachers, thus accounting for absences and refusal to do class work. He describes certain teachers as 'not being able to control the class,' indicating the extreme difficulty the inmate has over his own impulses. He is a dangerous individual for anyone—even hardened adult criminals—to be around. He is a very aggressive person and reflects little of the consequences of his acts. He is considered greatly socially hazardous. Exploration of institutional plans at this time would not be fruitful. Psychotherapy is not recommended."

In another evaluation, an equally bleak portrait of Sprinkle was presented:

"This is a violently antisocial individual. He is completely lacking in insight and has no ability to relate with others except to use or abuse them for his own hedonist goals. As the reality of the length of his incarceration is ingested, he will become increasingly desperate and will attempt to 'flee the field' either by an escape attempt, through self-destruction, or by decompensating into a psychosis. He has few inner controls now; he had few controls as a child or youth. He is considered highly dangerous."

In a psychological report dealing with the murder, Sprinkle's statements only remotely resemble the scenario he laid out for the governor in his quest of clemency:

My rappie wanted to sell this radio, but the Stukel boy didn't want it. James hit him and James dragged him into this field. James took some money from Stukel, but Stukel said it was his school money. James said you're going to have to fight for it. Stukel said he couldn't fight us both. I told him I would stay out of it. James hit him in the face. Stukel grabbed me and tripped, pulling me down too. I jerked away, got up and kicked him in the face. He fell back again. He stood up and looked at me. I said You want to fight me instead? He said I need my money so I'll fight you one at a time. I hit him in the face, then he hit me in the left side of the jaw. I hit him three times. James hit him and tripped him and he fell. Stukel started to come up and I hit him with an upper-cut.

James started looking around and saw these two irons bars attached to each other with a wire. He started waving one in the air and hit Stukel in the left side of the neck. I told James I was going back to the road because I was on probation and didn't want to get involved. I sat for about 45 minutes sniffing glue. I walked back in the weeds. When I got there Stukel was laying over a barrel completely naked and James was screwing him in the ass. I backhanded James for what he did. I got mad because Stukel could have hollered about what James was doing, so I hit Stukel. He just fell like a dead weight on his back.

James picked up the iron bar and he wrapped the bar around Stukel's shirt and pressed it against his neck, and he stepped on it with his left foot. Stukel tried to shove him off with his hands. I caught James in the left armpit and he fell. James picked up the iron bar and hit Stukel across the nose. Stukel was laying down, face up, then James hit him across the mouth. James rolled him over on his stomach and picked up the cement block, lifted it over his head and then hit the boy on the back of the head. Then James ground a cigarette into Stukel's back and we left the scene.

Four years after arriving at Pontiac, Billy Rose Sprinkle was granted a transfer to the Joliet Correctional Center so that he could be closer to his family. But two weeks after landing in Joliet, Sprinkle told *Joliet Herald News* reporter John Whiteside that two attempts had been made on his life, and that he was seeking another transfer.

"They are going to get me," Sprinkle said in the 1975 interview. "I don't want to stay in this jail. If I do, it's my life or someone else's."

More than thirty years after the article ran, Ray Stukel is still disgusted by its contents, placement, and timing.

"The story made it sound as if Sprinkle was a poor martyr, about how he was being mistreated in prison, how he was afraid for his life. On the front page! On Easter Sunday! It spoiled our Easter. It was like they were treating him like he was Jesus Christ ... Sprinkle!"

In the article, Sprinkle claimed he received a typed death threat: "We have been waiting for you to come back to Joliet. You will be either killed or poisoned."

Sprinkle told Whiteside that he wrote a letter to Gov. Walker asking to be transferred from Joliet back to Pontiac, and that he enclosed the threatening note but that it was stolen from his cell along with cigarettes. Sprinkle also claimed that an inmate tried to stab him, and that he was clubbed by another. Warden Fred Finkbeiner told Whiteside that there was no evidence to corroborate Sprinkle's accusations, and that the inmate had changed his story several times.

In a Joliet Correctional Center memo regarding Sprinkle's claims, the same psychiatrist who interviewed the inmate when he was first incarcerated in 1968 detailed his conversation with Sprinkle seven years later regarding the death threats:

"The inmate alleged he was attacked—an attempted stabbing and that he was struck on the head with either a club or a brick. I could find no evidence of trauma to the left side of his head where he was allegedly struck. Likewise, there is no evidence of any stab wound. I have known this man ever since 1968 when he was first interviewed at Will County in a notorious crime, and it can be stated that the resident cannot be considered a reliable historian."

The *Joliet Herald News* article provided a public forum for Sprinkle to once again claim his innocence—this time in the victim's hometown newspaper.

"My rappie did it," said Sprinkle, who was granted his wish and transferred back to Pontiac. "I'll never forget my rappie's face—white and pale—and his eyes when he walked over to me and said, 'I had to kill him.' I was wrong in letting my rappie fight with him. I'm sorry it happened, but I'm not a murderer—that's why I can talk about it. I remember his mother crying in court. I saw her anger for me. Someday I would like to go to his mother and dad and try to explain to them what I feel now. They would probably shoot me."

16

A Fantasy World

A year after returning to Pontiac, Billy Rose Sprinkle was charged with aggravated battery for his involvement in the gang-related, non-fatal stabbing of Pontiac inmate Richard Brockunier in September 1976. Court records depict Sprinkle as a co-conspirator who did not do the actual stabbing, but facilitated the commission of the crime. The aggravated battery case against Sprinkle went to a bench trial, and Livingston County Judge William Caisley ruled in favor of the state.

When you're a judge in central Illinois' Livingston County, home to the Pontiac Correctional Center, you preside over an abundance of cases with defendants known by names and numbers who wear jumpsuits and leg irons, so it was just another day on the bench for Caisley when Sprinkle appeared before him. The judge doesn't recall the specifics of the case, but he does remember one person who sat in the courtroom, eyes fixed on the defendant.

"The boy's dad, I recall him being there every day," Caisley says. "Most families of inmates, if the inmate is charged with another offense committed while in the penitentiary, they just don't show up. But Mr. Sprinkle was there, and him being there was out of the ordinary."

At sentencing, Judge Caisley asked inmate Sprinkle, who did not testify during the trial, if he would like to address the court. He nodded and read from a handwritten note, proclaiming his innocence, blaming his conviction on ineffective counsel, and accusing a corrections official of framing him.

Then, in an unorthodox measure, Judge Caisley extended an invitation to crusty Ed Sprinkle to address the court. He took advantage of the opportunity and declared his son's innocence—not for the 1976 aggravated battery but for the 1968 murder.

"Your Honor, the state's attorney, he brought up the prior conviction, and I appreciate the offer to speak. That boy," said the sixty-year-old Sprinkle, pointing at his twenty-two-year-old son, "he was convicted by telling the truth. The deceased boy was smacked by Billy two thousand feet from where the boy was found dead, and this boy Billy, being fourteen or fifteen years old at that time, rode nine miles on a bicycle, came back to pick up the radio. That other boy actually killed the boy, and the court drug Billy down the sewer with the other kid. If that ain't the truth, so God help me, God be my witness. We have been to the Supreme Court. We have been to the appellate court, and we are going back."

Judge Caisley then turned his attention to Billy Rose Sprinkle, issuing a one- to ten-year sentence that would be "served consecutively following the sentence out of Will County."

The day after sentencing, Sprinkle wrote a letter to the Livingston County clerk of the circuit court seeking a retrial. He was denied, and two weeks later he wrote to Judge Caisley, claiming his innocence on the aggravated battery charge and insisting that gangs are planning to take his life:

I want to say that some people hold anger and resentment against judges and courts who send them to the prison, Mr. Caisley I have no such feelings. You are a judge and you have a job to do, I believe you did your job well but I must say once again that I had no part in the aggrivated battery case of which I was convicted. I am still in segregation, I was released back to the general population but returned to segregation the following day on my own request. I had some words with a few gang members here, A copy of the investigation report somehow got in the hands of some of the residents.

Now because of it the gangs and myself are having a misunderstanding, Yes there is a "hit" out on me because of it. In the report on this incident I told officials who the gang chiefs are and who I see stab Brockunier. That is a copy of what some inmates have. I refuse to tell my father because I dont want him worrying or getting upset.

Mr. Caisley all elce is well with me. Thank you for your servises.

Sprinkle continued to write to Judge Caisley and, in one letter, it's possible the inmate was trying to place himself in a more favorable light in advance of a parole hearing:

Judge Caisley, I found an injured baby pigeon, washed it, forced fed it and nursed it back to health. I raised this bird from a baby, I turned it loose twice but it came back. Sooner or later the officials will take the bird and turn it loose and it will die, It a part of me now. Would you contact the Humane Society and inform them of this matter? To turn it loose would be a sentence of death. In case you dont remember me, I was in your court for Aggrivated Battery. I go back to the board again in August. There have been a lot of things going on here inside these walls, theres been a lot of bad publicity but there is also a lot of good things happening all the time. I feel saving this pigeons life was a good thing, not wanting to see it hurt or die but knowing some orga-

nization can take the bird and give it a proper home would be the humanitarian thing to do.

Two days after conspiring to stab Richard Brockunier, Billy Rose Sprinkle received a disciplinary "ticket" for refusing to be interviewed by penitentiary officials. To this day, Sprinkle isn't receptive to interviews, especially by reporters looking into his life. But Sprinkle does plenty of talking in letters to the parole board in which he consistently says that he is innocent of *all* charges against him.

Chicago-area native and former Pontiac inmate Mike Altschul thinks he knows why Sprinkle will never own up to his sins. Altschul, the man who was convicted of stabbing fellow inmate Brockunier and who lived under the same roof as Sprinkle for four years at Pontiac, made three trips to Illinois penitentiaries. Altschul, whose charges ranged from aggravated battery to forgery, reflects upon why Sprinkle would elect to maintain his innocence.

"In prison, either you're adaptable or you're not, and what's most important is trying to be as honest about your circumstances as possible," says Altschul, who was released from prison at thirty-four in 1979. "You just had to be for real. Being real is not only admitting or not admitting your wrongdoing. I don't mean that you stand up and under all circumstances you absolutely have to tell the truth. What I mean is, Sprinkle never quit living in fantasyland. He never realized who he was, what he was, and I understand that because I've known people that were in similar situations, where you've got a kid who murders, and once he understands what he did, he can't deal with it, so he doesn't. He has a whole denial thing going on, and he somehow justifies what he did."

Altschul says most inmates regretted their actions but not Sprinkle.

"Most of the guys I knew in those days weren't brash enough to think that what they did didn't matter. We all knew it mattered. Some of us tried to do something about it—some of us didn't. Look, I did three sentences. It's not like I woke up the day after I ended up in the penitentiary the first time. I was still willing to take the risks. I will say that I had a buried conscience, not that I had no conscience. There were times that my conscience would bother me. I'd think about how I let people down. Now Billy, he had some real bad personality conflicts going on within. He was one of the few individuals you'll run across in a lifetime of meeting people that really doesn't have a conscience—at least he didn't when I knew him. He cared not for anybody but himself."

It was in 1975 when Altschul met Sprinkle at Pontiac. Altschul was a member of the Vice Lords, a white, prison-only branch of the infamous black gang. And although Sprinkle tried to present himself to Judge Caisley as a non-gang member who was being threatened by gang members after the stabbing, Altschul says that Sprinkle was a high-ranking member of the Vice Lords.

Ask Altschul if he did the stabbing in '76, and he doesn't flinch: "Yes, I did."

Ask Altschul what role Sprinkle played, and he answers with the same assuredness: "Actually, he ordered it. He determined that it needed to be done, and it was done. Sprinkle was a second-in-command, like a deputy chief, and he ordered that to happen. It happened going into the school building, and Sprinkle was just inside the doors, and Brockunier was on the stairs. And I came up the stairs and plunged a spoon knife into him. And Sprinkle was there in case Brockunier tried to come down the stairs. And he was there to make sure it happened the way he ordered it."

Asked why Sprinkle ordered the stabbing, Altschul says, "It was probably something foolish like disobeying an order."

Altschul says Sprinkle was adept at avoiding trouble in prison.

"Billy Sprinkle had a façade of being a tough guy, but I never saw him stand up to anybody that he didn't have control or rank over. If someone not of his affiliation said something to him, he was not a tough guy. I know that I was not at all intimidated by him."

Altschul and Sprinkle were gang affiliates at Pontiac, but they were not friends, and they did not discuss the 1968 murder. "What I heard was that the murder took place and that he was responsible for the activity of it," Altschul says. "I heard there was a pipe being used rectally. I was disgusted by it. And because of it, people wouldn't associate with him, and it kept him from getting good jobs. Normally, people with those sorts of long convictions—after some time of being model inmates—they end up with plum jobs. The administration allows these people to work their way up. But the administrators were aware that Sprinkle was a no-good dog."

17

The Bottom Line

The head-turning headline "Boys Begin 75-90 Year Sentence for Murder" appeared on the front page of the *Joliet Herald News* on January 7, 1969. The words seemed to stamp an exclamation point on the fates of two young murderers who would be kept from society for the remainder of their lives. But when you read between the lines of the Illinois statutes, the truth becomes explicitly clear: Even though Billy Rose Sprinkle and James Perruquet received lengthy sentences, they weren't going to stay in prison from adolescence to the afterlife.

In 1969, the indeterminate form of sentencing utilized in Illinois was a two-number system, with the bottom number (seventy-five in this case) representing the minimum number of years before Sprinkle and Perruquet would be eligible for parole consideration, and the top number (ninety) indicating the maximum number of years they could be incarcerated.

Indeterminate sentencing is remembered by some as the bait-and-switch era featuring a numbering system that seemingly gave judges unlimited discretion at sentencing. But, in reality, the obscenely long sentences being doled out were little more than window dressing.

In the 1960s and '70s, opponents of the indeterminate system pointed to its infrastructure of credit mechanisms that allowed criminals to become parole-eligible in incredibly short periods of time. They wondered: Where is the truth in advertising? But the truth is indeterminate sentencing was exactly as advertised—indeterminate.

When Judge Orenic issued the murder sentences of seventy-five to ninety years, he could have given Sprinkle and Perruquet one million to two billion years, and they still would have been eligible for parole consideration in—unbelievably—eleven years and three months.

John Groves calls it an accident that he served as chief records officer for the Department of Corrections for fourteen years.

"I was a sergeant in the guard hall at Pontiac," says Groves, who retired in 1993. "The guy in the records office had a nervous breakdown. And the warden said, 'John, you know a little bit about parole dockets. Would you mind going back there and helping us out?' I went there in August of '65 and never went back. It was a fluke, a niche that I fell into and enjoyed."

John Groves

Groves, who was named the DOC's records chief in 1979 and was in the docket trenches during the controversial indeterminate sentencing era, reminisces about the format as if he were talking about an old friend.

"I thought indeterminate sentencing was a good tool for the criminal justice system. With indeterminate sentencing, there was a range there, room to work. They could parole him, and if he did not abide by the parole, he could be brought back to serve more time."

The harsh reality of indeterminate sentencing is that in 1969, when Sprinkle and Perruquet received seventy-five to ninety years, the bottom number dropped to twenty years—for parole-consideration purposes—even before they left the courtroom. And that twenty-year figure did not take into account time off for good behavior, which explains the parole-eligibility projections for Sprinkle and Perruquet of eleven years and three months.

Groves breaks down how the DOC calculated parole-eligibility numbers on indeterminate sentences, such as Perruquet's and Sprinkle's, with a bottom number of seventy-five years:

"The bottom number translating from seventy-five to twenty years was by law, and statutory good time was awarded upfront, which works out to eight years and nine months. So, when you subtract the eight years and nine months of good time, the twenty years becomes eleven years and three months. Now this eleven-three figure could be revoked by the director of the DOC, so if an inmate did not abide by the institution's rules, then the director could revoke good time. And the eleven-three did not mean that he was going to go out then or that he was even going to go before the parole board—it just meant that if he got all of his good time, the eleven-three is the minimum time in which he could go before the parole board."

The indeterminate sentencing formulas remained static from February 1, 1952, to January 1, 1973, when compensatory credit was thrown into the mix, further lessening the time that inmates would wait before becoming eligible to be heard by the parole board.

"In 1973, the Legislature passed the Unified Code of Corrections," John Groves says. "So, in addition to the statutory good time [eight years, nine months] that the inmates earned upfront, now—based on their conduct—they could earn an additional seven and one-half days per month compensatory good time."

Martin Rudman, who prosecuted Sprinkle and Perruquet, was no fan of indeterminate sentencing, and he says the formulas became more confusing in '73.

"The system got out of control to the point where no one could calculate what the good time was because the DOC was piling good time on top of good time," Rudman says.

With statutory and compensatory credit cutting back time from both ends of sentences, Sprinkle and Perruquet were eligible to have an audience with the parole board sooner rather than later. Based on statutory credit alone, Sprinkle and Perruquet were candidates for parole consideration in the eleven-year, three-month figure. Then, in '73, when compensatory credit entered the fray, they were in position to let the good time roll even more. Eligible to earn the seven and one-half days per month, or three months per year, the inmates were capable of knocking down their parole-eligibility wait from the original seventy-five years to nine years and nine months!

Taking statutory and compensatory credit into consideration, along with the three months and twenty days of time served before sentencing, the murderers garnered the shockingly early parole-eligibility dates of:

Nine years and six months for James Perruquet.

Nine years and eight months for Billy Rose Sprinkle—even with the felony conviction while in prison.

The year 1978 is significant for more than being the year in which Sprinkle and Perruquet became eligible to be heard by the parole board. It is also the year that Illinois Gov. Jim Thompson implemented "Class-X" legislation, which discarded indeterminate sentencing in favor of determinate, specific-length sentences, a switch that did not affect Sprinkle and Perruquet.

The two-number system was displaced by one-number, flat-time sentences. The indeterminate system's upfront statutory credit was replaced by day-for-day compensatory credit, allowing inmates to knock off one day for every good day spent in prison, and be automatically eligible for release without having to face a parole board. The parole system was basically abolished, and the parole board was supplanted by the Prisoner Review Board, which had no say as to when determinately sentenced inmates would be released. But in addition to handling indeterminately sentenced inmates' parole hearings, the PRB would now review records of determinately sentenced inmates up for release and, if necessary, attach conditions.

John Groves is the first to admit that he had to sharpen fewer pencils after the move to determinate sentencing.

"If you got a twenty-year sentence, you did ten years, then got out, that's cut and dried. He does not face the parole board. Now, the 1978 changes did allow the PRB to offer determinate release dates to those sentenced under the indeterminate laws with sentences of less than twenty years, so Sprinkle and Perruquet never got that option."

George Stampar didn't plan on a career in corrections. It just worked out that way. In 1947, the twenty-three-year-old began teaching physical education at the University of Illinois at Chicago. Five years later, Stampar left UIC to become a parole officer. Stampar so excelled at handling parolees that in 1961 he became the DOC's superintendent of parole, and four years later, he made the leap to assistant warden at the Stateville Correctional Center, north of Joliet, where he became intimate with indeterminate sentencing.

George Stampar

In June 1967, mass murderer Richard Speck was sentenced to die in the electric chair for slaying eight student nurses in Chicago the previous summer. But in June 1972, the U.S. Supreme Court suspended the use of capital punishment. With the death penalty no longer an option, the DOC introduced the thirty-one-year-old Speck to indeterminate sentencing in the form of eight consecutive sentences of 50 to 150 years.

George Stampar was at Richard Speck's side in a Peoria courtroom when the names of the eight victims and the indeterminate numbers were repeated.

"We had a state plane pick us up just down the road from Stateville at Lewis College," recalls Stampar, who retired in 1985.

Stampar was given the assignment because he regularly dealt with Illinois' most notorious inmate.

"Speck never bothered anybody," Stampar says. "He lived in what was designed as 'The Hole,' the isolation building. The execution chamber was in the same building. In fact, his bed was against the execution chamber wall, but he couldn't have cared less."

Stampar says Speck displayed an impassive demeanor during the re-sentencing proceedings.

"Between sessions, the judge was taking his time," Stampar says. "And Speck says, 'Why don't you go in there and tell the judge to do his thing and get it over with?'"

On the plane trip back to Stateville, Stampar played with the numbers regarding the indeterminately sentenced Speck's eight 50- to 150-year sets, each with the standard parole eligibility of eleven years and three months based solely on statutory good time (compensatory good time would not enter the picture until the following year).

"Speck had served time from the day he was arrested," says Stampar, referring to the nearly seven years that Speck had been incarcerated. "So I says to him, 'Richard, you know that in four or five years, or whatever it might have been, you're going to go before the parole board.' He looked at me as though, 'What planet did you come from?'"

After Stampar returned to Stateville, he dispensed the Speck parole-eligibility bombshell to the media, knowing full well that few reporters understood the intricacies of indeterminate sentencing.

"The reporters were calling and I was telling them, 'Speck's going to be eligible for parole in four or five years,' and they were thinking, 'There's something wrong with that guy at Stateville.' So they started calling Springfield and found out it was true. Everybody was saying, 'This guy at Stateville's saying Speck's coming up for parole,' and they're saying, 'That can't be, the prison's going to fall apart before Speck ever gets out.'"

The reality is that Stampar's prediction, with an assist from the compensatory good time introduced in '73, was accurate. Speck came up for parole just four years after his date with death was converted to an indeterminate sentence, and he was resoundingly denied each year until he suffered a heart attack and died the day before his fiftieth birthday in 1991.

Former Sen. Edward Petka, who for a decade ran the Will County state's attorney operation in the 1970s and '80s, understands the disappearing-numbers act that was indeterminate sentencing. "It was almost smoke and mirrors," says Petka, who championed victim's rights and spearheaded the passing of tougher crime laws over two decades as an Illinois lawmaker.

In November 1977, Henry Brisbon, Petka's poster boy for indeterminate idiocy and architect of the "I-57" murders, received the astronomical indeterminate sentence of one thousand to three thousand years for the execution-style murders of a young couple in Cook County four years earlier.

Brisbon's 1973 Interstate 57 rampage began in Will County. The then-seventeen-year-old Brisbon forced Betty Lou Harmon to climb naked through a barbed-wired fence before killing her with a shotgun blast. On the same night in Cook County, Brisbon ordered newly engaged Dorothy Cerny and James Schmidt to lie facedown before shooting them in their backs. Brisbon was not charged in the Will County murder because it would have been senseless in the wake of the sentence in the Cook County case, but jurors were allowed to hear the brutal details of the first murder. Brisbon was not eligible for the death penalty, which had been reinstated, because he was seventeen at the time of the murders. But one year after going to prison, Brisbon fatally stabbed a fellow Stateville inmate, and Petka used the death-penalty phase of that trial to expose the shortcomings of indeterminate sentencing.

The jury returned a death-sentence verdict after Petka showed jurors color photographs of the "I-57" victims, informing them that even though Brisbon had been sentenced to one thousand to three thousand years for the '73 murders, he would be eligible for parole in eleven years, three months.

The Illinois Supreme Court overturned Brisbon's death sentence, ruling that Petka's actions—showing unrelated crime-scene photos of the "I-57" murders in the Stateville murder case and stating parole-eligibility numbers—may have prejudiced the jury.

In a rehearing of the penalty-phase arguments on the Stateville case, a jury again delivered a death sentence to Brisbon. But in January 2000, Illinois Gov. George Ryan placed a moratorium on the death penalty. Then, in January 2003, Ryan commuted the sentences of Brisbon and 163 other death-row inmates to life in prison without parole.

Petka does not distance himself from the comments he made three decades ago.

"Brisbon's lawyer ingeniously argued that he's never going to get out. In my rebuttal, I said he'd be eligible for parole in eleven years, three months. It was reversed because of my remarks, and he had to be retried."

Asked if he regrets making the parole-eligibility statement, Petka says: "No, because they're truthful. The argument that was made by the other side was that, 'He's got twelve hundred years in prison, he's not going anywhere.' And I pointed out, 'Well that's not true. I mean he's eligible to be released next week.'"

Now the Supreme Court said that even though it's true, it's prejudicial. It would have been better left unsaid, but it was in response to an uninvited comment."

Petka still believes that executing Brisbon would be justifiable

"Brisbon is a walking testimonial of why we need the death penalty," Petka says. "He stopped two cars, one of which had a young couple and ordered them in the ditch, told them to 'kiss their last kiss,' then shot them in the back. With Betty Lou Harmon, he inserted a shotgun into her vagina, pulled the trigger and while she was writhing in pain put the shotgun underneath her face and literally blew her head off."

Petka's predecessor, Martin Rudman, understands the frustration Petka felt when he exposed the ludicrousness of the parole-eligibility formulas, but he isn't surprised that Petka's words resulted in the reversal.

"The theory was, the jury was not supposed to concern itself with when people got out," Rudman says. "Either give them the death penalty or don't give them the death penalty. And don't start giving them a lot of numbers."

And never tell them the truth about indeterminate sentencing.

18

If These Files Could Talk

The formidable Prisoner Review Board files of Billy Rose Sprinkle and James Perruquet have that been-around-the-cell-block look, feel, and smell to them—faded and parched with the musty scent of something you would find in Grandma's attic. Tucked away in the PRB's modest headquarters in the state capital of Springfield, 145 miles southwest of Joliet, Sprinkle and Perruquet's files overflow with paperwork, and for every two letters of condemnation, there are ten of commendation, pleas for leniency mixed with certificates for everything from finding Jesus to completing substance-abuse classes to raising funds for the Jaycees.

John Shelley

With a tenacious father working on Sprinkle's behalf, support letters began pouring into his file in the late 1970s—some from the most unlikely of sources, the most surprising of which was Will County Sheriff John Shelley:

I knew Billy Sprinkle before his incarceration. I have known the Sprinkle family for many years and find in them a loving, caring people. It was more than a decade ago when young William Sprinkle committed an act which everyone condemned. I, too, was appalled that such a terrible crime could be committed by one so young. However, time has been on William Sprinkle's side. He has had the time to reconsider his actions, to receive help in redirecting his priorities, and time to gain a new lease on life. It is now time that Mr. Sprinkle is asking for. The correctional system has given him most everything that it has to offer. Now he is asking for the time to make his newfound dreams of the good life a reality. William will have the support from family and the assistance of many in trying to attain his dream. He is still young enough to begin a new life and I'm sure that he would like a chance to try.

John Shelley, who was fifty-one when he wrote in support of Sprinkle, is forthright four decades later in articulating why an officer of the law would seek the release of a murderer.

"I knew the people, and when they need a favor, they come to you. Ed came to me, and I did it. I don't have any regrets. The boy was young, and I thought he had a chance to make it."

Shelley does recall some uneasiness over the decision because he and his late wife, Marilyn, were friends and neighbors of Debbie Stukel's in-laws, Walt and Vera Skrtich.

"It was a bit of a dilemma, but I felt it was the right thing to do at the time," Shelley says.

When Debbie Stukel discovers that Shelley wrote in support of Sprinkle, she can barely complete a sentence.

"I don't understand ... why would he be defending him? I don't know what to say. What he says about the Sprinkle family, that they are a loving, caring family, is that totally fabricated? This is like out of left field ... a total surprise. My husband, Gregg, knew the Shelleys well because they had a son, Guy, and they had a band and Gregg used to play drums. And when these letters were written, John Shelley ... he had to know by that time I was married to Gregg. The parents were neighbors and friends having coffee together!"

From 1950 to the early 1960s, LeRoy Van Duyne owned a barber shop on the depressed Northeast Side of Joliet, the same neighborhood where Ed and Grace Sprinkle settled with their family after moving from Michigan in 1958.

"Every afternoon, Grace Sprinkle would walk by with two of the most beautiful blond-haired twins you ever saw," recalls Van Duyne, referring to brothers Steve and Stanley, who are actually a year apart. "She'd get them duded up and they'd go to the tavern on the corner, and she'd have a few beers and wait for her old man to come home."

Ed Sprinkle became one of Van Duyne's regular customers.

"He was a kind of rough-and-tough guy," Van Duyne says. "One of the things that I remember about him is that he carried a gun. He never brandished it. I just heard that he carried one. I think his kids probably got in trouble by not being taken care of—their mama not watching them while their dad was out working."

In 1965, Van Duyne entered local politics. In '74 he was elected to the House of Representatives, and in his sixteen years in office he never forgot the people of his blue-collar district. One such constituent was Ed Sprinkle, who persuaded the congressman to write a letter to the PRB:

I am writing on behalf of Billy Sprinkle, who was a very young boy when his crime was committed. Since that time he must have developed somewhat at least. His father tells me he has done very well. If there is anything that Billy has going in his favor, please give him the benefit of the doubt.

Asked about the letter nearly a quarter-century later, Van Duyne doesn't recall the letter or being asked to write it, but without being shown a copy, he accurately describes its superficial complexion.

"I place a hell of a lot less importance on that than a lot of people would," Van Duyne says. "I used to write those types of letters for a lot of people. They used to come in and say, 'My boy is this and my son is that and I need a recommendation for a job or I need this or that,' and if I knew them I would write some kind of non-committal-type thing, just to satisfy them and not only that but to try and help them out if I could without jeopardizing myself."

When Billy Rose Sprinkle was sent to prison, his mother, Grace, could not bear to see her son behind bars, so she chose not to visit him.

"When Billy was in the joint, she just sat there in the chair and grieved herself to death," Lorraine Sprinkle says. "She said, 'One day I'll be sitting in this chair, and he'll come walking down that driveway.'"

That day never came.

In May 1980, Grace Montana Sprinkle died at fifty-nine of cirrhosis of the liver.

Three months later, the Will County state's attorney's office wrote its first letter objecting to her son's parole consideration:

Enclosed you will find a copy of the State's Attorney's Statement of Facts containing the particularly heinous facts relative to the crime committed in Will County by Billy Rose Sprinkle and his co-defendant, James Perruquet. It is the feeling of the State's Attorney that Billy Rose Sprinkle and his co-defendant should remain in jail for the absolute maximum time allowed by law.

In his own letters to the PRB, Sprinkle was persistent in his attempt to gain his release and consistent in his claim of innocence:

The law says an adult cannot be held responsible for what he did as a juvenile. I was tryed as an adult but only in the eyes of the court. I was arrested at 14. I was a child, high on beer and airplane glue. I did not kill David Stukel. I was "NOT" allowed a polygraph test. If I am granted a parole, I will not be a return offender. I want to work, I like to work. I have many offerings of love, help and residency. I beg your office to give me every consideration for parole.

Like his father, Sprinkle was proficient at soliciting support from unlikely sources such as Pontiac guard D. Gear, who wrote a glowing assessment of the inmate's work ethic:

I have had a chance to observe Resident Sprinkle in day-to-day activities. Resident Sprinkle has taken night courses at the Pontiac high school to improve his education. Resident Sprinkle has been assigned as cell house help for about nine months. In his capacities as cell house help he has been assigned as a painter and other jobs as needed. He is respectful, trustworthy and responsible. Resident Sprinkle is a good worker with a great disposition. He handles every job task in a professional manner with a good attitude. If I owned a business I would hire him to work for me.

Ed Sprinkle doggedly covered all the angles in his crusade to have his son set free—from rounding up character references from men in high places to gaining assurances of post-prison employment from a man who had the power to cut corners, painters' union officer Herman W. Prescott:

This is to inform you that I am the Secretary-Treasurer of Painters District Council No. 30. Our jurisdiction covers a five-county area and if Billy Sprinkle is to be released from custody on parole, I will issue him a journeyman's card to do painting within 30 days of his release, and he will enjoy all the rights and privileges of any of our members. Several members of his family are members and have very good work records and are well qualified journeymen painters. It is my wish that you will give consideration to this matter.

Lawman John Shelley and Congressman Leroy Van Duyne weren't the only heavy hitters recruited by single-minded Ed Sprinkle to fill his son's PRB file with support letters. A person with perhaps more clout than either a sheriff or a politician was Tom Vinson, the public defender turned judge who wrote a passionate and prolific plea for his former client's release:

I, as Public Defender of Will County, represented Billy Sprinkle in defense of the charge of murder brought against him. The events of this case are clearly recalled, and I have no difficulty writing this letter, although my duties as public defender ceased more than 8 years ago, when I was appointed circuit judge. The crime, of course, was a most serious one and the sentence, although severe, was clearly in line with the seriousness and nature of the offense. The events were matters of public concern, and carried in detail by the local news media.

Billy Sprinkle and his co-defendant were very young offenders. I am sure that the character of Billy Sprinkle has changed since his terrible crime. I could never subscribe to the thought that the seriousness of the crime should, of itself, determine a lifetime behind bars. If his time behind bars has caused him to grow up, I would certainly want him on parole.

I have been asked to comment as to the public reaction if Billy Sprinkle were put on parole. In my opinion, it would be carried as a news item by the Joliet Herald News, certainly without violent comment, and the effect on the public would be about the same as a pebble thrown in our local Deep Waterway. Those that were in this area at the time would vaguely remember and turn to other and more interesting news. With our changing population, most of our present public would not remember and would care not at all.

We can make better use of the cells in prisons than keeping one in who was a boy at the time of the crime, and who has become a potentially good citizen, while behind bars, paying for his crime with more than 12 years of his life. Only those who feel that every criminal, except one of their family, should be behind bars forever, would have a different view. If the facts warrant parole, Billy Sprinkle should be out. If his life behind bars does not warrant parole, he must stay in until it does. I can only hope that the facts are in his favor.

A generation after Vinson's letter was written, the Stukels are stunned when informed about the letter and the judge's pebble-in-the-waterway statement. Debbie Stukel has the most difficult time digesting Vinson's comment that Will County residents would not recall the case, and she is equally perplexed that the words came out of a judge's mouth.

"I think this judge doesn't know people at all because something like that murder, no matter whose child it is—you remember! And he was a judge? That's amazing. They're supposed to be protecting the general public. These are people who are paid to look out for us. No adverse public reaction? What world are you living in? What air are you breathing?"

Former public defender Sam Andreano defends Vinson's prediction of a muted public reaction.

"I'm sure that some people would have remembered the case. By comparison, with Will County changing like it is today, people probably don't know what happened five years ago. At one point, I guess that [former state's attorney and congressman] George Sangmeister's name was known to everybody. Today, I bet twenty-five percent don't know him because fifty percent of the people living in this community didn't live here ten years ago. That's part of growing as a community.

And people that were eight at the time of the murder, and all of a sudden they are voting age, they wouldn't remember this. In a different vein, I'm driving the other day, and all of a sudden I see dump trucks and they've destroyed Loscheider Field. Loscheider Field was a big deal in the '70s because [William] Loscheider was a Joliet policeman who was killed in the line of duty, and now, thirty years later, we abolish the ballfield that is his memorial stadium? And we've got a mayor who was a policeman that worked with the guy!"

Billy Rose Sprinkle

On July 14, 1981, Ed Sprinkle's relentless pursuit of his boy's freedom was rewarded when the PRB approved the inmate's parole on just his fourth try.

On July 27, 1981, one month after Thomas Vinson's letter reached the inmate's file, the twenty-seven-year-old Sprinkle breathed the air outside of prison for the first time since age fourteen.

19

The Long Way Home

In the spring of 1978, James Perruquet was busy soliciting support letters from family and friends. Perruquet did not have a bulldog like Ed Sprinkle in his corner. He didn't have a sheriff vouching for him, but his file did receive a stream of support letters from relatives, including a heartfelt one from his mother, Hazel, who admitted that she should have done more for her son when he was a child:

I'd like to write this letter to ask that you give my son a chance to come home. We all miss him and want him. His father has been ill and he wants to have his boy home before he passes on. I fear that I will never do the things for James that I did for my other sons. My boy is a man now and needs a new clean life. I only wish I could erase the years that led to James imprisment. I think a hundred times a day how I could have prevented all this grief. I will help my son as much as anyone can humanely. I would have the time to give James the guidens he needed years ago. Please send our boy home.

Another blood connection, cousin Debbie Barclay, who made frequent visits to Menard from her southern Illinois home, made a valiant effort to have the PRB see Perruquet in a better light:

I'd just like to say that I believe he has matured and developed into a decent caring human being over his last years. He's both excited and looking forward to a second chance at living a clean fulfilling life. He has talked with me about the crime he committed and told me that he wants to really make it up to his family for the grief he has caused them.

James was a young immature boy when his crime was committed and he understands the seriousness of the crime now. James has been locked up and taught new ways through the young years of his life, he is now a man and would like to try on the outside world as an adult. His family and friends are willing to guide him and help him rehabilitate. Everyone here realizes it will be difficult for James to adjust his life and ways to civilian life. But we are all willing to help guide him so that he can have a fulfilled life.

I think that for James and his family that its important that he not be away any longer than absolutely necessary. James is in his best years for starting fresh right now. I'm sure he could find work very easy. And he would have his family all home and behind him one hundred percent. We all miss him very much and are looking forward to his homecoming.

The first protest letter filed by the state's attorney's office possessed far stronger language than any Will County letter of objection that landed in Sprinkle's file:

James Perruquet should not be paroled, based upon the hideous facts surrounding his victim's death. We do not feel that there can be any other decision, other than to deny James Perruquet's parole. The victim, David Stukel was a good student, never in any trouble, and never stayed out late at night. He was walking home from high school when James Perruquet and Billy Sprinkle accosted David Stukel. Perruquet forced David Stukel to commit acts of fellatio and pederasty with both himself and Billy Sprinkle.

After these acts were completed, David Stukel was brutally beaten by these defendants with their fists and kicked with their feet. Then Perruquet and Sprinkle beat the victim about the head, facial area and the body with a metal rod. Perruquet began to viciously beat David Stukel with a concrete block. Both defendants then just left the victim laying in the field.

The agony, pain and humiliation that David Stukel must have suffered before he died is too great to imagine. James Perruquet exhibited his fiendish nature through his response to this inhuman and senseless killing in that he, several minutes later, bragged to two other teenagers as to how he had killed his victim, and, in fact, showed them the blood stains on his hands and shoes. He, at no time, exhibited any remorse over the killing of David Stukel.

There can be no circumstances that would justify the parole of such a cold-blooded fiend.

Public defender-turned-judge Vinson also vouched for Perruquet. But the letter carried neither the length nor profundity of the one he wrote for Sprinkle:

I vividly recall the case. It was a very tough one for all concerned. I sincerely hope that James has grown up and sincerely hope that he is worthy of release. He was very young when the crime occurred.

Of course I have had no contact with him since he went to prison, and thus have no basis for opinion as to whether he should or should not be released. I do know full well, however, that no matter how terrible the crime, or the emotion at the time of sentence, if one does grow up and has the makings of a good resident outside prison, the severity of the crime should not stand in the way of release. James has now gone from youth to manhood, and if the authorities believe he should be released, I would certainly join in the effort.

No defense counsel has much, if any, weight in influencing release, whether or not that counsel has become a judge. But for whatever, if any, good this letter will have, it is gladly written..

Like Sprinkle, Perruquet received support from a high-ranking public servant—Illinois State Representative Bruce Richmond from downstate Murphysboro. And like Representative LeRoy Van Duyne's letter for Sprinkle, Richmond's was a token display of support for Perruquet:

I have been asked by one of my constituents whose integrity I admire to write this letter in support of James Perruquet's efforts to be paroled. I understand that James will be eligible for parole in the fall. He evidently has been working hard, going to school and in general doing all that he should. Any consideration given to this request will certainly be appreciated.

Perruquet also received support from a woman who fell in love with him from afar—pen pal Linda Matthews, who moved 250 miles from northern Illinois to an area near Menard. Unfortunately for Perruquet, Matthews grew weary of maintaining a relationship with an incarcerated man and returned to the Chicago area, but not before seeking Perruquet's release in a letter to the PRB:

I'm writing for a request of parole for resident James Perruquet. The crime he was charged and convicted on, was indeed a serious one. It will never be forgotten, but in time will be forgiven. I feel he has paid his debt to society, in full! He committed the crime as an ignorant child! He is now and has been an intelligent, responsible adult. He's learned his lesson, and has paid a very high price. Twelve years out of the important part of his life. Now he's asking you to grant him what every man wants and needs, a wife, a home, a family, and most of all, his freedom!

I began writing James over year ago. I found he was intelligent, kind, understanding, unselfish, and compassionate towards others. I left my home, friends, and job, just to be near him when he got out. I have a full-time job as a secretary. Now my last wish is to have him come home, so we can begin our life together. That, my friends, is all in your hands. I can only hope and pray you make a just and fair decision.

Like Sprinkle, Perruquet was not shy about filling up his file with self-penned letters. In one letter, Perruquet, who had been granted a transfer from Menard to the minimum-security Vienna Correctional Center, provided a litany of accomplishments while behind bars:

What I was convicted of was very serious. Now 12 years later, and being a 26 year old adult, I have understood what I have did, and still regret being a part of such crimes. I've been away from my family for along while. I'm sorry, theres nothing I really can do but ask for foreigivness. Since being with the department of corrections, I have worked as a Knitting Mechanic and a Sewing Machine Opertor. I become a member of the Institutional Chapter of the Jaycees. I became Chairman of all the money making programs and a Director of the Board of Director's, and Vice President. I was awarded a Membership for Life, to the Sharp Memorial Jaycees, and the U.S. Jaycees. I accomplished getting my GED. I stayed in "A" grade.

In a letter to the PRB, attorney E. Michael O'Brien, who was retained by the Perruquet family, states why his client should be paroled:

Subject to being paroled, petitioner will reside at the Faith Hope Love in Christ Halfway House located in Peoria, Illinois. In the past this Honorable Board has seen fit to parole several persons to the Faith Hope Love in Christ halfway house with excellent results. Local parole officer Howard Courtney has reviewed the background of petitioner, including recent psychiatric report and has granted Petitioner through his legal representatives to inform the Board that he has no objection to accepting Petitioner as a parolee. Petitioner first asks this Board to consider that he was only 14 years old when convicted. Petitioner admits his complicity in the count of murder but denies his involvement in the sexual charges. Petitioner states that there is nothing he can do to bring to life the victim and that if there is anything to be gained from this tragedy it is for Petitioner to seek every opportunity available to make himself a person worthy to release and an asset to the community, which Petitioner has done.

Petitioner's parents are elderly, in poor health, and are in need of support from Petitioner, who has shown guilt and remorse for his involvement in the offense to virtually everyone he has come in contact with. Petitioner would ask this Honorable Board to note that in his most recent psychiatric evaluation the testing psychologist stated that at this time there is no clinical reason for denying parole.

James Perruquet

Unlike Sprinkle, Perruquet, even with the hiring of a lawyer, admitting culpability for the murder, and having a clean psychiatric report, was not released on his fourth try.

Or his fifth.

Or his sixth.

But on July 6, 1983, nearly two years after his co-defendant left prison, the PRB approved the release of James Perruquet.

Two weeks later, on July 19, 1983, the twenty-nine-year-old Perruquet entered the free world.

20

Sending a Message

Standing five-feet tall and weighing less than a hundred pounds, Ethel Gingold is never the most imposing figure in the room. But as a humanitarian, she is a heavyweight. Gingold fights for the forgotten, and crusades for civil rights and civil liberties with equal fervor. As a champion of equal rights for minorities, Gingold, who is white, doesn't merely talk the talk—she walks hand-in-hand with her black brothers and sisters as a longtime member of the NAACP.

Growing up Jewish in Terre Haute, Ind., Gingold learned firsthand about intolerance, and she vowed at an early age to fight for the oppressed.

Gingold points to the black-and-white photograph inside her Springfield home that features a white baby beside a black baby.

"That's the way I've always envisioned society," Gingold says. "They're birthed and they're just so good, then they learn all this hate when they grow up."

In her fifties in the early 1970s, after enduring a divorce and looking for a challenge, Gingold earned a master's degree in criminal justice and joined a prison watchdog organization. Gingold, a loyal Democrat, eventually was appointed to the Prisoner Review Board by Republican Gov. Jim Thompson—a decision that Gingold calls "an act of God."

Ethel Gingold was in the PRB conference room in Springfield on three occasions when inmate Billy Rose Sprinkle came up for parole, voting twice to deny his release and approving it in July 1981, when he was set free.

Gingold voted against James Perruquet's release three times, but she issued a dissenting opinion in 1982, when six members voted to deny his release. The full board did not hear Perruquet's case in July 1983, when his release was approved by a panel that did not include Gingold.

A quarter-century after casting her "yes" votes for Sprinkle and Perruquet, Gingold discusses the case, which, on first mention, she does not recall. After poring over the facts of one of the hundreds of cases she ruled on, Gingold is shaken by the shocking details of the David Stukel murder.

"It was such an insidious crime. I couldn't get over it when I read it. And in retrospect, I wondered how I even voted for their release," says Gingold, who was sixty-two when she approved of Sprinkle being released.

"I really do wonder about that decision because of what they did to that young boy. I really cried when I read about the case. I've thought about the facts. I'm just trying to figure out what my rationale would have been. I'm sure their ages played a part. It was a really violent, vicious crime. It was despicable."

In July 1981, Gingold was the lone woman present at the hearing in which Sprinkle's release was granted. And she was joined by at least two board members with law-enforcement backgrounds. When informed that Sprinkle's release was approved even with the inmate picking up a felony conviction for aggravated battery while in prison, Gingold says, "I'm amazed that those law-enforcement guys went along with that."

Gingold, who says she was inclined to see the best in people, always did her homework before casting a vote.

"I just used to try to consider everything, their background, the support they would have upon release. I was just very careful. I tried to be fair. I've always tried to believe in rehabilitation, but with a really violent, vicious crime, maybe some of them should never be released. I was very careful because I was always worried about recidivism."

Billy Rose Sprinkle was imprisoned for just twelve years and ten months. James Perruquet was incarcerated for fourteen years and ten months. Why Sprinkle and Perruquet were released in so few years is the more puzzling question, but why Sprinkle walked first also warrants scrutiny. While incarcerated, Sprinkle and Perruquet had nearly equal numbers of "tickets" for minor infractions such as unauthorized movement, disobeying an order, loud TV, or possession of contraband—usually involving the transfer of cigarettes. Perruquet received twenty-one such tickets; Sprinkle had twenty, but he also was the possessor of two major tickets for the aggravated battery conviction and for assaulting a fellow inmate with a pipe.

How did Sprinkle, who was housed in maximum-security cell blocks and who was considered by psychiatrists to be a danger to himself and to others, overcome those major tickets and exit prison two years before Perruquet, who was not diagnosed with psychoses, who was not charged with a felony while behind bars, who was not a gang member, and who spent the majority of his time in minimum-security settings while in maximum-security prisons?

There are myriad factors that worked in Sprinkle's favor, the most significant of which was the endless campaigning by Ed Sprinkle. His ability to persuade Will County power brokers to stand up for his wayward son was a remarkable achievement. Another element that placed Sprinkle in a better light was the transcript of the confession having been a fixture in Perruquet's file, not his. When PRB members reviewed the files before casting votes, with Perruquet they were confronted with his impersonal account of the brutal murder in which he takes sole responsibility for smashing David Stukel's head with a cement block. With Sprinkle, details of the crime were limited to the statement of facts. Conversely, when Will County assistant state's attorneys, who were not part of the office's regime at the time of the murder, conducted research to compose Sprinkle's protest letters, they had the statement of facts to draw from but not necessarily Perruquet's confession. As a result, Perruquet's PRB file contained much harsher protest letters.

The charming Sprinkle provided the right doses of repentance and rhetoric during parole interviews, while the unpolished Perruquet had difficulty expressing himself. And even though local law enforcement believed that it was the streetwise Sprinkle who instigated the sexual assault and murder, that information was not part of the court records because, with no trials, there were no testimonies. In addition, Sprinkle's felony conviction in prison, although certainly a blemish that should have resulted in a longer prison stay, did not automatically add more time to his sentence as the presiding judge had indicated.

"A lot of the courts were still under the old interpretation that a consecutive sentence was a true consecutive sentence," says former DOC chief records officer and indeterminate sentencing authority John Groves. "With a one-to-ten, Sprinkle's sentence would have gone from seventy-five to ninety years to seventy-six to one hundred, and it wouldn't have affected his parole-eligibility date. And an aggravated battery against another prisoner doesn't carry much weight. Had it been an officer, that would have been a different story."

After Sprinkle and Perruquet were sentenced, reporters surrounded recently elected State's Attorney Louis Bertani, who read from a prepared statement:

"This brings to a close the legal proceedings surrounding one of the most heinous murders committed in Will County in years. The two youthful defendants, without any provocation from their victim, brutally beat him to death. I recognize in recommending this sentence that it is a long prison term for the two young defendants. I believe that in cases of this type the message must be clear to all those who remain in the community that those who contemptuously disregard the value of life will be prosecuted to the fullest extent of the law, and my office will continue to recommend stern punishment in all cases where contempt for the law is shown."

Bertani's well-intended post-trial rhetoric would ring hollow in July 1981 and July 1983—when Sprinkle and Perruquet walked out of penitentiaries.

In the early 1980s, with support letters in the files of Sprinkle and Perruquet overwhelmingly outnumbering letters of objection, the playing field was rendered even less level by a clerical error. Sometime after sentencing in 1969 and before Sprinkle and Perruquet became eligible for parole in 1978, the PRB made a documented request for the names and addresses of the victim's survivors, but Will County did not respond, leaving the Stukels in the dark regarding parole hearing dates for their son's murderers. As a result, while Sprinkle, Perruquet, and their families campaigned for freedom, Ray, Marilyn, Debbie, and Nancy's voices were not heard.

"They never once called us," Ray says. "If they would have called, I would have been there. They were supposed to let us know. 'You will be notified, Mr. Stukel.' Yeah, right!"

Asked if they would have protested in person, Marilyn says, "I know we would have been there. Those boys need not have been let out into society."

"We would have been there, if we had been given that option," Ray says. "We're still waiting for call one. We were told they would never get out. What a lie that was! With these two little bums, they come up for parole and—whoosh!—they turn them loose! If I was sitting on the parole board and I was passing judgment on someone that took a life for no reason, like these little clowns did, they would never get out. They took a life. They were the persons that did it, and they admitted it."

Ray turns his attention to the supposedly lengthy prison sentences.

"The numbers? What does it all mean? Nothing! Seventy-five years and another thirteen years for deviate sexual assault. I was told that because of the viciousness of the crime that they would never be let out."

The releases of Sprinkle and Perruquet were especially tough on Debbie and Nancy.

"I was angry," Debbie says. "My kids didn't have an uncle. They would have had some cousins. That was all taken away. I remember thinking, 'They're going to do the same thing to somebody else.' You just knew that they weren't sorry or reformed. That's just who they were because they were such young kids to be that way, so you knew as adults that they were only going to get worse."

"My brother's gone forever, and they're back out living a normal life," Nancy says. "I felt a lot of anger. Just talking about it now brings up a lot of pain."

Although Debbie says that the inmates should never have been released from prison, she now believes that it was a blessing that her family was left out of the parole process more than a quarter-century ago.

"With them being in prison and us not knowing where they were mentally, they might have come out and taken it out on my parents. Their lives were taken away. And maybe they would think, 'I'm going to take that away from them, too.' I want to say they're human beings, but they're not really human beings. You don't know if they would be sitting there all those years thinking, 'I'm going get revenge as soon as I get out.'"

The fact that the co-defendants were freed in 1981 and 1983 does not reflect negatively upon the state's attorney's office. But it is an indictment of the indeterminate sentencing formula. Prosecutors in the indeterminate sentencing era used the term "sending a message" when talking about the period's two-number system. But in the cases of Sprinkle and Perruquet, that message did not translate to decades of time in the system.

"A seventy-five to ninety is not a slap on the wrist in anybody's book, but anything short of a death sentence would not have kept them in for life," says former prosecutor Martin Rudman. "There was no life sentence back then. All you could do was send the parole board a strong signal with the bottom number. When sentencing judges gave seventy-five to ninety years, what they were really saying to the board was: 'If I wanted him to be eligible first time out of the box, I'd have given him a twenty.' The seventy-five years tells them that we thought this was a bad case."

Former investigator Dennis Jaskoviak didn't have much faith in the "message method" of sentencing.

"There are some people that get the message and ignore it. You know, it's supposed to be a fair and objective means of ensuring justice for everybody, but them getting out, I don't consider that getting the job done. I wasn't happy with it, but try to look into the minds of some of the judiciary types, and you'll give yourself a large headache."

Indeterminate sentencing expert John Groves says the numbers didn't always send the intended message.

"In Chicago, in Cook County, if a kid committed murder, they might give him a twenty to forty. If he was in St. Clair County, if he was sentenced for armed robbery, Judge [Harold] Farmer down there, he'd give 'em seventy-five to one hundred—for armed robbery! He was a hangin' judge. Now Will County, they used a little more discretion, so a seventy-five to ninety had some significance. But when the board looked at it, they weighed it and said, 'Well, if he had been in Cook County he would have got this type of sentence.' What the seventy-five-year sentence would have told them is, 'Well, had he been in Cook County, he would have got a forty."

Former public defender Sam Andreano takes a practical view of the short prison terms for Sprinkle and Perruquet.

"Everybody was getting out in about that length of time, regardless of their sentence. No one was staying in for twenty years. It was a horrible crime. If they serve twenty years or they serve thirty years … maybe some crimes have no redeeming number. The problem back then, we were facing such a crisis in the prison system where they were so overcrowded, and murderers were getting out in twelve to fourteen years."

Martin Rudman puts the issue into historical perspective.

"When Mike Orenic became a judge and George Sangmeister was elected state's attorney in '64, the criminal justice system at the local level and at the state level was conservative. In the eight years that followed, the system at the state level went the opposite direction and became liberal. When we all started, the people who went to prison were called inmates. Ten years later, they were residents. It started out warehousing, then rehabilitation. Then over the next thirty years, today the system is more conservative than when we all started. It's gone back to recognizing that there's no magical rehabilitation just by using words and having concepts. So when these fellows were coming up for parole, you have to put a perspective on what was going on at the state level. It didn't have an impact on the local level—because when you get a sentence of seventy-five to ninety, that's significant. But what was happening at the state level was a different ballgame."

21

"In the Middle of the Night"

In the movie *Rudy*, a Notre Dame Stadium groundskeeper tells Dan "Rudy" Ruettiger: "You're five foot nothin' and you weigh a hundred and nothin' and with hardly a speck of athletic ability." The movie is based on Joliet's Ruettiger family, an East Side, middle-class clan of fourteen children—all of whom have been nicknamed "Rudy" at one time or another—a family that in the 1960s lived one mile east of David Stukel.

Rudy is the story of undersized overachiever Dan "Rudy" Ruettiger, but it could have been about his younger brother Francis, David Stukel's best friend.

Dan, an author and motivational speaker, and Francis, a Joliet detective, defied overwhelming obstacles to reach seemingly unattainable goals—Dan beating the odds to play twenty-seven seconds for the Irish as a walk-on, and Francis powering his way to a bucketful of amateur weightlifting world records.

In 1968 when he entered high school, Francis Ruettiger was even smaller than David Stukel. He stood just four feet eleven and weighed less than a hundred pounds, but that did not stop him from competing in football, wrestling, and baseball. By his senior year, Francis was all of five feet four and weighed 135 pounds.

Ruettiger, who hasn't grown an inch since his high school days but now weighs 180 pounds, keeps the *Joliet Herald News* article detailing David Stukel's murder in a drawer in his office at Rudy's Gym, his weight-training center just west of Joliet. Francis doesn't keep the article to remind him of how his friend died. He keeps it to preserve the memory of how he lived.

"I feel good when I think about David and the fun we had," Ruettiger says. "The article inspires me to talk to kids about how short life can be, and that no matter how hard things get, you always have to realize that you have a life and a lot to look forward to, and that you better make the most of it. I always think about what David would be doing if he were alive. He'd probably still be in the area because he loved Joliet. I've always wondered what it would be like to meet his wife, his kids. I think we'd still be real close friends to this day, and he'd probably be a godparent to one of my kids. Knowing Dave, I think he'd be in some type of business. He wasn't the most aggressive person, but I can see him wearing a suit and tie, very successful, nice family, and kids with the same personality he had, very giving, very loving."

With Francis Ruettiger's physical makeup these days, you'd be hard-pressed to knock him off-balance. But his eyes moisten when he talks about childhood days spent with David Stukel.

Francis Ruettiger and David Stukel at their eighth-grade graduation.

"Dave and I were very close," says Francis, unable to hold back tears. "There's not a day that goes by that I don't keep him in my heart and my prayers. When I got the call on that Tuesday morning that he'd been murdered, I cried for two weeks. I was devastated."

Francis always thought of David as a brother, not that he needed another sibling to compete for second helpings at the Ruettiger dinner table.

"David was like an extension of my family."

Francis and David spent eight years together at St. Mary Magdalene.

"It took a lot to get David mad. A coach could be screaming at him, and he'd be smiling," Francis says. "He was a blast, a good kid. Never heard him cuss. Never saw him smart off to his parents. He had a lot of love for them. Dave never got in trouble. He was the good kid, the good student. I was just the opposite. I'd try to sit next to him so I could see his papers!"

Francis and David were inseparable in grade school. But for high school, David headed to East High, the polished public school, and Francis opted for Providence, the modest Catholic school three miles east of St. Mary Magdalene. But before high school began, Francis and David got together for a sleepover at the Stukels.

"It had to be a couple weeks before he was found dead, maybe the week before," Ruettiger says. "I spent the night. I was there all day Saturday. We went to the quarry and went swimming, jumped off the cliff into the water, had a great weekend, just doing things kids did, watching TV, playing baseball. I had dinner with his family. We played in his room. It was wonderful, and for years I replayed that weekend in my mind. I would sit back and think, 'At least I got to share that weekend with him.'"

A month after David's death, Francis was drawn to the crime scene.

"I rode my bike over to the place where David died without my parents knowing. I just wanted to be there. Even after high school, I went over there a few times, just to sit and think about what might have been going through his mind and how I could have helped if I had been there."

Francis believes that David would have done well in sports in high school and that based on the size of his feet, plus the height of his father and older sister, that he would have grown considerably.

"He was a good athlete," Francis says. "And unlike me, he was going to be tall. I thought of him growing to be six-two or six-three."

Those overachieving Ruettiger boys always did aim high.

On a chilly evening in February 1986, twenty-six-year-old Fred Hayes, a five-year veteran of the Joliet Police Department, was working the midnight shift, breaking in thirty-one-year-old rookie Francis Ruettiger.

"That night was the first night that I let Fran drive the squad car. That's a big step with rookies," says Hayes, who is now Joliet's chief of police. "I remember giving the wheel to Rudy. He seemed nervous but excited that I was giving him the chance to break loose."

Officer Francis Ruettiger

Hayes and Ruettiger were just beginning the shift when they received the report of a burglary in progress at Certified Foods on the East Side.

"I'm flying there because I'm all excited about going to a burglary," says Ruettiger, who was making a career change after being laid off by Caterpillar.

"Rudy was making sure that we were getting there quickly," Hayes says. "He wasn't reckless, but we got there quick, and we had called for the Fire Department to get some ladders because they were on the roof."

The two burglars, who had busted a hole in the roof with a pick ax and tripped a motion detector as they lowered themselves into the store, climbed down the ladder and into the hands of officers.

"When we're putting the bracelets on them, I can see Rudy is acting pretty emotional," Hayes says. "He seemed agitated, and he was kind of rough on the guy, not to where he was punching the guy or hitting the guy, but he was kind of manhandling him. I remember stepping in and saying, 'OK, OK, we got them' and I'm thinking, 'What's up with this?'"

The complexion of the night changed in a heartbeat for Ruettiger. The adrenaline rush of speeding to a crime scene for the first time was suddenly squelched by the shock of coming face-to-face with Billy Rose Sprinkle.

"I had no idea who it was because I had never seen the kid before," Ruettiger says. "And then when he was identified as Billy Sprinkle, the emotions I felt, the rage I went through when I heard that name—everything that happened to David came flooding back."

After the thirty-two-year-old Sprinkle and his nineteen-year-old nephew, Ronnie Sprinkle, were arrested, just two-tenths of a mile west of the Sprinkle homestead, Hayes addressed his partner's behavior.

"Rudy is still really charged, so that's when I started asking him, 'What's going on here?' And Rudy starts telling me that one of the guys had killed his friend. I started to tell him, 'Hey, you've got to be careful because you're going to come across people that you know—you may someday have to arrest a next-door neighbor, so you've really got to watch your emotions.' But Rudy starts telling me a little bit more about what had happened to his friend. And after hearing what he had to say, I thought, 'Wow, that under the circumstances Rudy's reaction was a little more reserved than probably most people would have been.' There isn't a way to prepare for a chance meeting like that. There's a brutal murder, it's your buddy, you've probably moved on but it's in the back of your mind, and all of a sudden, in the middle of the night, it's thrown in your face."

Sprinkle was brought to the Joliet City Jail, where he told investigators that he was on the roof trying talk his nephew out of burglarizing the store, but an eyewitness saw two men climbing to the roof at the same time.

"It took everything … to not go in there," says Ruettiger. "I just had to stay out of the interrogation. I had some not-so-good thoughts going through my head. I probably would have lost my job if I had the chance to get close to him."

After Sprinkle's parole was approved in July 1981, he sent a thank-you letter to the PRB:

Dear Mr. William Kauffman PRB director

I appeared before the Prisoner Review Board yesterday 7-14-81. I found out today that I have been granted a Parole.

Sir, I write to you giving thanks. Please see that all Board Members receive my personal thanks.

I came to jail at the age of 14. I'll be 28 Dec 28-81. I will not ever return to Prison, I promise you Mr. Kauffman I will do everything I possibly can to be a model citizen.

For my father, brothers and sisters and from myself, I thank you and all Board members.

I will work regularly, attend church services regularly.

May God Bless You and Yours sir.

Sincerely

C-15277—Bill Sprinkle

Upon leaving prison, Sprinkle was funneled into the Model Ex-Offender Program in Joliet, but he did not magically become a model citizen. Just nine months after writing the thank-you letter to the PRB, Sprinkle was a suspect in a burglary at a restaurant, but he was not charged. One month later, Sprinkle was arrested on an assault charge after a fight outside a liquor store, but the victim opted not to press charges. A year later, Sprinkle was arrested for driving under the influence of alcohol; illegal transportation of alcohol; failure to signal; and improper lane usage. He was ticketed and fined. Just two weeks after being hit with the multiple driving violations, Sprinkle was arrested for "theft under $300," but the charges were dropped.

Sprinkle's rap sheet remained clean for more than two years—until he and nephew Ronnie climbed to the roof of Certified Foods and tripped an alarm that signaled a parole violation.

While indeterminate sentencing did not guarantee long jail terms, it did give the PRB extreme latitude in keeping parolees such as Sprinkle and Perruquet under a microscope. As long as an indeterminately sentenced inmate was not discharged from parole stipulations, he remained on parole—conceivably for life. With Sprinkle not having received his complete discharge from parole for the murder of David Stukel, any conviction or behavioral problem could result in a violation and a return trip to prison. And that was precisely the case in February 1986 when Francis Ruettiger arrested Billy Rose Sprinkle.

Sprinkle's bail was set at $10,000. But after state's attorney Edward Petka reviewed the facts of the 1968 murder, Sprinkle's bail was raised to $100,000.

A "hold order" was issued by the Department of Corrections, leaving no doubt: After four and one-half years as a free man, Billy Rose Sprinkle was returning to prison.

22

On Vacation

In 1975 in the southern Illinois town of Royalton—just up the road from James Perruquet's hometown of Herrin, fifteen-year-old Desiree Vreeland married high school sweetheart William Bailey and had his baby, Billy. At the time, Desiree did not know James Perruquet, but she was friends with Karen Perruquet, the wife of James' older brother Joseph, who spent much of his teenage years bouncing around Illinois juvenile jails before committing a burglary that sealed his first trip to the penitentiary.

Joseph was twenty-three when he was assigned to the Menard Correctional Center, home to twenty-one-year-old James Perruquet.

James and Joseph Perruquet at Menard in 1975.

"Karen had been visiting Joe," Desiree says. "So Karen says, 'I've got a brother-in-law that needs some friends on the outside—why don't you go up and see him?' So me and my husband, William, we would go up and see James."

Desiree and William would regularly visit James and find creative ways to cast sunshine into his otherwise dreary life, such as the day William surprised the inmate with a one-day marriage license with the names "Desiree" and "James" typed on it.

"We saw James for a while, but William decided he didn't want to go see James anymore," Desiree says. "We agreed we wouldn't go, but I snuck up there a lot after my husband stopped going, and we were writing letters. My husband had a feeling that I was sneaking up there to see James, so he brought a picture of me up to Menard and asked the guards if I'd been going up there, but I didn't care—I was interested in James."

Desiree gradually drifted apart from William and divorced him. She stopped communicating with James, too, and eventually married again, but that didn't last. Then, when Perruquet was paroled in July 1983, he headed to Royalton and hooked up with Desiree, a twenty-three-year-old single mother with a seven-year-old son.

James and Desiree Perruquet

Four days shy of his one-year anniversary of leaving prison, James married Desiree, this time with their names typed on a legal document.

James began taking classes at the local community college, and it was the perfect start to a new life. But there was a detractor in the background.

"My second husband, Charley, had been a prison guard," Desiree says. "And he always told me, 'Desiree, you don't want to be with this man. I've seen it happen many times. The man's out here on vacation, and he'll be back.'"

Desiree became obsessed with that prediction.

"James was a good father. But what Charley said was in the back of my mind, so when James started talking about wanting a baby, I kept telling him I didn't want to get pregnant. I said, 'I'm afraid you'll end up back to jail.'"

Despite her concerns, Desiree decided to grant James' wish to father a child.

"I couldn't get pregnant. So me and James and my son got down on our knees and held hands, and we prayed for a baby. And within six months, I was pregnant."

James David Perruquet Jr. was born January 25, 1986.

A month before his son's birth, James Perruquet decided to take care of unfinished business—a meeting with Sprinkle for the first time on the outside since they were fourteen. In a letter, Perruquet discusses that reunion:

You know, it was just something I had to get out of the way, see how Billy was doing. Basically, if you look at it, from the time before we ended up in prison together till I got out, him and I had kinda been like brothers more or less, even though we never seen each other and we didn't write each other or anything. But this whole deal kinda tied us together. Me and Desiree was together that day. We looked him up in the phone book and called him. We went out there and we seen Billy for a little bit. Billy and I was happy to see each other and to be free. We hugged. He looked the same and I don't think he really changed by the way he talked. Still a tough guy. I seen

Billy's dad. They took me in and showed me pictures of his sister Doll, what she looks like. I was a little uncomfortable because all these years I let Billy make it seem as if I was the soul person in all of this—I was dedicated to Billy and my story because of his sister Doll. We was boyfriend and girlfriend. But seeing Billy, it was like a weight lifted off me, something I had to put behind me for good.

While in the East High neighborhood, Perruquet returned to the scene of the crime, unaware that the high school had closed in 1983 after operating for just nineteen years, a victim of declining enrollments and its wrong-side-of-town location. The East High building had been converted into a heavily guarded, state-run technical school for troubled teens. In a letter, Perruquet discusses driving up to where the back parking lot leads to Hill Street and the old Frtiz farm:

I didn't even know East High School was now some sort of military deal. We come up Mills Road, drive around the school, through that parking lot back there. There was a gate where Hill Street starts. I stopped, I got out, walked over there and I was shaking and everything and just thinking. Some military dude come up and asks me What are you doing? I said I thought this road was still open I ain't been up here in awhile. I could feel the presence of what happened there. It's in my heart still, something's there, something's still wrong. I was being drawn back. I lost my life there—in Joliet. When I went back, it scared me. I always thought, if I got out I want to go back over in that area, something's keeping me from letting it go. But I was scared maybe of facing the truth. And it looked so much alike in that area. At least in my mind it still did. But I never did try to come back in the other way. I left and never came back.

Two years after James Perruquet was released from prison, parole agent Booker O'Neal recommended that Perruquet receive his discharge from all parole stipulations for the murder of David Stukel, but the PRB rejected the request. Three months later, O'Neal again sought the ex-inmate's complete discharge from parole, but the PRB again said no. Despite those setbacks, Perruquet seemed to have his life in order, but, like Sprinkle, his world crashed in 1986 when he too was charged with burglarizing a store. And with son Jimmy just seven months old, Perruquet returned to prison.

Asked to discuss the case, Perruquet writes that he did not burglarize Charles Stilley's mom and pop used furniture/appliance store in the southern Illinois town of Energy:

I paid the lady the money for an air conditioner. I had a receipt. I left and word got around that they were looking for two guys, one with blond hair, one with dark hair who bought an air conditioner then robbed the store and was driving a blue car, which I was driving a brown car. My brother-in-law has brown hair and I was dark haired. The police came and interviewed us and a few days later they arrested us. They want to send me back to prison on some trumped up charges. I don't even know how you burglarize a store when it's open? This lawyer kept telling me that we got it beat.

Three months after Billy Rose Sprinkle was sent back to prison, James Perruquet returned to the penitentiary a bitter man, but he channeled that negative energy into trips to the prison's law library. Desiree divorced James and moved on with her life, reuniting with—but not marrying—ex-husband number two, Charley, and she had his baby, Kyle, while James was in prison.

Despite the loss of his wife, Perruquet, with the help of fellow inmates, kept his focus on the law books, miraculously located a precedent in a 1925 case, and filed an appeal. In September 1988, attorney Thomas A. Lilien handled Perruquet's appeal, and the appellate court ruled in the inmate's favor.

"The question was: did he commit a crime of opportunity, or did he plan to commit a crime before he went in?" says Lilien. "He had gone there to buy an air conditioner and he purchased it, so it wasn't that he was totally up to no good, but he then apparently snatched some money while the store owner was away from the cash register getting the air conditioner. But it was charged as a burglary, not as a theft. The conviction we were fighting was a burglary, and to commit a burglary you have to have the intent to commit the theft when you go in."

In October 1988, the PRB declared Perruquet a non-violator, and he was released from prison after serving twenty-eight months. Perruquet was thirty-four and desperate to get his life back. He reunited with Desiree, even though they were divorced, and he managed to keep his record clean for the next year.

In September 1989, Larry Fired, Perruquet's new parole agent, filed for his complete discharge from parole stipulations for the 1968 offenses, and one month later—possibly to make amends for the wrongful conviction—the PRB approved Perruquet's discharge from parole supervision.

Although Perruquet stayed in prison for two years longer than Sprinkle, he accomplished something Sprinkle had not been able to do—be granted a discharge from parole for the murder of David Stukel.

Desiree is no longer married to James Perruquet, but she is still fond of him. "I still love him. I'll always care for James because James is a good man, the best family man I've ever been with. James was in tune with my children like no other man. He's a very good father. James was caring. He would cook for the kids, clean, play with them. He always wanted to take them to Six Flags or to the zoo or something. He was real good with my older son, Billy. He got him into sports. James was into the picnics, going to the parks—all that excited him. He was just like a kid himself."

Desiree describes James as gentle and mild-mannered.

"James was just dealt a shitty deal in life, I think, but he rarely displayed a temper. One time his mom came to me and said he stole a hundred dollars from her. When he came home from work, I asked him if he did that, and he said, 'No.' And I said, 'Don't lie to me! Did you steal her money? You were over there earlier in the day.' Well, finally, I got him to admit it, and I said, 'You're going to take that money to her, and you're going to apologize to her.' He said, 'No, I can't do that.' I said, 'Why that's your mom!' He said, 'She don't care about me.' So I went and picked up the phone. I said, 'Either you take the money back to her, or I'm gonna call her and tell her to come over and get it.' And when I did that, he went to grab the phone and said, 'No you're not calling her,' and I jerked the phone and it popped him right in the nose. And he got mad, and he smacked me and gave me a black eye. That's the only time I saw him get angry, and I pushed him all the time. Believe me, I pushed that man. I pushed him to the extreme that he should have gotten mad at me many times and he didn't."

Desiree says that alcohol and drugs were not an issue during her marriage to Perruquet.

"There were never alcohol problems with James," Desiree says. "He didn't drink alcohol much. Very seldom. Didn't like drugs. I'm being totally honest because this was back when I was twenty-three and I still smoked weed, and he just didn't like it. He told me, 'If that's something you got to do, do it, but just leave me out of it.' He didn't like it. It made his head feel strange. He told me he used to drink a lot of alcohol when he was a young kid up in Joliet. But when I got him, after him getting out of prison, if we went out, he'd drink Coke."

With Desiree constantly prodding him for information, Perruquet reluctantly discussed the murder with her.

"I asked James, 'Why did you guys decide to kill him?' And he said that they were messed up on glue and whiskey. I said, 'So you just decided to kill him?' And he said, 'Yeah.' And I said, 'What was that like, killing somebody?' He said, 'I don't want to talk about this. I've lived with this all my life.' And I said, 'I need to know. Was the boy begging for his life?' And he said, 'No, he didn't say much.' James said he didn't feel any emotions while murdering the boy, but that when he sobered up he was upset."

Perruquet attempted to appease Desiree's desire to understand why David Stukel was murdered, but her curiosity was insatiable.

"I wanted to know from him," Desiree says. "The stories that I heard about the murder were horror stories. I had heard that they had cut off his privates, stuck them in his mouth, put cigarette burns all over his body. He said that wasn't true. He said he was very sorry for what he did do but that all that stuff wasn't true."

Even though the appellate court overturned James Perruquet's burglary conviction, he did not re-enter society in a positive frame of mind.

Perruquet writes that he came out "salty"—prison slang for being bitter and angry:

I felt like I lost everything—all those young years being with my son. I was salty because I was doing good out there. I was going to school, making something of me. Even though I won two years down the road, things between me and Desiree had done fell apart. I got out and started living with her but I just didn't give a damn anymore. I thought the world owed me something now, so I just started stealing and not living right.

Desiree agrees that after James was released from prison on the burglary charge, he was a changed man.

"He just couldn't stop stealing. If we went to the store and had the money in our pockets, I guarantee you we would leave and he would have something else that we didn't pay for. I said to James, 'You're welcome to stay here, be the kids' dad, but I'm not going to be with you in that way,' so it was like we were brother and sister."

The relationship officially ended when Perruquet was arrested for retail theft in Herrin in August 1990.

"James was trying to steal a camcorder and was using my son as camouflage," Desiree says. "We were shopping for Kyle's third birthday party, getting the plates and candles, and James decides he wants a camcorder because he wants to camcord the party. I'm like, 'We can't afford that.' And I said, 'I got a funny feeling somebody's watching you,' and sure enough, when he walked out, they got him. He went back to prison, and Kyle had to have a party without James."

Perruquet was out on bail for stealing the camcorder in Williamson County when he was caught stealing in Franklin County. In September 1990, Perruquet was convicted of retail theft for stealing the camcorder, and was given a five-year sentence to run concurrent with a three-year term for the second retail theft. Less than two years after his burglary conviction was overturned and just ten months after he was discharged from his association with the 1968 case, Perruquet's self-destruction resulted in his third trip to prison, his first as a determinately sentenced inmate. He was released two years later, and in January 1993, with Desiree out of his life, the thirty-eight-year-old Perruquet headed to the last place one would expect—Joliet, where he landed after niece Cecelia Perruquet—sister Fern's twenty-two-year-old daughter—invited him to move in with her.

In a letter, Perruquet explains how he met and fell in love with wife number two—Tammie Lou Troyer:

I was hanging out with someone who lived by Washington Junior High. While spending the night there I meet Tammie, who in my eyes was beautiful and I fell in love with her right off the bat. She was living with her ex who was a drunk and was abusing her and her kids. Three weeks after moving to Joliet, I found myself standing up for Tammie and wanting to take her and her two kids out of the abusing home. Tammie and the kids never needed to live like that again. Days after I first met Tammie, I found us living in a hotel. I was worried that Tammie's ex would find us and hurt one of them so we take off to Southern Illinois. We moved to Marion and for a couple weeks everything I try or did fell in. We was living in a car. So I started stealing and returning things and getting money back for it and we started living in a hotel.

On July 27, 1993, James, thirty-nine, and Tammie Lou, twenty-nine, were married in Marion in the southern reaches of the state.

Two months later, Perruquet was convicted of yet another retail theft, and another "vacation" came to an end.

23

Family First

James Perruquet walked out of prison for the fourth time in September 1994 and reunited with second wife Tammie Lou, who had moved 205 miles northwest of Marion to the central Illinois town of Eureka, eighty-five miles southwest of Joliet.

James, Tammie Lou and her young children, Ashley and Nathan, moved into a trailer on Lot No. 80 of the Timberland Mobile Park in Goodfield, six miles south of Eureka.

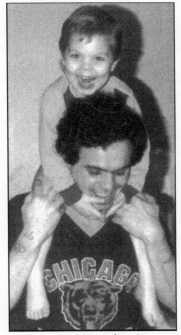

James Perruquet and son Jimmy

At forty years old, James Perruquet vowed to never again jeopardize his freedom. He took a job as a cashier at a convenience store, and he never missed a shift, walking or riding a bicycle two miles to work in all types of weather so that Tammie Lou could have the car.

Perruquet was on top of the world.

He loved and adored Tammie Lou. He was making money, helping raise nine-year-old Ashley and four-year-old Nathan, and cultivating long-distance relationships with namesake Jimmy and Desiree's children, stepsons Billy and Kyle. When Tammie Lou responds to a question about James' personality and his relationship with her children, it's as if she had compared notes with Desiree.

"He's very sweet," Tammie Lou says. "He would do anything for anybody. His family always comes first. He loves his children. They love their dad."

Based on Tammie Lou's loving portrayal of her husband, it would seem to confirm that all is right in James Perruquet's world. But Tammie Lou's assessment of James was not in response to a writer's question. Her answer was in response to a query by Woodford County public defender Diana Barber and was culled from the two-foot-high stack of 1,200 pages of Case No. 95CF 44: Illinois vs. James Perruquet for the murder of Christopher Hudson.

On April 10, 1995, Desiree Perruquet drives the nearly two hundred miles from southern Illinois to Goodfield to bring nine-year-old Jimmy to his father's trailer home for spring break.

Four days later, James tucks Jimmy, Ashley, and Nathan into bed around eight o'clock.

James and Tammie Lou envision a quiet evening—frying catfish and watching TV. But those plans disintegrate over James' suspicion that next-door neighbor Chris Hudson has been flirting with his wife and that she has not rejected those advances.

Despite not being regarded as a drinker, Perruquet consumes six wine coolers during the course of the evening, then confronts Tammie Lou about her relationship with Hudson. There are several flareups between James and Tammie Lou throughout the night. Hudson hears the commotion and makes a series of phone calls to the Perruquets, inquiring about Tammie Lou's well-being and offering to protect her.

At nine o'clock, Hudson calls 911 and reports a domestic disturbance at the Perruquet trailer, but when Woodford County officers arrive, Perruquet and Tammie Lou assure them that everything is under control. After the officers leave, the arguing escalates, and shortly after midnight, Hudson intervenes. He shouts to Tammie Lou through the unlocked screen door: "Are you OK?"—then tugs on the door handle. Perruquet screams, "Stay out of this" and unsuccessfully struggles to keep the door shut.

Perruquet, who later would say that he felt as if he'd been stabbed in the stomach, storms out the door, knocks Hudson to the cement patio, and stabs him multiple times.

Perruquet then says to the bloodied and barely conscious Hudson, "C'mon, buddy, we've got to get you to a hospital." Perruquet bear-hugs Hudson and begins dragging him to his car. But Perruquet panics, lowers Hudson to the ground, jumps in his car, and flees.

Hudson dies of internal bleeding at a local hospital an hour later.

The next night, Perruquet is arrested near Eureka.

The knife is never found and public defender Diana Barber insists that Hudson initiated the confrontation and stabbed Perruquet in the stomach, and that Perruquet, in self-defense, stabbed Hudson with his own knife.

In October 1995, James Perruquet took the stand at the Woodford County Courthouse and was cross-examined by State's Attorney John B. Huschen. The exchange became the heart of the prosecution's case:

Mr. Perruquet, got any explanation how Chris Hudson received seven stab wounds to his body while he was laying on your patio?

"No, unless ... no."

You have any explanation for that?

"No, I mean, according to my neighbor there were only three stab wounds when I left."

You're saying that somebody else stabbed him?

"I can't say."

You have no recollection of how Chris Hudson received the stab wounds?

"I do not remember having a knife in my hand. I do not even ... I remember very faintly, like, OK, like where neighbors started breaking us up, letting each other go. Other than that, from the time I come out the door and hit the ground till when they started breaking it up, I do not remember."

You don't remember anything?

"I don't."

You don't remember thrusting your arms towards his body?

"No."

You don't remember having a knife?

"No."

In the most controversial aspect of the trial, Perruquet's revelation that he doesn't remember the stabbing sabotages his public defender's self-defense strategy. Prosecutor Huschen, now a circuit court judge in Woodford County, recalls being shocked by the defense's flawed approach.

"He doesn't remember the actual stabbing. But the defense attorney was trying to show that the defendant was acting in self-defense because the victim came to the house and was banging on the door, and that he was just protecting himself and protecting his house. But you can only claim self-defense if you admit to doing the act! You know, 'I stabbed him, but I stabbed him because I was afraid he was going to kill me.' But you can't say, 'I don't remember what happened, but whatever I did do it was in self-defense!' The biggest issue of the trial was that point. And I think it ultimately ended up, 'He didn't remember what happened, and if you don't remember what happened, how can you plead self-defense?'"

Huschen says that Perruquet's behavior after the stabbing did not reflect the actions of a man defending himself.

"His wife was messing around in some fashion with the victim, and he and the victim had a fight about it. They're arguing and he basically comes flying out of the trailer with a knife, they fall on the ground and he stabs him. He dragged him towards his car. And the suspect says that he was dragging him to take him to the hospital. So if that's the case, why drop him? And the defendant also throws all of his clothes away. He goes to Wal-Mart to buy all new clothes, and he stabbed himself to make it look like it was self-defense."

In a letter, Perruquet describes his version of the deadly encounter:

Tammie and me, we never argued violently at any point. We raised our voices and I covered her mouth so I can get a word in. I was not out to do anyone any harm. It all came to me, unwanted. Chris was told by numerous people to stay out of it. He made threats to me and others heard him and he came to my home after being told by both of us to stay out of it. I never went looking for him. Chris knocked on the door. I opened the door and see Chris and tell him to leave. I slammed the door, trying to lock it, when Chris jerks the door open. I tell him it's none of his business and pull the door shut. Chris gets into a tug-a-war with me over the door. I felt a sting on my side and come flying out the door. I really don't recall stabbing him. You know how you can close your eyes and picture yourself doing it? I can't remember that. I remember I hit him with my fist a couple times because he forced me to come out of the house. I figured he was hurt. That's when I tried to take him to the hospital. I had to get in the car, turn on the ignition before I could hit the button to open the hatchback and that's when I got spooked and ran.

In the 1960s, the murder rate in Will County was low, averaging five or six deaths per year. But homicides in sparsely populated Woodford County are downright rare—whether it was the 1960s or today.

"They don't happen very often," says John Huschen, Woodford County's state's attorney before becoming a judge in 1996.

"The Perruquet case was the only murder case I had during my eight-year term as state's attorney. I can count the murder cases in this county back to the '60s when my dad was state's attorney," says Huschen, whose father was the county's top prosecutor from 1960 to 1972, a twelve-year stretch in which just three murders cases were tried.

"My predecessor as state's attorney, who was state's attorney for eight years, inherited one murder case," Huschen says. "It was a retrial of a murder that occurred a tenure before him. Then he had another, and he didn't have to try it because the guy killed himself in jail."

With murder cases so rare in Woodford County, one can understand why its citizens and public servants were a bit rusty in October 1995, when Perruquet stood trial. When the jury was presented with deliberation instructions, everything got lost in translation. As a result, after a weekend of discussions, the confused jurors returned not one verdict but a trifecta of the most serious guilty verdicts—first-degree murder, second-degree murder, and involuntary manslaughter.

"Jury instructions were given improperly," Huschen says. "And the verdicts were returned wrong. If the jury found him guilty of first-degree murder, they had no reason to find him guilty of the other charges."

The next day, Judge Richard Baner reinstructed the jury, which deliberated for six hours without reaching a verdict. But the jury needed just one hour the next morning to return a guilty verdict on the most serious charge—first-degree murder—assuring that Perruquet would spend the rest of his life in prison, and—in the trial's death-penalty phase—would be in the battle of his life for his life.

Huschen figured a date with the electric chair was a long shot. But when Will County's Ray Van Dyke, the detective who worked the David Stukel case, took the stand in Woodford County and walked its citizens through the 1968 murder, the prosecutor realized the jurors no longer had an easy decision.

"When they found him guilty of first-degree murder, I had the distinct impression that they thought, 'We'll impose life, no big deal,'" Huschen says. "But when they learned the particulars of the prior murder, you could tell that they were like, 'Now what do we do?' There was certainly more than one juror that had reassessed their positions as far as the ease for which they were going to get through the third phase of a capital murder trial."

Huschen says the jurors weren't alone in being affected by the details of Perruquet's first murder.

"The 1968 murder is the most serious and gruesome murder that I'd ever heard of. I thought it was downright disgusting. And I think that was the reaction of the jury. It was like, 'Oh, no! This isn't gonna be as easy as we thought.'"

Despite Van Dyke's testimony, it took jurors just three hours to spare Perruquet's life.

"They did the right thing," Huschen says. "I didn't think it was warranted based on the facts of the second murder, with the girlfriend and boyfriend element, the fight. It was authorized by statute to argue for the death penalty because of the prior murder, but that doesn't mean I don't have personal beliefs."

24

"A Gentler Spirit"

In April 1995, central Illinois resident Dave Johnson opened the Sunday *Peoria Journal-Star* and read about James Perruquet being charged with murder. Three days later, Johnson made the short drive to Eureka to visit the man he had lost touch with for more than a decade.

In the early 1980s, Johnson was assistant director of the Peoria-area halfway house Faith, Hope and Love, which cared for ex-offenders and also provided ministry in prisons. In '81, Johnson became acquainted with Perruquet during a visit to the Vienna Correctional Center in southern Illinois.

"I met James during one of the weekend retreats," says Johnson, who was twenty-five when he met the twenty-seven-year-old inmate.

"I got laid off from my truck-driving job. I'd been doing that for about three or four years. And I was a part-time policeman during the same time in South Pekin. One of the judges that had been involved in Faith, Hope and Love asked me if I'd be interested in going to work there."

After they met at Vienna, Johnson believed Perruquet had a genuine desire to change.

"With my law-enforcement background, I'm not much of a sucker," Johnson says. "Ninety-eight percent of the people that are in prison are just cons. But James was different. He never asked me for money. He never asked me for anything that would benefit him. I've been around thousands of convicts, and James just has a gentler spirit. I would go to visit James, and I would take my youngest daughter, Kristi, who was five at the time, and I trusted James with my daughter. I'd let James live in my house today."

Johnson's fondness for Perruquet is evident when he talks about the inmate's seemingly selfless nature.

"James played chess in prison, and he had won a trophy," Johnson says. "And he took his trophy, and he changed it around a little. There was almost an angel-looking figure on it, and he pasted a picture of Kristi on it and sent it to her, and it read, '*My No. 1 Angel, Kristi.*' Another time, he quit smoking. Well, just before Christmas along comes a box in the mail with presents for everybody in the family, or as much of a present as James could get from prison. James took his cigarette money and bought Kristi a doll and sent something for me and my wife, and then he started smoking again."

When James Perruquet stabbed next-door neighbor Chris Hudson to death, Dave Johnson had no idea that his friend was living just fifteen miles away.

"If I would have known, I would have been helping him out," Johnson says. "I testified at James' parole hearing in 1983, the one that was successful. Then I kept in touch, and the first time he got married [to Desiree], I drove down to southern Illinois for his wedding. After that, seeing him was sparse, and then it just kind of dwindled away to nothing."

Johnson doesn't believe that Perruquet should have been convicted of first-degree murder in the Woodford County case.

"Given those circumstances, I probably would have defended my home, too," Johnson says. "This was clearly a case of self-defense."

When the trial began, Johnson was there every day.

"It's interesting how people that I talked to at the trial felt about James. He worked at a gas station, and the owner said James would walk to work in a blizzard, and that he would let James watch the store while he was on vacation, and there'd never be a nickel missing."

Before and during the trial, Perruquet openly discussed details of the case with Johnson.

"James talked about not remembering all the details, and I absolutely believe he was being honest with me," Johnson says. "The guy he killed was an ex-convict, too, and a punk, a drug guy. James had been drinking, and he's not a typical drinker. And what I heard is that the guy was taunting James about the fact that he was sleeping with Tammie."

Even though Tammie Lou took the stand in the death-penalty phase and praised James, Johnson believes she could have prevented him from being convicted of first-degree murder.

"I think she was afraid that it would all come out about her relationship with this guy, and she'd have to put up with chastisement from her mother. She didn't want to be dragged into the dirt. I know James doesn't want to believe she cheated on him, but if I was going to put money down, that's the side I would go with."

When Dave Johnson sat through James Perruquet's murder trial, he got a firsthand look at the legal representation his friend received and was not impressed. For that reason, Johnson is spearheading a relief effort for Perruquet.

"I would like to see James' sentence reduced, anything that would let him get out of prison before he dies," Johnson says.

The main thrust of the appeal is insufficient representation—that public defender Diana Barber based her case on self-defense, then inadvertently sabotaged that strategy by allowing Perruquet to testify that he didn't recall stabbing Chris Hudson.

"James' attorney made a lot of mistakes," Johnson says. "This was a self-defense case, and I think James had a good shot at proving it if he had a competent attorney."

Don Pioletti, who was the Woodford County public defender in 1995 when his assistant, Barber, handled the Perruquet murder trial, presents another scenario for the foiled self-defense strategy.

"I'm not sure it was a tactical error on Diana's part," says Pioletti, who did not participate in Perruquet's defense. "The error on her part might have been putting him on the witness stand, but at the same time, if you're going to claim self-defense, you have to put him on the stand, and it might have been that she put him on the stand and then, all of a sudden, his testimony takes her by surprise, because they do that. Even though you're the defense attorney, defendants think for themselves. And it might have been that he was the one doing the thinking at the time, and he thought wrong. I can't imagine Diana making that mistake on her own without help from him. She was a very capable attorney."

Although Pioletti defends Barber, who has left Woodford County, he says that Perruquet might have a sound basis for an appeal.

"I think there are some issues that possibly are legitimate, and because the jury instructions were done wrong, that could be a mistrial right there," Pioletti says. "And regarding the self-defense, if the attorney is found to be the one who actually was going with self-defense, and she had him testify that he didn't know what happened—man, you can't do that because the defendant has to know exactly what happened when you're in the self-defense mode."

During the trial, after the improper jury instructions resulted in the inconsistent first verdict, Judge Richard Baner allowed the defense to eliminate either second-degree murder or involuntary manslaughter from the jury's options. Involuntary manslaughter—with a sentence of probation to five years—indicates a person acted in a reckless manner that caused the victim's death. Second-degree murder—with a sentence of four to twenty years—is a crime of passion.

Johnson was present for the crucial closed-door meeting with Barber and Perruquet that resulted in the defendant electing to eliminate second-degree murder, leaving first-degree murder—a premeditated act—and involuntary manslaughter as the jurors' only choices.

"James was confused by the advice given to him by Diana Barber," Johnson says. "When James went in to consult with her, he asked that I come too, and she was absolutely useless. In fact, she said, 'I wash my hands of this.' She said, 'Dave, you and James are going to have to decide.' I was appalled. She didn't want to be responsible. James and I were forced to make the decision, and the gamble was this: If you say you'll go for manslaughter, does that give the jury the easy way out because he did kill the guy? And in their minds they might just say, 'OK, we'll give him manslaughter.' Or do they push for the first-degree murder, which in my mind and in James' mind, there wasn't enough evidence to convict him of that. How could it be premeditated if the guy's coming in James' door? So James opted to throw out second-degree murder and leave in manslaughter and first-degree murder, and that's what he got convicted of—first-degree murder! He got a life sentence when really it should have been involuntary manslaughter—or not guilty for acting in self-defense."

Despite Diana Barber's alleged shortcomings in defending Perruquet during the trial, her argument in the death-penalty phase helped keep Perruquet out of the electric chair:

"You learned a lot about James Perruquet. This is a man who worked hard. This was a man who was trying to make it in the world outside prison, and that's a world he had hardly ever seen. He called his employer the day after Christopher Hudson's death to apologize for not being at work. This is not some evil person who's here to wreak havoc upon the land. This is somebody who was trying to get his life put together. He loved his children; you heard the mobile park manager talk about how he helped her with many things around the trailer park, but most particularly how he helped take the kids to recreation night at the gym, spent time playing with the kids, transported them back and forth, never caused any problems as a tenant. Then what happens? What happens is some degree of betrayal by his wife, which leads to the continuing confrontation that came up between Christopher Hudson and James Perruquet. Christopher Hudson's conduct provoked the actual altercation that took place. Without what had gone on between Chris and Tammie, between Chris and James, this whole incident wouldn't have happened. Chris was right there. He kept getting in James' face, kept revving it up, kept calling on the phone, kept pulling that door open. These are all things that led to Christopher Hudson's ultimate death. These are the acts that somehow caused a man who was trying very hard to make a living, to take care of his family, who loved his wife and who loved his children, to get into an altercation. I can only ask that you think carefully about what type of case deserves a death penalty and what type of person deserves a death penalty. I submit that you cannot find either of those things present in the facts of the case or in the person of James Perruquet."

In seeking intervention by Illinois Gov. Rod Blagojevich regarding James Perruquet's second murder conviction, Johnson has recruited former Faith, Hope and Love director Michael Learn to present the case to the PRB.

Johnson has confidence in Michael Learn's ability to expertly present executive clemency cases, and that faith is not based on Learn's credentials. Learn doesn't have a bachelor's degree and at times talks as if he has spent more time in a poolroom than a courtroom.

"I'm a paralegal, but I got special permission from the PRB in 1983 to plead executive clemencies," says Learn, who would need to convince the PRB that Perruquet's conviction was rife with blunders for the appeal to reach Gov. Blagojevich's desk.

"James' 1995 case is a classic self-defense case," Learn says. "The guy's beating on your door, trying to get in your house. And at crossroads in the proceedings, his lawyer let James make up his own mind. Well, James doesn't have the wherewithal to make those kinds of decisions."

Learn has rare insight into the criminal mind, and it's not just because he was the leader of a ministry that provided guidance to convicts and ex-convicts. Learn acquired his knowledge the hard way.

"I'm not the boy next door," Learn says in introducing his criminal past.

"I'm a big believer in personal responsibility, and I did what I was convicted of doing, mostly armed robberies," says Learn, who knows firsthand that prison can obliterate one's spirit.

"Prison is basically a never-ending, almost crushing existence of monotony punctuated by occasional bursts of violence. Prison is like having a wet blanket over your face—it suffocates you if you can't find something to occupy yourself. And in cases where they sentence people to an inordinate amount of time, like James, you wake up and say, 'I got to get out of here!' Prison can destroy you. It's vicious. But then because you survive it, you start getting numb to it. I remember the day I saw a kid getting stabbed at Pontiac, and they threw him off the gallery.

He fell nine stories, splattered down on the bottom, and I turned to my friend and I said, 'Sam, you got any coffee?' When you get to that point, you've got a problem."

Learn likes to quote from ex-convict Eldridge Cleaver's book, *Soul on Ice*, when talking about the paralyzing effects of prison.

"What Eldridge Cleaver said was, 'You don't grow in prison, there's nothing to grow into.' In other words, you go into prison when you're fourteen, like James did, and you come out when you're twenty-nine, but you're still fourteen, and there's no way to catch up. You are not equipped for so many different things. And that was one of the biggest problems with James. He got out; he had support; he did well. You want to be somewhat independent; you want to chart your own course—that's human nature. That's what happened with Jimmy. When he got away from his support group, that's when the problems started. Then later on, when he tied up with this girl, everything went south."

Learn has a unique vantage point from which to examine the lives of Perruquet and Sprinkle.

Learn spent seven years behind bars with Sprinkle at Pontiac, and while running Faith, Hope and Love, he gained insight into the mind of Perruquet.

"Billy was no punk, I'll give him that," Learn says. "Billy is verbal. Billy can be quite charming when he wants to be. But Billy came from a very dysfunctional family, and you hate to be judgmental, but Billy is about the closest thing to Beverly Hillbilly-type people that you're ever gonna meet. Billy was always in trouble for making hooch or trying to get some reefer or doing something stupid, but then again, who wasn't. It's the penitentiary, you know. It's not like you're sitting around reading Dostoevski."

Learn believes that Perruquet was "along for the ride" in the murder of David Stukel.

"James is not a leader. James is the type of person that reacts to what's going on; he doesn't start it," Learn says. "James was shy and easily intimidated. Now Billy was a very aggressive kid. James pretty much got dragged along in that whole thing. Having said that, James damn sure knew better than to stay there once Billy started what he started with that kid—that's on him. I know Billy and I know James, and James was not the point man."

Informed that Sprinkle has repeatedly denied participating in the sexual assault and murder, Learn says, "If you're waiting for Billy to fess up, it's gonna be a long time. See, back in the day, if you get caught in the bank with money in your hand and a smoking pistol and a dead guard at your feet, you plead not guilty. You take a jury trial: not guilty. After they sentence your butt: not guilty.

You're never guilty because as you go through the system, given the nature of a trial and the appeal process, the more chances there are for things to go wrong for the state, so you're never guilty. So Billy's never gonna fess up. You can forget about that."

In January 1980, Michael Learn walked away from the penitentiary and into Faith, Hope and Love, where he would rise from resident to running the show.

One of the most gratifying aspects of Learn's post-prison life has been assisting worthy inmates, first at FHL and later through filing clemency petitions.

"It's a miracle that they let me do it," Learn says. "I'm the only ex-convict that's ever been allowed to plead anything before the board."

It's also somewhat of a miracle that Michael Learn is alive. A year into preparing Perruquet's appeal, Learn's work came to a standstill when his heart literally stood still.

"They basically brought Michael back from the dead," Dave Johnson says. "It was a massive heart attack. Initially, the doctors told me he'd never leave the hospital, and for a while they were convinced they ought to pull the plug."

"I got beat up pretty bad, and I've had seven heart attacks over ten years," Learn says. "This one was the worst—about half the muscle of my heart died."

Despite his failing health, Learn isn't giving up on his ability to help inmates such as James Perruquet gain their freedom.

"The PRB is the court of last resort. If we blow it there, we are—rather James is—going to die in prison."

25

Fueling the Rage

There are several parallels between James Perruquet and Billy Rose Sprinkle. They endured deplorable childhoods as middle children with seven siblings. They were incarcerated at fourteen and made return trips to the penitentiary eighteen years later on burglary charges. And on the outside, they each fell for women with the same first names—Tammie Lou Troyer and Tammy Brooks.

The moment that Tammy Brooks laid eyes on Billy Rose Sprinkle, in November 1981, she was attracted to him. Tammy was a seventeen-year-old high school dropout and single mom with a seven-month-old baby boy living in an apartment on Joliet's East Side. Sprinkle was a twenty-seven-year-old ex-convict, four months removed from prison and living at hid dad's house.

"The girl and her boyfriend living downstairs from me were going to pick up food stamps. We had to stop by his job, and I saw this gorgeous man standing outside. And he finally came over and started talking to me. Then he started coming over to visit. At first I ran away from him because he had a girlfriend."

Six months later, Tammy again ran into Billy.

"We were together from that day on," says Tammy, who

Tammy Brooks at 17. at the time was moving to another apartment on Joliet's Northwest Side. Billy left his father's home, and he moved in with Tammy and her son.

"We were a pretty good distance from his dad's house, but he was over there every day," Tammy says of the apartment she shared with Billy six miles from the Sprinkle homestead.

"Billy felt a need to be at his father's side. He told me many times that his dad had high expectations of him and expected him to pick up wherever he left off. Billy was gone every day, and I had nowhere to go. I didn't have a car, a phone. I had a young child, plus I was in love. That was the most innocent love I've ever felt. I believed that there was nothing or no one that could ever come between us."

Billy and Tammy eventually gave up the apartment and landed at the Sprinkle homestead, in the smaller of the two homes, a move that Tammy would live to regret.

Tammy, now living in Tennessee, says Billy's alcoholism and temper were a lethal mix.

"Billy would snap real quick when he was drinking," says the five-foot-two Tammy, who weighed less than one hundred pounds as a teenager. "He would get cocky and downright mean. He never seriously hurt me, but he terrified me. And I don't know if it was intentional or not, but he would hurt me where it wouldn't show. The first time he raised a hand at me, the last words out of my mouth were, 'If it's going to make you feel more like a man to hit me, then go ahead and knock yourself out,' not knowing he would actually do it. I had never been hit before. It knocked me halfway across the room."

After moving into the second Sprinkle home, Tammy was frightened by everyone in Billy's family. "They would get drunk and get to arguing. That part of my life—it amazes me that I even lived through it!" Tammy says. "I was more afraid of the family than I was of Billy, and I was more afraid of his sister Lorraine than I was of anybody in the family. She'd throw a punch just as bad as any of the boys. She didn't take crap off anybody, and I envied her for that because I was always so scared and so timid, and every time Billy would come at me, you know, I'd crouch down in a corner and just cry and cover my head and say, 'Please don't hit me. Please don't hit me.' One time, Billy and his nephew Ronnie had come home with blood all over them. They were drunk, and they told Lorraine about these guys at the quarry that beat the hell out of them. Lorraine went up there, and Billy and Ronnie said she had these guys on the edge of the cliff with a sawed-off shotgun. One of them said something, and she told him, 'You better shut your damn mouth or your buddies are going to be picking your head up on the other side of the quarry!' And I don't doubt that it happened because I know how crazy she was. One time, we pulled into the parking lot of a liquor store. I was in the passenger's seat, and this guy walked up to the car and he stuck his head in the driver's-side window and said to Lorraine, 'Oh, baby, I'd like to have your ass on a silver platter.' And she reached under the seat and pulled out a thirty-eight and laid it on her lap and said, 'Yeah, mother fucker, if you don't get away from my car, I'm gonna have your goddam head on a paper plate!'"

While living at the Sprinkle homestead, Tammy feared for her safety within the family's inner circle, but she felt completely insulated from the outside world.

"One of the things that I did like about living there was that even though the house was in a bad neighborhood, I could have slept in my front yard stark-naked and nobody would have come near me because people around there knew the Sprinkles were nuts."

Tammy came into Billy's life after Grace Sprinkle died.

"All I was told about his mom was that she was mean as hell but that she had a big heart, and that she had great big boobs and carried a twenty-two between them," Tammy says.

Asked if she saw any nurturing at the Sprinkle homestead, Tammy pauses, then responds, "Sometimes things seemed good and everybody was being a family; then other days, I'd watch them try to beat each other with shovels."

Tammy says that when Billy was sober, "He was as good as gold. Billy only hit me one time when he was sober. We got into an argument outside the house, and he knocked the shit out of me and dragged me by my shirt across the lot, across the driveway, and up the stairs into the house."

In conversations about his life in prison, Sprinkle told Tammy that he frequently used drugs and drank alcohol. Lorraine believes that her brother became an alcoholic and drug addict while behind bars.

"There was many times that I went to the joint to visit him and Billy was stoned," Lorraine says. "When Billy got out of prison, he was a monster. He was a little boy when he went in, and shit happens in there. He was very hardened when he came out. He never confided in me what happened to him in prison, but it's like he could never have sex with his wives unless he was drunk after that. And he just couldn't overcome the alcohol when he got out. When the alcohol enters Billy's body, he is like Jekyll and Hyde, and he would beat the shit out of Tammy."

Asked if she knew about the murder early in her relationship with Billy, Tammy says: "He told me his side of it. Billy said he walked into the barn behind his father's house and caught some kid raping his younger sister, Doll. He told me the kid was seventeen. Billy told me they cut the boy's penis off and stuffed it in his mouth, and shoved a lead pipe up his ass."

You can circle the date September 17 on Billy Rose Sprinkle's sociopathic calendar. He was arrested for murder on September 17, 1968. On that date in 1974, Sprinkle assaulted a fellow inmate with a lead pipe. And on September 17, 1976,

Sprinkle orchestrated the stabbing of a fellow gang member while inside the Pontiac Correctional Center.

Finally, Sprinkle had reason to celebrate on a 17th of September, when in 1985 he and common-law wife Tammy introduced Amanda Rose Sprinkle to the world.

Although Sprinkle passed down the name "Rose" to Amanda, the name's history remains a mystery, even though Lorraine says her brother was named after former baseball star Pete Rose. The Pete Rose revelation initially made sense. Ed Sprinkle once lived in Kentucky, across the Ohio River from Riverfront Stadium, where Pete Rose played for the Cincinnati Reds. But Rose would not have been in left field in 1953, the year Billy Rose was born in Michigan. In fact, when Billy Rose came into play, Pete Rose was four months shy of his thirteenth birthday.

When she was nearly full term with Amanda, Tammy realized that Billy wouldn't be changing his ways.

"A week before Amanda was born—I told Billy that I was leaving," Tammy says. "I had my son by the hand. I walked up to the side of the road, and Billy grabbed me and threw me down. He was drunk and he tossed me in the ditch."

Tammy and her unborn baby were not injured. But even after the birth of Amanda and with the responsibility of fathering a four-year-old stepson, Sprinkle continued his descent into alcoholism and physical abuse.

"I was scared to leave Billy," Tammy says. "There were times when I wanted to call the police, but if I called and he went back to prison, I was terrified of what his family would do to me."

Five weeks after Amanda was born, Tammy says she watched Billy "shoot up cocaine in my kitchen."

The next week, Billy sent Tammy running to Tennessee with her two children in tow.

"It was Halloween in 1985. Billy came in drunk and started to hit me," Tammy says. "I was holding Amanda, and I told him, 'Don't you dare hit me with this child in my arms!' He told me he would burn down the house with me and my kids in it. The next day, I called my mother, and she came and got us while he was gone. My mother put me and the kids up in a motel until we got a bus to Tennessee—it was November the fifth of 1985, three o'clock in the morning that we got there."

Tammy Brooks left Sprinkle six weeks after Amanda was born. Less than four months later, Sprinkle was arrested on the 1986 burglary charge and sent back to prison.

Tammy Brooks has always had a stubborn streak. "I was a rebellious little brat in high school. I was too busy doing my own thing, so I didn't graduate, and I didn't get my GED until I was twenty-six."

Tammy's hard-headed nature might explain why less than a year after she left Billy, she inexplicably returned to the Sprinkle homestead with her two children in December 1986 while he was serving the burglary sentence.

"I have to knock my head into the wall fifteen or twenty times before I get it," says Tammy with a laugh. "Apparently, it took everything that I went through for me to be who I am today, and I don't have a problem with who I am anymore. I arrived on Christmas Eve and left on Valentine's Day. I was considering getting back with Billy, but I don't know if I was really trying to get back with him or that I was looking for another escape route out of whatever hell I had created for myself."

In February 1987, Sprinkle, believing that Tammy was again in his corner, portrayed himself in a letter to the PRB as a model family man:

I did 4 years and 7 months on Parole with no problems. I kept a steady, good-paying job. I was a responsible family man, with a child and common law wife. I'm positive my former parole agents will vouch for me as to being dependable, trustworthy, honest, respectful and responsible. I have a child—17 months and a boy whom I plan to adopt. My fiance—Tammy Brooks and I are planning marriage. While on Parole I was a good, law abiding citizen and a asset to the community. I'm no thief, liar or vagabond.

Loyal to her brother despite his return to prison, Lorraine Sprinkle picked up her ill father's banner and wrote to the PRB in October 1987:

Our father is in failing health. Ed Sprinkle has a serious heart condition, complicated by high blood pressure, diabetes, emphysema and severe arthritis. Our mother died when Billy was quite young. We would like Billy to have the opportunity to spend some time with his father while it is possible, and we ask that you give this information careful consideration in your deliberations.

In November 1987, a Will County assistant state's attorney wrote a protest letter that had stronger wording than any letter that landed in Sprinkle's file during his first run through the system:

The murder and deviate sexual assault performed on the victim was extremely brutal. Your department previously determined the inmate was fit for parole and paroled him in July 1981. Your decision to parole him was obviously not well-founded in that he committed a burglary while on parole. The inmate has proven he is a dangerous individual with a history of violent crimes, and parole in this case is totally inappropriate. He should have to complete his sentence as it was originally set in 1969.

Burned once, the board denied Sprinkle's first parole bid, in November 1987.

Two months later, on January 11, 1988, Ed Sprinkle—Billy's greatest supporter and the patriarch of the Sprinkle family—died at age seventy-one.

"Dad died when Billy was back in the joint," Lorraine says. "Billy was dressed nice in a black suit, but he was in chains. And the state made us pay for the suit."

After a year of inactivity in Sprinkle's file, in November 1988 he was again denied parole.

When Tammy Brooks walked away from the Sprinkle family for the second time, in February 1987, she returned to Tennessee but stayed in touch with Billy, who had transferred to Menard.

"He was writing me and telling me how much he loved me, but I never intended on getting back with him. I did what I could. I'd send him some money, but I finally had to tell him, 'I'm raising these kids. I can't keep sending money because it's taking food out of my kids' mouths.'"

While Sprinkle continued to profess his love for Tammy, he was courting Sharon Bartley Cole, who became acquainted with Sprinkle through his cellmate's mother.

Sharon sent letters, visited, and fell in love with Billy, and on March 10, 1989, thirty-five-year-old Billy married forty-six-year-old Sharon inside the walls of Menard.

"It really caught me off-guard when I heard Billy had gotten married," Tammy says. "That really floored me because he had been writing all those love letters to me. It just made me mad that he lied to me."

Nine months after Billy married Sharon in a jailhouse ceremony, the PRB denied Sprinkle's release for the third time. But Sprinkle did receive a transfer from maximum-security Menard to minimum-security Danville.

In October 1990, Sharon Sprinkle praised her husband in a letter to the PRB:

Billy has attended an alcohol abuse program. He is enrolled in school. During the water shortage, he was helping to make life more comfortable for his fellow inmates by carrying water to the cell houses. Every day he works on the yard detail, where he mows grass, plant flowers, trims shrubs. Billy has not had any problems adjusting to the routine of this facility. He has not received any tickets. Taking into account that he has been incarcerated most of his adult life, I think that he has done a wonderful job of adjusting. I am Billy's wife. I am employed as a secretary at a hospital. If Billy is paroled, he has a very Loving Wife who will stand beside him and a stable home to come to.

In November 1990, the Will County state's attorney sent a venomous letter protesting repeat-offender Sprinkle's parole consideration:

Billy Sprinkle's criminal history indicates a complete disrespect for humanity. He was convicted of Murder and Deviate Sexual Assault. He continued on his criminal path of human destruction. It is obvious that Sprinkle is a menace and a severe threat to society after being convicted of heinous crimes. Billy Sprinkle was free to make decisions which controlled his actions, yet Billy Sprinkle chose to break the law. Billy Sprinkle should never be paroled until his sentence is served in full.

Despite the potent protest letter, Sprinkle was paroled in December 1990.

26

One Victim after Another

In December 1993, parole officer Nancy Bowman filed papers to have Billy Rose Sprinkle removed from parole stipulations on the 1968 conviction, but Sprinkle was denied, and he responded by immersing himself in his two standbys—substance abuse and abusing women. Throughout the '90s, Sprinkle's wife, Sharon, provided a loving environment and diligently went to work. He reciprocated with infrequent employment and frequent beatings. Sharon's trailer on a dead-end, gravel road in Springfield was no longer a safe haven, and she finally gained the courage to flee to Texas in October 1997.

"Sharon never had him arrested for smacking her around," Lorraine Sprinkle says. "She told me that the first time he hit her, he said, 'You ever tell Lorraine, I'll beat your brains out! I'll kill ya!' And that's because I told Billy, 'If you ever hit her, I'll kill you!' She was so terrified of him that she never told me—until after she left for Texas."

While Billy was able to keep his abuse of Sharon a secret from Lorraine throughout most of the '90s, his problems with alcohol, just as was the case in the early '80s after being released on the murder charge, surfaced on his rap sheet.

In '95, he was charged with leaving the scene of an accident, and in '96, he was arrested for driving under the influence of alcohol. But he was not declared a parole violator on either occasion.

Lorraine witnessed her brother's steady self-destruction.

"When he'd come to see me, I'd tell him on the phone, 'Billy, if you're drinking, don't bother coming,' and Jesus Christ, he came to my house drunk. He pulled up and fell out of the goddam truck, fell flat on his face! My kids were little so I went out there, and I slammed him up against the garage. I said, 'No! This shit ain't going on, so get your happy-ass back in the truck with your little wife and go home!' He's like, 'I ain't good enough to come in your house?' I says, 'That's not the point.' I says, 'I told you before, don't ever come in my yard drinking.' He made Sharon go out and sleep in the truck with him. He treated her like shit. I wouldn't treat a dog like that."

Sharon, who acknowledges the beatings but chooses not to talk about them, officially shed the Sprinkle name in March 1999. Her ex-husband likes to tell the PRB that it was he who divorced her because she was a cocaine junkie.

"What Billy says is not true," Lorraine says. "He wants to lay the blame on somebody else. It's always somebody else's fault!"

Connie Nudo lives in a cozy two-bedroom bungalow on Cincinnati Avenue in Grandview, a village in Springfield, home to the PRB. When she looks out of her back-door window, past one of her gardens, she sees the vacant lot where Billy and Sharon Sprinkle once lived.

"In 1994, I had come to live with my dad who was ill," Connie says. "We'd sit in the backyard and I'd say, 'Look at that nice-looking guy. I'm going to go over there and ask his mom if I can get introduced to him,' and I found out later that it was his wife! Thank God I didn't do it."

Connie's dad died in '96, and she was alone for a year, occupying her time with her gardens, pets, and innumerable illnesses.

"I've got emphysema, arthritis, asthma, and chronic bronchitis," Connie says. And, almost as an afterthought, she says, "I've got cancer, too. Colon cancer."

Shortly after Sharon left town, Connie was introduced to Billy Rose Sprinkle.

"Billy was friends with my neighbor Dorothy Glass. I was at Dorothy's house, and Billy stopped by," Connie says. "I told him to come over for coffee sometime. The bank was repossessing the trailer after Sharon left, and he said, 'I guess I'll have to go to the Salvation Army.' I said, 'You can stay here, sleep on the couch till you get a job.' About three months later, we become lovers."

Connie says the first two years of living with Billy were blissful, so they married on June 7, 1999.

Connie was fifty-one. Billy was forty-five, and the honeymoon lasted three months.

"When we met, Billy wasn't drinking much, just beer," Connie says. "He never drank heavy, never drank vodka, never smacked me. If he didn't drink, we got along. At first, he was perfect. Then, after you get married, they think they own you. And then the hard liquor started coming down his throat, and that's when the beatings started. He hurt me bad a few times, but I didn't turn him in because I didn't want him going back to prison."

While taking away Connie's dignity, Sprinkle also was stealing her late father's tools to finance his drinking.

Billy and Connie Sprinkle on their wedding day.

"My dad was a tool man, and I mean he had everything underneath the sun," Connie says. "Well, one day I couldn't find the hedge clippers. I said, 'Billy, you seen them hedge clippers?' And he says, 'They're out in the shed.' I had a hunch, so I stopped in the pawn shop, and I went right to them! I said, 'Who brought these in?' He said, 'Your husband.' I said, 'How much do I have to pay to get my tool back?' I had to pay $5, and he only got $4 for them. I set the clippers in front of Billy, and I says, 'You said you didn't know where this was—you took them and got money for booze!' He said, 'Somebody probably broke into the building and took them down there.' And I said, 'No, Billy, he told me it was you!' One day I started looking around and seeing a lot of other stuff gone, so I walked down to the pawn shop and I seen it all right there! I wasn't about to buy my stuff back because it would of cost me too much. And I knew if I brought it up, I'd end up getting hit."

While Sprinkle was pawning tools and beating his wife, he also was showering her with love.

"He showed me love like I'd never seen," Connie says. "He followed me around like a little bitty puppy dog and would do everything for me, but when he'd drink vodka, it made him violent."

Connie says her husband's increase in alcohol consumption was in response to their declining health.

"I started having problems breathing, and then there was his hepatitis C. It dries up your liver and turns it to sand, but he would drink vodka right out of the bottle—gulp-gulp-gulp-gulp—and it made him crazy."

Connie Sprinkle believes she knows why husband Billy switched from beer to vodka as his drink of choice. And her theory has more to do with his conscience than his hepatitis C.

"He wanted to forget—and the beer wouldn't do it," Connie says.

With steely resolve, Sprinkle has for decades denied sexually assaulting and murdering David Stukel. In letters to the governor and to PRB, as well as in psychological reports, he has claimed that he sat by the road while Perruquet committed the crimes. But in the privacy of his home, with Connie by his side and no parole votes hanging in the balance, Sprinkle tells a different story.

Asked if she believes that her husband committed the murder, Connie says, "He told me he did it. I think he tries to put in his mind that he didn't do it so it don't bother him worse, but you can tell it bothers him by the way he sleeps. He'd talk a lot about it in his sleep. He'd say, 'I'm sorry.' He'd wake up in a cold sweat. He told me he'd dream about it over and over—he'd be running, trying to get away from it, and he never could get away from it."

Sprinkle has often discussed the murder with Connie.

"He would cry about it when he was drinking, and he cried about it when he was sober. He feels bad about it. You could see him at times, staring at nothing. He'd say, 'I can't change it. We weren't planning on killing him. I didn't mean to do it.'"

The motive that Sprinkle shared with Connie is the same version he told to Tammy Brooks.

"He said the guy they killed had raped his sister. Billy told me he didn't sexually assault the boy, but that he cut his dick off. He said that he had to plead guilty because, 'They was giving us the death penalty.' He said he didn't know that wasn't true until it was too late."

Asked if she thinks Billy sexually assaulted David Stukel, Connie says, "I do. Billy's probably afraid to admit it because he can't forgive hisself."

In April 1999, Billy Rose Sprinkle was arrested by Grandview police for failing to register as a sex offender. He was instructed to bring a sex-offender registration card to parole officer Nancy Bowman's office within two weeks.

Exactly two weeks later, Sprinkle drank vodka before walking into the service center and becoming confrontational with Bowman. Sprinkle refused to take a balloon alcohol test, then bolted, ignoring Bowman's order to stop. Officers went to Sprinkle's home and administered a Breathalyzer test, which he failed.

In her report, Bowman recommended that Sprinkle be returned to the DOC to await a PRB hearing, and that he receive substance-abuse counseling while in lockup:

"I am asking that he be ordered to attend sex-offender and substance-abuse counseling," wrote Bowman. "His violent history, coupled with alcohol, puts him at a high risk to re-offend."

Sprinkle was held at the Graham Correctional Center southeast of Springfield for forty-four days, during which time he underwent substance-abuse counseling.

The PRB showed leniency by not declaring him in violation of his parole stipulations, but it did add sex-offender and addiction counseling to his parole order. A week after his release, Sprinkle began receiving alcohol-abuse treatment, first on an inpatient basis, then as an outpatient.

"The first thing he did after he came home from Graham, he said, 'Let's get some booze!'" Connie says. "Billy went through a lot of classes, but that don't mean nothing. They made him go up here to the Triangle Center. He was staying up there and went through that. After that he was only going to classes at night. As soon as he'd get out, he'd get a bottle before he'd come home."

The drinking and beatings escalated over the next two years, and in May 2001, Connie, convinced that her life and Sprinkle's rage were on a deadly path, called his new parole officer, Teri Myers. Parole officials came to the Sprinkle home, and he was returned to Graham to await another hearing. Three weeks later, the PRB surprisingly tossed him a second stay-out-of-jail card.

"He was drinking real bad, and I was tired of being hit," Connie says. "I hoped it would wake him up. But two days after he was out of Graham the second time, he was drinking again! He was drinking real bad, then it got even worse. I was scared in my own house. He had me so scared that I was afraid to breathe, to even let any air out, afraid he'd take that away."

Connie Sprinkle shakes her head as she reflects upon the events of Saturday, July 28, 2001, the day Billy Rose Sprinkle engaged in a drinking marathon, consuming four pints of vodka and four quarts of beer and chasing it all with a death threat.

"I was outside fooling with the flowers," Connie says. "Billy pulls up on his bike and falls off. I looked at his eyes and could see clear through them. We went inside and Billy started saying, 'It don't hurt for me to drink.' I said, 'It don't hurt you to drink, but you don't have to set there drinking that f-ing vodka!' He starts talking about my [adult] son Vince, and I said, 'Shut your f-ing mouth!' He said, 'Bitch, shut your mouth or I'll fucking kill you!'"

Against her better judgment, Connie screamed "Bullshit!" before attempting to escape.

"He grabbed my hand. He pulled. I pulled. It took a lot but I got loose, thank goodness. I didn't know he tore my right arm out of the socket. And I didn't know the screen door was locked. I hit the door and smashed through it."

Cradling her injured right arm with her left arm, Connie raced across her front patio and down the street to neighbor Dorothy Glass' house.

"I told Dorothy what happened, and she called the cops," Connie says. "I told her, 'I don't want to put him in jail, just tell him to go away and never come back!'"

A Sangamon County Sheriff's Department officer arrived at Dorothy's house just after Billy showed up on his bicycle.

"Jim, Dorothy's husband, was in the driveway," Connie says. "I was behind the screen door. Billy threatened to kill Jim and Dorothy. Billy started to go up the driveway, and Jim says, 'You don't want to come up here, Billy, because you'll be messing with the wrong person.' Jim's three times the size of Billy, and Billy backed down. As soon as Billy came up into the driveway, the cop pulled up right behind him, so I screamed, 'Tell him I don't want him around my house anymore!' The cop says, 'You're going to have to come out, I can't hear you.' Billy says, 'Please Connie, don't do this.' I said, 'Please? I've asked you, Please don't drink, and you do it anyway.' The cop told Billy to go and not come back. He got on his bike, fell off, then left."

After the officer left, Connie remained at her neighbor's home, where she was told by another neighbor that Sprinkle returned home with more alcohol. Connie immediately called Teri Myers, Billy's parole officer.

"I says to Teri, 'He's going to kill me if you don't come and get him!'"

Agent Myers called the police, who rushed to the Sprinkle home and administered a Breathalyzer.

The results were staggering.

"They said he should be dead," Connie says. "It was clear to the end of the scale."

Connie Sprinkle has endured a tough existence, practically from birth. "When I was young I got mentally abused by my mom. For some reason, she didn't like me," Connie says in a near-whisper.

Connie is a good woman who has attracted bad men into her life. She stands by Billy despite her instincts and in spite of the beatings. In one breath, she calls Billy the love of her life and, in the next, a monster. She is an enabler who seems unable, or unwilling, to flee from her tormentor.

Connie sits at her circular, four-seat kitchen table, points to the chair to her left and says, "It's Billy's chair. He won't sit anyplace else because he can see both doors. Must be from being in prison—he wants to see everything that's going on."

Once, while sitting in his chair of choice, the five-foot-eight, 175-pound Sprinkle begged for forgiveness the day after hurling a cast-iron kettle at his five-foot, 125-pound wife, striking her above the left knee and knocking her to the faux-wood linoleum floor of her spotless kitchen.

"There was a knot on my knee, and it bruised halfway up my leg from my knee," says Connie, displaying the pan that is too bulky and heavy to steady in one hand. "I could not even walk on it. To this day it still hurts. If I stand on my feet too much, it's like I got needles sticking in it."

As the beatings became routine, Connie decided to show neighbor Dorothy Glass her wounds.

"I was down at Dorothy's house, and I felt some pain in my chest, so I go, 'Holy shit!' and Dorothy says, 'What's the matter, Connie?' I says, 'Billy's got a habit when he's angry of grabbing my boobs and pulling down on them, and he puts bruises and scratches on 'em.' Dorothy says, 'Lemme see, Connie,' and I showed her and she said, 'What the hell!' Dorothy knew that Billy had hit Sharon a few times, but she had no idea he was like this. He never hit me in the face. Sometimes I wouldn't even say a word, and he'd just jump out of the chair, come over and grab me and start choking me. Every time he got me, he got me from behind. His fingers were right in my throat, both hands around my neck—it takes the energy right out of you, knocks me out of the chair and onto the floor, then he starts doing whatever he wants."

Connie describes the ways in which she was beaten by Billy as if she were passing down a family recipe.

"He'd throw things at me. Push me. Punch me. Shoot, he'd do anything; he'd do everything—just try to hurt me. He always hit me in places that you couldn't see, so I showed Dorothy. I wanted to show someone what he did to me—just in case."

Billy's clothes are washed, folded, and neatly arranged in a chest of drawers in the front bedroom of Connie's home.

"I washed them all once, then washed them again a few months later—you know how clothes start to yellow just a bit when they sit in a drawer," says the dark-haired Connie, cigarette in hand and dressed in a gray sweat suit.

The clothes Sprinkle wears these days are prison blues, courtesy of the Department of Corrections, where he landed for the third time in his life after threatening to kill Connie. But despite everything her husband has done—the drinking, the beatings, the revolving-door relationship with the DOC—Connie talks about keeping his clothes clean even as she rattles off a laundry list of his transgressions.

"He never had a steady job. Billy's always telling people how much he's worked and how hard he works. Well, his work record does not show it! Look what he's worked, it ain't much," says Connie, displaying his Social Security employment history. "Billy is a lazy ass. The longest he worked while living here was one month. He worked one week at Springfield Iron and Metal, got hurt, and sued. And he took the first, smallest offer they gave him because he wanted some booze money. His drinking and not working got me to selling this, selling that, and things went down from there. I asked for a raise at work. I was cleaning houses, and they wouldn't give me a raise, so I quit. I didn't realize I wouldn't find a job for a while. Then Billy goes to prison, and I'd wondered, 'How am I going pay the bills?'"

Despite the hardships Sprinkle has inflicted upon her, Connie still cares for him, even though she changes her mind from one day to the next regarding whether to keep him in her life.

"I guess I still love the butthole," Connie says. "You know, even with what he did to me, I still worship the ground he walks on. I love him to death."

27

"Sleepin' Dog"

Ray Stukel, upon absorbing the news that his son's murderers have been in and out of prison for over four decades, and are once again incarcerated in Illinois penitentiaries in the new millennium, says, "Now, here's a case of the victim's family being victims. As a taxpayer, I'm paying to feed them, clothe them, keep them healthy, keep a roof over their heads. Do you know what it costs to keep a prisoner in a nine-by-twelve cell? You can keep a family of four in a house and pay all their bills for what it costs to keep one lousy prisoner in prison."

Ray Stukel has a right to be cynical—and bitter. He wasn't asked for his opinion regarding the Sprinkle and Perruquet plea bargains; he wasn't notified when his son's murderers came up for parole; and he left the courthouse in January 1969 believing that Sprinkle and Perruquet would be incarcerated for life.

Despite the judicial system's shortcomings, George Stampar, the former assistant warden at Stateville, believes that the Stukel family not being informed about yearly parole hearings was not such a bad thing.

"The family of a victim has to live through the murder again every twelve months," Stampar says. "Let's say the inmate is coming up for parole in September. The victim's family gets a letter in July. All the memories flood back. You don't want to see the prisoner. You want no part of the process. You can't tolerate to even think about it. Then the day comes and you think, 'I don't want to appear in person at a prison.' Family members are extremely reluctant to go to a prison. And if they choose to write a protest letter, they ask themselves, 'Can I write a letter that would sufficiently explain how I feel and convince them to not let this guy out? Do they really read them?' The fact is, they might not read all of them."

Stampar says another emotion that a victim's family commonly experiences is fear.

"It's always there," Stampar says. "When you think of what they did, when you think of what they might do—you know, 'You're the ones that held me in there. You fought my release for all these years. I gotta do something to ya. I'll torch your house or something.' It's tough stuff."

George Sangmeister, the Will County state's attorney at the time of David Stukel's murder, agrees with Stampar's assessment of the victim's family fearing retaliation.

"Any time you've dealt with somebody who's committed a homicide, and you're going to be doing something, testifying or protesting at a parole hearing, I imagine you have some trepidation about doing it because you already know what they're capable of," Sangmeister says.

When Ray and Marilyn Stukel learned Billy Rose Sprinkle would have a parole hearing in November 2002, they displayed moderate interest in protesting his release.

"If they called me, I'd go down there and say, 'Hey, he killed my son, he doesn't belong any place but in prison,'" Ray says. "There's only two options they should have had from the start—execution or life in prison—no parole!"

"We could write a letter," Marilyn says.

"I'll tell you what I'd write," Ray says. "If you can't bring my boy back, then he doesn't belong out of jail. Keep him there until my son comes back!"

"Well, they've heard that one before," Marilyn says.

"Well, why don't they listen?" says Ray, his voice and blood pressure rising. "The system is no better now than it's ever been. Right now, what the parole board is looking at is this: 'Let's look at the money we save by him being out of prison.'"

"I feel, who's gonna listen?" Marilyn says.

"It doesn't matter what we say or write," Ray says. "If the parole board thinks it's going to save some money, they're gonna turn 'em loose."

In February 1986, moments after bungling burglars Billy Rose Sprinkle and nephew Ronnie tripped the silent alarm at Certified Foods, two-tenths of a mile west of the Sprinkle homestead, store manager Ken Clymer was roused from sleep by a late-night phone call from the alarm company.

"The burglars had cut a hole in the roof, and one of them stepped right on a motion detector coming down. They weren't exactly rocket scientists," Clymer says with a laugh.

There have been many times over the past two decades when laughs haven't come so easily for Ken Clymer.

Clymer and the Stukel family are linked by more than Sprinkle's rap sheet. Clymer, like the Stukels, knows all too well the pain of losing a loved one in a senseless and disgusting manner. Five years after the Certified Foods burglary, Clymer's sister, forty-nine-year-old Judy Zeman, was raped and brutally murdered by Edward Moore Jr., who had been hired by the family to paint the interior of their home in Morris, the same city where Debbie Stukel resides.

"My sister was a pretty tough lady," Clymer says. "The guy robbed her. He raped her. He beat her. He bound her with duct tape, then doused her with gasoline and set her on fire. She managed to pull herself off of a woodpile. She had burns over almost ninety percent of her body, but she crawled to the driveway, nearly one hundred feet … she crawled all that way."

Ken Clymer has never met Ray and Marilyn Stukel, but he understands what they went through and are going through. He saw his parents endure the same pain.

"You want to see people age before your eyes—have one of their kids get murdered," Clymer says. "I don't know how a parent gets over that. They don't. And it doesn't matter how old the kid is. If you're seventy-five years old and your kid is fifty, they are still your kid. Your relationship is still as a parent. You will be healing for the rest of your life. Somebody gets murdered in your family, and no Christmas, no birthday is ever going to be the same."

Clymer isn't surprised when told that the Stukel family rarely discusses David's murder among themselves.

"We didn't talk a lot about this as a family either," Clymer says. "It is still such a painful subject that my brother-in-law and I probably have only had conversations about things that have happened concerning my sister half a dozen times, and we're as close as any brothers would be. I mean, how do you verbalize something like that? My sister wasn't just murdered, she was butchered. How do you have a discussion with your brother-in-law about anything concerning it?"

Magnifying the family's horror in dealing with Judy Zeman's slaying was the fact that Edward Moore Jr. was writing harassing letters to the family from Death Row.

"My brother-in-law was getting taunting mail from the guy," Clymer says. "Generally, prisons don't screen the outgoing mail. They screen everything that comes in to check for contraband, but they don't look at what goes out, and he used to do stuff like send Christmas cards to my brother-in-law."

In one of the letters, the inmate wrote: "I will be keeping in touch with you … like it or not … you have not heard the last of me."

Eventually, the prison began screening Moore's mail. "They would look to see where it was going and wouldn't let him mail anything to my brother-in-law's house," Clymer says.

Because of the intimidation the Zeman family endured at the hands of the murderer of its matriarch, Debbie Stukel had no interest in writing a protest letter in advance of Sprinkle's November 2002 hearing, and she discouraged family members from doing so as well.

"When the guy was harassing the family from prison—the system, they've gone too much the other way for the criminal versus the family," Debbie says. "I don't trust the system. The family couldn't get the guy to stop harassing them from prison. Nancy and I talked about how my parents were treated, even in the courtroom, by Sprinkle's family. And they'd gotten harassing phone calls asking for David. Just cruel things. I don't want my parents to go through anything like that again. And now Nancy is concerned about her children too. They're right next door. I'm concerned about what they might do to our parents. Their family was terrible to us back then, so who knows what they might do now."

Nancy Stukel did not want any part of determining Sprinkle's fate in 2002.

"I'd like to see him stay in, not just for what he did to David, but for what he might do to the next victim. Someone who could do what he did—that magnitude, the way he murdered—could do it again. And there are a lot of Sprinkles out there. I went to school with his brothers and sisters. If we protest and then he gets out, where would we be if he decided that he wanted to retaliate? After all these years, you want to put it behind you and start living a fairly normal life. We shouldn't have to go and say he should be in jail forever. It should be automatic."

After weeks of contemplation, Ray and Marilyn decided not to protest Sprinkle's release—in person or on paper.

"We don't want to focus on them," Marilyn says. "I'd just like to see them stay in prison for the rest of their lives."

"They aren't worth the effort," Ray says.

Asked if there is a specific reason why they decided not to write protest letters, Ray says, "The girls are not in favor of it. With families like that, you never know what they're going to do, so we'll let that sleepin' dog lie."

28

Everything but the Truth

I drive the final leg of a 280-mile trip from Chicago to Billy Rose Sprinkle's Prisoner Review Board interview at the Big Muddy Correctional Center in Ina, just east of Interstate 57. The rising sun casts a reddish hue over Rend Lake, which nestles up to Illinois Route 37, just east of the institution. It is a brilliant sight on this warm, picturesque fall morning.

Big Muddy, population 1,860, is located just south of the small town of Ina, population 2,500.

I arrive at 8 a.m. for the 9 a.m. hearing, and I am told by officers in the reception area to get comfortable, that the PRB officials won't arrive until 9 and won't get started until after they've had their coffee.

A corrections officer standing in the sunlit waiting area peers out one of the many windows and spots an inmate driving a tractor on the institution's front lawn.

"That's the first time I've ever seen an inmate drive a tractor here!" says the officer to no one in particular. "Should have had old Johnny Blue do that. Johnny was arrested for stealing combines. He'd be perfect for the job!"

Everyone enjoys a good laugh.

Even while sitting in the safety of a sterile waiting room, a few feet from freedom, it's disconcerting to hear gates slamming, the sound muffled by the occasional freight train rumbling along the tracks across Route 37.

At 8:45 a.m., PRB members Barbara Hubbard and Milton Maxwell enter the waiting room, make small talk with the officers, then are escorted into the penitentiary.

Billy Rose Sprinkle is a veteran of institutional life, a man who probably has no trouble sleeping the night before his parole interview, the precursor to the PRB session in Springfield seven days later, when his parole fate will be determined by the board. I am a first-time parole interview observer who naively assumes that one parole candidate will be heard on this day. I discover at 9:30 a.m. that eighty-nine Big Muddy inmates still under the indeterminate-sentencing umbrella will be interviewed.

At 10 a.m., visiting hours begin, and an officer inspects magazines in the possession of a young female.

"Is this a tattoo magazine?" inquires the officer.

"No," replies the young woman.

"Is this devil-worship?" asks the officer.

"No," replies the woman.

At 10:55 a.m., an officer informs me that the hearings are running late, and that Sprinkle will not be heard until one o'clock.

At 12:15 p.m., three shackle-free inmates—wearing wide smiles and gray sweat suits, and accompanied by a lone guard—enter the reception area from within the institution. The thick metal door slams behind them, and one-by-one they state their name, inmate number, and date of birth. One inmate, with a cigarette tucked behind his ear, looks out the window, squints as he admires the glistening blue sky, and says, "I never thought this day would come."

At 1:15 p.m., after a five-hour wait, my name is finally called.

I am quickly escorted down hallways, past two security checkpoints and into a waiting area, where I find myself twenty feet from Billy Rose Sprinkle, who is sitting outside the two interview rooms, in the last of nine perfectly aligned orange-colored plastic chairs. I sit in the first chair. I had never seen Sprinkle or talked with him. And I do not make a connection, or eye contact, on this day.

Even though we are the only people in the waiting area, Sprinkle's steely blue eyes focus on the wall ten feet in front of him.

Sprinkle wears a short-sleeve, light-blue denim shirt from which his muscular forearms emerge. He has the sun-worn, ruddy complexion of a construction worker. His thick, brown hair is neatly brushed back off his forehead, and a rubber band corrals a short ponytail above his starched collar. Strands of gray hair converge at his temples, and his bushy eyebrows look like silhouetted mountain peaks. He weighs 175 pounds, but at five feet eight, he has grown just two inches since the murder. His abbreviated legs inside navy blue baggy pants seem disproportionate to his elongated torso.

As if in a meditative trance, Sprinkle seems unaware of the handful of inmates accompanied by two guards who pass through the area. And he is oblivious of the muted sounds of inmates pleading for their freedom behind interview-room doors on the other side of the room.

Veteran PRB member Barbara Hubbard enters the waiting area, calls out my name, introduces herself, shakes my hand, and invites me into the first of the two interview rooms. I sit in the first of two plastic chairs, just left of the door. Hubbard rises from her desk, leaves the interview room, and returns with Billy Rose Sprinkle, who walks less than a foot in front of me and sits down three feet to my left without acknowledging my presence. During Sprinkle's interview with Hubbard, she grills him regarding his relationship with David Stukel:

State your name and number.

"My name is Bill Sprinkle—C15277."

Mr. Sprinkle, I see that you were on parole from December 1990 to July 2001. What do you attribute your recent return to prison?

"I'm married now, to Connie. We bought a house. She can't work. She's got cancer real bad. I started drinking when I found out about her cancer. And then I quit for a long time. I went into the Service Center in Springfield. I was worried about my ex-wife giving me—I had an HIV test, and they told me, 'No, you're not HIV, you have hepatitis C,' and they said there's no cure for it. It's a death sentence, so I started drinking. I didn't know how to deal with it."

Were you working?

"Yes, I've always held a job."

Where were you last working?

"Springfield Iron and Metal."

How long did you work there?

"June of 1999 'til when I came back here in July 2001."

Have you participated in the mandated conditions for drug and alcohol counseling?

"Yes, in my file there should be a certificate from Triangle Center. It's a mile from where I live."

Do you have children?

"I've got a daughter, Amanda."

How old is she?

"Sixteen, September the seventeenth."

Does she live with you?

"Off and on. She's living with her mom in Tennessee. And I see her usually during the summers."

Do you view yourself as being stable within the community, other than the drinking? The drinking caused some problems. You're not attending substance-abuse programs, well, you did go earlier. What made you quit going?

"My wife's cancer and then finding out about my liver condition. I'd get my beer, set in my yard, and drink."

So that means that you were not going to work?

"I would drink when I'd get off work. I handle a lot of heavy equipment, and I would never go to work, how do you say, intoxicated or hung over."

You did last out on parole for a ten-year period. But the fact remains that in a parole existence you're still doing your sentence. And that extension of the institution within the community means that you have to follow rules, too. The seventy-five to ninety years suggests the serious case that you were involved in. Who actually did the murder and who actually did the deviate sexual assault? Tell me what happened.

"It was a fight over a radio. And James Perruquet kind of got carried away. I was a lookout man, and I thought it was just going to be a fight, and it turned into a murder. I had a fight with him, with the victim. After that, I was standing out by the road. And then when I went back there, I seen the body laying there."

You came into the adult division at seventeen. Did someone get hurt in the facility where you were? Let's see. I can't locate it ... you were in protective custody in 1977. Why?

"I wouldn't cooperate with the gangs. I had an assignment where I had free movement, and different gangs wanted me to run stuff for them."

Here it is ... in 1977 you were found guilty of stabbing someone in prison. Tell me what happened there?

"That was related to the gangs."

You were part of a gang?

"Oh, no, no. Never."

Tell me how you got accused of stabbing someone?

"It was the Vice Lords. I worked in the general hospital, and they wanted me to move drugs through the hospital. I wouldn't do it, and they sent two guys after me. They jumped me, and later a friend of mine got into it with a guy, and I jumped in on that because it was one of the same guys that attacked me."

Why should this board believe that you would be a good risk for release at this point?

"I did everything I can to prove I'm not a violent person. On parole, I never had any problems with anybody. And they've never had a problem with me. I've always tried to help people. I've never messed with narcotics, any kind of stolen property. I didn't associate with any cons. I did everything I could to be a good citizen. I wanted to be better than the people that had never been arrested."

When you came back to prison as a violator, were you trying to be returned?

"No, I had medical problems. I didn't know how to cope."

It sounds like more than just the fact that you were not going to drug counseling. There was a call to the operations center. Here it is: "The subject had come home drunk and was threatening to kill his wife. Deputies arrived. The subject took off. He returned and his wife called his agent who arrived at his house. Deputies administered the Breathalyzer, and Mr. Sprinkle blew a point-thirty-five." So it appears that you had become explosive within the home. Now you have a letter from your wife. Is that where you plan on going back?

"Yes, ma'am."

Why would that be a good plan?

"I've never—in all the years we've been together that was the first incident between us. I've never threatened her, I've never—I don't believe in putting a hand on nobody anyway, especially my wife. And she had never seen me drunk before, and it scared the hell out of her. And the day I got here I signed up for the alcohol-abuse program, and I've been in that program ever since."

Was your co-defendant paroled?

"Yes. I never had no contact with him, then he showed up at my house. I made him leave. I called the police and said, 'I don't want him here.'"

You did know this victim, the victim in this case, is that correct?

"No."

When you came in, they did an evaluation, and you said that you had met this individual in the past.

"He had been to my house. He had been there a couple times with my brother, my sister, riding the horses."

You said you didn't know him.

"I just seen him."

If he's been at your house, you had to have known him.

"Yes."

Why were you and your friend antagonistic toward the victim? Why did you fight him?

"He was whipping my buddy's ass."

OK, is there anything that you want the board to know?

"I'm not a threat to nobody, nobody in society, nobody in prison, nobody living or dead. I've done a lot of soul-searching. I have a wife out there. I've got a life. I've got immediate employment."

Where would you work?

"I could go right back to Springfield Iron and Metal. I can be working within three days. I'm trying to turn my life around. I've got God in my life; my wife knows this. I have a church two blocks from me that I want to attend."

You were paroled in '81, and then you came back and committed another crime, burglary. And then when you got released, you came back even again. What would you tell those board members who released you?

"If I would have never started drinking, I wouldn't be sitting here today. My interpretation of an alcoholic was somebody living in a doorway, eating out of dumpsters. I didn't believe I had a drinking problem. And when I got actively involved in the program, I realized that anybody can be an alcoholic."

I've tried to give you a fair hearing today, Mr. Sprinkle. Is there anything more you want the board to know regarding your original crime?

"Yes, I just wish to God it never happened. It was senseless. I live with this every day, so I can't imagine how the family lives with it. I never did nothin' to no one. There's nothing I can do to change what happened. I wish I could, not just for me but for everyone involved. I've got a lot of remorse, a lot of sadness. I try to put myself in the family's place; I can't do that. And then, you say you're sorry, but it's like that's not enough. If I could do something to change it, I would do anything. I just want to say, I don't know if I'm going to be granted parole or not, but I have contacted the Triangle Center, and they have a program there, outpatient classes, one mile from my house. And they have an alcohol program, and when you're involved in it, you Breathalyze every time you walk in the door. And when I'm working, you never know when they're going to show up and give you a Breathalyzer. If I was paroled today, my meetings would start forty-eight hours after I go home."

Billy Rose Sprinkle rises from his chair, passes in front of me without looking in my direction, and exits the room.

He has spoken, but he has not spoken the truth.

Not about the sexual assault.

Not about the murder.

Not about abusing women.

Not about narcotics.

Not about the severity of his alcoholism.

Not about stealing.

Not about the reunion with his accomplice.

Not about his relationship with his daughter.

Not about run-ins with police.

Not about his gang involvement in prison.

Not about his shoddy work record.

Not about his employment prospects.

Not about much other than his name and number.

One week after Sprinkle's November 2002 interview at Big Muddy, PRB Chairman Anne Taylor, legal counsel Ken Tupy and board members Arvin Boddie, Victor Brooks, James Donahue, Robert Dunne, Craig Findley, Susan Carol Finley, Barbara Hubbard, Jorge Montes, and Norman Sula gather in the conference room in Springfield.

At 8:35 a.m., I sit in a small waiting room just inside the front door of the PRB headquarters. I am a rapt audience of one, my eyes fixed on a tiny black speaker resting on an end table.

Barbara Hubbard's voice emerges above the speaker's crackling:

"Mr. Sprinkle was fourteen at the time of a very brutal crime. Mr. Sprinkle had problems in the juvenile system, and he was shipped to an adult institution earlier than planned. He was paroled in 1981 and was returned as a violator in 1986. He was paroled again in December 1990. He had been on parole from 1990 until his return to prison in 2001 as a parole violator. He had two other parole violations and was allowed to resume his parole—they were technical violations. He has had a lot of incidents of abusing alcohol. In July, he was brought back in for an incident with his wife. There had been a criminal charge filed against him by his wife for domestic battery, but no charges were pursued. As I reviewed this case, I look at the seriousness of the committing offense. I think the board—back in 1981—probably considered his youthful age at the time of his conviction, so they granted him a parole. The fact that he came back in 1986 is a concern for me, in addition to the fact that he has come back before this board on technical violations, in April 1999 and again in May 2001, followed by the incident with his wife in July 2001.

"Considering all the history that Mr. Sprinkle has had with this board since 1968, his criminality and recidivism, I move that parole be denied."

Hubbard's motion carries—nine in favor; one abstainer.

When I call Ray Stukel to get his reaction to the PRB's ruling, he says that he is just sitting down to enjoy a plate of bacon and eggs.

At 5 p.m.

When you've been retired for more years than you worked, you're entitled to have your eggs any way you want them, any time you want them. Ray also has earned the right to speak his mind, especially when it comes to matters involving the PRB.

Ray, who retired at forty-seven, five years after his son's murder, doesn't tap-dance around issues. Informed that the PRB denied Sprinkle's parole by a nine to zero vote, with one member abstaining, Ray responds, "I want to know who is the one who abstained from making a decision because he's somebody that can't make up his mind."

When Ray is informed that the system worked—that the board's discussion emphasized the murder of his son—it is of little consolation.

"Something better work!" he says.

When Debbie Stukel receives news of the inmate's parole denial, she is more pragmatic than her father.

"I am not a vindictive person, yet I think that if they let him back out he would hurt somebody else, and I wouldn't want anybody else's family to go through what we did."

Told that Sprinkle has denied participating in her brother's murder, Debbie replies, "Then he can't be sorry for what he did. Maybe in his mind he didn't do anything wrong—'I was beating up this kid. Gee, that's too bad, he died.'"

When Nancy Stukel hears the news of Sprinkle being kept in prison, she is relieved.

"It's good, it's real good ... for another year anyway."

29

"He Never Deserved to Die"

The land on which the Stateville Correctional Center sits covers 2,264 acres of former farmland two miles north of Joliet. With three-tenths of a mile of gently rolling, grass-covered hills, mature trees, and vibrant flowers, the front entrance to the sixty-four-acre maximum-security penitentiary could be mistaken for a national park if it weren't for the roadside display of large, white concrete letters on a backdrop of crushed black rocks that form the word:

S-T-A-T-E-V-I-L-L-E

Richard Speck, John Wayne Gacy, Nathan Leopold, and Richard Loeb all did time behind the ominous and omnipresent thirty-three-foot walls enveloping this historic penitentiary. Entering the gatehouse is the first step in penetrating this fortress that houses 2,800 inmates, half of whom are murderers, including inmate A-10300, James David Perruquet, serving a life sentence for committing two murders twenty-seven years apart.

After being thoroughly searched, visitors exit the gatehouse's back door and are greeted by fifty yards of fresh air—the last breath of freedom before entering the foreboding ashen monster, its harshness tempered by the administration building's red-brick walls, which stand in stark contrast to the concrete that sprouts from its sides like gigantic wings. Inside the foyer, visitors traverse a winding, ornate staircase with marble steps to the second level, home to the warden's office and the first security checkpoint.

Gate 1 is an iron door with thick bars covered with decades' worth of gray paint. Gate 2, also covered with multiple coats of gray paint, is twenty yards away.

The two gates are never open at the same time.

After passing through Gate 2 and spotting inmates wearing a variety of colored jumpsuits and milling around beyond yet another gate, I am ushered into a tiny, tired interview room that houses a nondescript brown table and worn plastic chairs. A large, glass-block window at the rear of the room allows streams of light to brighten the room.

I sit alone.

Unable to tune out the chatter of inmates and the clanking of cell doors, I struggle to collect my thoughts as I await the arrival of James Perruquet, who after months of writing letters from his Stateville cell, has agreed to be interviewed in person.

I am apprehensive about meeting the man whose reprehensible behavior is the reason I am here and David Stukel is not. That thought is still ruminating in my mind ten minutes later, when the five-foot-six, 190-pound Perruquet enters the room wearing a light-blue, short-sleeve denim shirt, navy blue pants, and at least twenty pounds of baggage around his midsection.

James Perruquet grasps my hand, gives it a firm shake, and offers a smile that reveals gaps east and west of his two front teeth. Perruquet's wide, fleshy face is anchored by a double chin, and he has tattoos of an eagle on one arm and Deputy Dawg on the other. The tip of the middle finger on his left hand is missing. He has marble-like green eyes and thick, gray-splashed brown hair tailored on the top and sides but bushy and hanging over his collar in the back. His salt-and-pepper moustache and goatee are neatly cropped, and the rest of his face is freshly shaven. He doesn't look like a man who for ten years has shared an eight-by-ten cell with a fellow murderer. He does not display the desperation of a man condemned to life behind bars.

When I ask Perruquet if I may take his photograph, he pivots forty-five degrees to his right, the Pavlovian response of a man who has spent three-quarters of his life in the custody of the Department of Corrections.

Perruquet is cordial and willing to talk about all aspects of the 1968 murder, even though he says that discussing it is excruciatingly painful. He says that living with the memory of murdering David Stukel is often an unbearable burden. With a tape recorder capturing his every utterance, a contrite Perruquet, near tears at times but rarely pausing, apologizes for his role in the murder and agonizes over its ramifications. It is a discourse on remorse that Perruquet has been waiting nearly four decades to articulate.

"David Stukel never deserved to die," Perruquet says slowly and calmly, clasping his hands and gently shaking his head. "And I'm sad I was a part of his death."

Told that he and Sprinkle were seen laughing outside the Will County Courthouse by Ray Stukel in 1968, and that he and Sprinkle bragged about the murder to two boys soon after leaving the crime scene, Perruquet says, "We wasn't happy about what we did. We didn't think we were tough or that we did something terrific. We didn't really understand the significance of it. We was two punks. We were fourteen-year-old kids. With the black kids, we was asking them for money, and that's when Billy told them we just killed a boy. They was telling us we was in big trouble, and Billy said, 'We don't care. We just killed someone, and we'll kill you, too.' Billy told them not to say anything or we'd come back and get them. Billy was cool-headed about everything. I was scared, jumpy, saying, 'Let's go.' But being around bad-ass Billy, I felt like somebody."

Perruquet says that over time he realized the magnitude of his behavior that day.

"I look for answers about this all the time, and I don't know if I'm trying to justify it in my mind or if I'm really trying seek out the truth," Perruquet says. "I try putting myself back to that day. It cuts into my heart and soul. I am very sorry, and I do pray for David's family every day. I think about it all the time—the fact I can't take it back. It eats at me. I don't have any pity for myself. I feel bad for David Stukel's family because what we did wasn't right. If there was any way we could take it back—and I'm not just saying that because I got caught and I had to do time. If I wouldn't have gotten caught, I think I would have ended up turning myself in because that's how guilty I do feel inside."

Perruquet refuses to expend energy worrying about those who question his sincerity.

"I've heard about people saying, 'They ain't got no remorse.' What is remorse? How do you show remorse? Was I supposed to cry and cry for the rest of my life because of what I did? I still hurt inside. I'm sorry. There ain't nothing else I can say. I killed a kid that never should have been killed. I'm going to live this out the rest of my life. There's times I still dream about it. And I can't believe that I did what I did. I didn't even know the kid, and I wasn't known for hurting people. I want to tell his family I'm sorry, but I know it ain't going to make any difference to them. They still lost their son. I've been forgiven by God, but I'm still torturing myself. I'm living in my own hell. I may not look like it. I may not sound like it. But take the worst thing that's ever happened to you, that you're embarrassed of, something that you torture your own self about—and add it a thousand times and that's how bad I feel inside. I'm my biggest critic on the death of David Raymond Stukel—that name's like second nature to me. I wish I could bring him back."

Perruquet says the reason he's talking about the case is twofold—to help David's family and himself. He believes that by sharing the truth, he might finally be set free—not from Stateville—but from a past that haunts him.

"I do sometimes pray that I never was born," says Perruquet, no drama in his voice. "But I was born, and I do regret how I lived my life. But it's not too late to clean up this messed-up life, even if I got to do it from prison. I want to be truthful. I feel like talking about this, getting it all out. I still picture that boy. I see him all the time in my mind. Now don't get me wrong, I don't sit around and ponder on it every day, but there will be times when all of a sudden it will just hit me. But every night when I say my prayers, I always pray for his family, and I hope that they get closure. I used to pray for his soul until I read the Bible and realized there ain't nothing I can do for David. I hope he is OK. But once he was done dead and gone, his soul was left up to God, so I pray for his family. I used to be afraid to admit that I was hurt over it. I know I got to let it go somewhere. I want David's family to forgive me for the heartache I've brought them. But if it takes my life to give them closure, then I wish to God that he would hurry up and take it. I'm really tired of living this life. And I'm not just saying it because I'm in here 'cause I felt like this on the streets, too."

Perruquet leans forward in his chair, lowers his voice, and confides that he once considered suicide to squelch his guilt.

"Nobody knows this, but I almost shot myself. I stole a gun, and I was going to kill myself because of what happened with David. The two reasons that stopped me—one was because my son Jimmy was just born, and the other was I know that I could never be forgiven by God if I was to kill myself. To me, that's like the ultimate sin, and there ain't no way you could ask for forgiveness 'cause you're dead."

Perruquet says he fully understands why the Stukel family would have been furious when learning that he and Sprinkle walked out of prisons in the early 1980s.

"I do, in a way, feel that Billy and I should of did more time for taking David's life. But how long will make it right—life? Then we should be put to death. But even that won't make things right. The seriousness of the crime is never going to change. The loss of David is never going to go away. He is always going to be missed if I live or die. How long is enough: ten, twenty, thirty, or life? They say there's always a reason for something to happen. Maybe me getting this life sentence is to finish letting me pay for what I did to David. I mean, my life, taking my life, spending my life here in prison is not going to change the situation. I regret my part in this. So how long will satisfy his family and friends' hurt and loss? I asked God for forgiveness for my part, and God gave me forgiveness. Now I will ask you all the same: Please forgive me for my part. It happened, and no matter what happens to me, it'll never make it right for anyone. God will deal with me for what I've did in my life."

"He had been my best pal. In one sense, he was also the greatest enemy I have ever had. For my friendship with him had cost me my life."

The statement above could have been made by James Perruquet about Billy Rose Sprinkle. But the words come from Nathan Leopold, and they refer to Richard Loeb. The quote comes from the book *Life Plus 99 Years*, which details Leopold and Loeb's 1924 thrill-killing of fourteen-year-old Bobby Franks in Chicago as he, too, walked home from high school. Sprinkle was Perruquet's closest friend, and although they would hang out for just sixteen months, their names would forever be linked. Like Leopold and Loeb, Sprinkle and Perruquet committed a heinous crime—one they most likely would not have done on their own. But unlike Leopold and Loeb, who were in their late teens at the time of the Franks murder, fourteen-year-olds Sprinkle and Perruquet were not privileged members of the community; they were not geniuses; and they did not plan their murder like their counterparts. But like Leopold and Loeb, once Sprinkle and Perruquet hooked up, their lives were destined to take a downward spiral and produce tragic results.

"I just started doing stupid things when I was with Billy," Perruquet says. "I started stealing and drinking because Billy was drinking with his older brother and his friends, and Billy taught me how to sniff glue. When we were kids, me and my brothers always used glue to put models together, but we never did sniff it. Hanging out with Billy is when I started drinking, and I became an alcoholic at thirteen."

Perruquet was no saint in his pre-Sprinkle days, but he insists that he wasn't a violent person.

"I gave my life to Billy in 1968," says Perruquet, who, like Leopold, tried to impress his partner.

"I did everything Billy wanted me to do—hit, kick, and help kill this boy who was going home and who never had no money. If I had never met Billy, I don't think I would have ended up in prison. I might have ended up in juvenile or something if I got caught stealing. The murder wouldn't have happened. I probably would have ended up getting straightened out somewhere along the line."

When Perruquet met Sprinkle, he figured a bully would be the ideal companion for an undersized outsider.

"Billy was stocky, tough. He was a perfect person for someone like me to hang out with," Perruquet says. "I was a little guy, and I figured a tough guy would take care of all the roughneck stuff. I never knew how to think for myself. I'd do things just to fit in with the crowd, trying to impress Billy. I wanted to be known as being tough like him when really I was a coward. Before I met Billy, I was always afraid to fight or stand up for myself. With Billy around, for the first time I had people afraid of me. Billy would tell me to prove myself. I'd have to go into a store, steal, then give it to him. Before meeting Billy, I only stole candy, but after that, I got a brave heart. I started doing things I otherwise wouldn't of, just to show him I could do it. There's no question that Billy Sprinkle was the worst influence I had on my life. Don't take me wrong, I did my share of stealing back then, but in a lot of ways, I was nothing but a puppet for him. I never knew or felt like I was a puppet then, because I believed he was my friend. I wanted to fit in no matter what to keep from being an outsider. I was a country boy, a square, so around Billy I would be bad even when I never wanted to be bad. People told me, 'Billy is nothing but trouble' and, as always, I never listened to them. No one could of told me Billy was the wrong guy to be with. I always wanted to hang out with him, do what he did. Now I can't blame Billy for my actions that day. I blew it. I messed up. I shoulda known better. But, like I said, the murder wouldn't of happened, at least on my part, if I hadn't been with Billy that day."

Asked to expound on Sprinkle's power over him, Perruquet recounts the day Sprinkle ordered him to harm a boy, and he willingly complied.

"Me and Billy was coming from uptown, walking down the tracks. There was a couple of boys who lived up there by the tracks, some real nice guys, too. And Billy and I'd been drinking all day—we stole alcohol out of a car. These boys come by and we knew 'em, and Billy said, 'C'mon, take a drink.' And they was like, 'No, we don't drink,' and they were very nice about it. And Billy said, 'If you don't, I'll have James bust this bottle over your head!' And about that time—whoosh!—I hit him on the head with a bottle and busted his head."

Although Perruquet and Sprinkle were inseparable, James never felt accepted by Billy's father, who relished watching his son grow up tough.

"I never spent much time at Sprinkle's house," Perruquet says. "I really don't think his dad liked me 'cause I wasn't tough, so he didn't want Billy around me. His dad always built Billy up as being the tough-type kid. To me, it seemed like the old man wanted him to be tough; he was proud of him being tough. The few times I did go over his house, they was all drinking, talking big stuff, the whole family. Really, outside of his sister Doll, the rest of them seemed like they always had to act bad. One time at Billy's house, after his dad had seen I was a puss, he had Billy fight with me. So Billy had his two young brothers help me fight, to show how tough he was. Three on one, and Billy beat all three of us up. It was me, Stanley, and Steve against Billy, and Billy put all three of us down hard while his dad was watching. And I remember after that his dad told me it was time for me to leave. Mr. Sprinkle was a know-it-all, always trying to make people believe he was tough. Even after I got out of prison and visited the Sprinkles, the old man still acted like he was the tough guy. He had a little money, at least it seem that way to me, and he acted like a big shot."

During a post-homicide discussion in jail, Perruquet says that Billy confided to him that his father routinely beat him.

"Billy said his old man used to clobber him a lot, punch him in the face," says Perruquet in a compassionate tone. "These are things we talked about in the county jail—that if he messed up, his old man would beat the crap out of him."

As a youngster, Sprinkle took out his anger on his classmates, and Perruquet was not excluded from the wrath of a boy who lived what he learned.

"I got beat up by Billy," Perruquet says. "Once, before I started sniffing glue, I sat with him and watched him sniffing, and he went off, went crazy on me. He hit me and tried drowning me. And he blamed the glue for what he done. Then once when we was sniffing together, he hit me and was going to push me in front of a train. Another time we was sniffing glue, and Billy went off on me at the quarry. He threw a rock at me, making me fall off the cliff and thirty feet down into the water. And once I stole a gun, and Billy took it and pointed it at my head, saying he would kill me."

Perruquet says the biggest mistake he and Sprinkle made was growing up too fast.

"I was stupid because I wanted to be with the big boys. We was both lost kids trying to find our way, and we found it in older people. We wanted to be older than what we really should have been and should have just been kids."

Perruquet talks openly about the physical abuse that he and his siblings endured while growing up.

"My parents whupped us and everything, but you know, I look at it this way: After so many years of being whupped and used to it, I kinda grew, I guess you could say, numb to it. If they took how my mom and dad whupped us back then and did it today, they'd be in jail for child abuse. They didn't mess around when it came to disciplining us. We got whupped—belt, chain, whip, switch, paddle, whatever. I mean, I was beaten—I couldn't put it no other way. And my parents, we was called idiots and stuff like that by them when we done something stupid. I wouldn't do that to my kids, do what my parents did to us."

Hazel and Earnie Perruquet's abusive behavior was triggered by their almost daily abuse of alcohol.

"The way they talk about what an alcoholic is nowadays, I believe Mom and Dad was drunks," Perruquet says.

Hazel and Earnie Perruquet raised not one but two career criminals—James and Joseph. When James landed at Stateville in 1995, he was reunited with older brother Joseph, with whom he had done time at Menard in the 1970s.

Joseph also is serving what is the equivalence of a life sentence—sixty years for rape, deviate sexual assault, and aggravated kidnapping for ransom in 1980. Joseph has a projected release date of 2041, when he will be eighty-nine. To further illuminate this cycle, two of Joseph's children are incarcerated—Joseph Jr. (an eighteen-year sentence for aggravated criminal sexual abuse, child abduction, and aggravated kidnapping) and Danielle (five years for drug possession).

Perruquet believes that his family's move from southern Illinois to Joliet was the springboard to his life of crime.

"When we lived in Herrin, as I remember it, it was cool, really cool. We all played together. We always had season tickets to the swimming pool every year down there. We would always ride our bikes out into the country, looking for swimming holes. We was adventure-type kids, but we didn't get out and cause a lot of trouble. We got in our little bit of trouble for going in somebody's apple orchard, stealing apples and stuff like that, or on Halloween putting dog do-do in a bag and setting it on fire and soaping windows. We did all the kid stuff. I never stole down there. All my mess-ups really came when we moved up to Joliet and I started hanging with Billy. I didn't have that kind of freedom until we moved to Joliet. Mom and Dad were strict, but they was both working, and they slacked up a lot here in Joliet."

The only time Perruquet discussed the murder with his parents came a couple of years after he was transferred to the penitentiary in the early 1970s.

"I was eighteen or nineteen," Perruquet says. "Mom shook her head, saying, 'James, how could you of did something like that? We raised you better than that.' Dad also shook his head, and you could see the hurt in his eyes. But when I talked about the glue and the booze, this kind of lost them both because they both drank so much back then that they never knew their son was such a booze hound and that I messed with glue."

30

A Split Decision

James Perruquet has known for forty years that Billy Rose Sprinkle's father tried to pin the sexual assault and murder on him, and he's well aware that Sprinkle claims to have sat by the road while he committed both crimes.

"Billy's still in denial," says Perruquet, who insists that he was so devoted to Sprinkle that the night of the murder he agreed to split the blame if caught. He says that is exactly what he did in his early-morning confession.

"My dad had just got home from work, and he had a confused look on his face when he got to the jail," Perruquet says. "It was a lost look. My dad hugged me and sat with me. I was scared, confused, and tired. I held my ground, not saying anything, and knowing and believing Billy would, too. Billy and I agreed to be strong and not talk, but if they knew it was us, then we agreed to take the blame 50-50. I was a very good guy this way with my friends, at taking the blame for whatever. When they took Billy in the room, they come out wanting a tape recorder, looking at me and saying 'Billy is telling everything.' They asked if I wanted to talk, and I turned to my dad and I said, 'Yes,' and I started crying. I went in, and I told them my story, thinking Billy had done the same thing, split everything down the middle. So everything I didn't do, I just added my name to, even if I didn't do it. What happened is true, but if you notice everything is half-and-half in the statement. In the confession, everything that happened is true up to one fact, when you get to the sexual assault, James Perruquet did not commit any sexual assault, and if there was any way to do a DNA test, you'd realize that I never had no sex with the boy."

Informed that in his confession he failed to give Sprinkle half the blame for crushing David Stukel's skull with a concrete block, Perruquet emphatically states that he was assisted by Sprinkle.

"I'm sure some of the things I said were slip-ups 'cause it's not like we had a lot of time to make our stories one hundred percent the same. But Billy never sat by any road. He was a major part of this deal—ordering me to fight the boy and

197

showing me how to hit him to knock him down, telling me to hit him with an iron bar, telling me to find something heavy to drop on him, showing me how to lift the cement block and drop it on him, and then hitting him with the block, too."

Shown copies of letters Sprinkle wrote proclaiming his innocence to Judge Orenic in 1969 and Gov. Walker in 1974, Perruquet says, "It's a bunch of bull! That ain't the way it happened. Basically, he's saying he didn't do nothin'. Let me ask you a question, 'Does Billy seem like the type that's not going to be involved? Is that how anyone has described him?' I am sure Billy and I both regret how and why this happened. And only two people know the truth. I've been trying to go back in time and let my feelings out as to what we did. If I could talk to Billy, I'd say, 'Don't let it go untold, the truth.' If Billy is looking for peace from this, he'll open up. But if he is in a state-of-prison mind, he'll take the truth to his grave. I call it trying to be too much like a con and hold it to his heart until death—let no one have the pleasure of ever hearing the truth."

Perruquet has a good idea why Sprinkle doesn't tell the truth.

"He has a chance for parole, so I'm sure he doesn't want to say anything that will hurt him. But to me, Billy is just a lost soul. For myself, I know I was part of all this. I wasn't a bad person back then or now. I just failed everyone when it came to getting around the wrong people, but it's not all Billy's fault. I shoulda known better. I want to live past this, and I'm doing my best to open up to the truth and pray that I get some peace from it all."

Just as Billy Rose Sprinkle claims that it was James Perruquet who sexually assaulted David Stukel, Perruquet has for decades said it was Sprinkle who acted alone in the commission of the sexual assault.

"I didn't know much about homosexuality—two guys being together or anything like that," Perruquet says. "I was dumbfounded by it. The boy was standing there naked and Billy asked me, 'Did you put the cable back up out front? Go check to make sure so nobody would think anything is going on back here.' I came walking back and I was feeling a little scared, more of Billy than anything else. Billy was behind David and Billy's underwear were around his ankles, and it seems as soon as he seen me he was done. He told me, 'It's your turn, go ahead.' Deep down, I felt it was wrong for boys to do boys, but I wanted Billy to like me, so I just said, 'I don't feel like it.' He said, 'OK,' and this give me relief from him being mad at me."

Perruquet, who claims he was a virgin at fourteen, says sex was the last thing on his mind that day.

"When we was looking for David's money, I thought the undressing of him was more to embarrass him. There wasn't, at least in my part, no sexual intent. You know, it seems like everything happened to me right in that area by East High. This neighborhood we was in was Billy's area. I was lost there. There was a girl who lived a block away, and come to think of it, that's why we came over there that day, the day of the murder, to see her, the girl that Billy raped a week or so before in the same spot."

Perruquet claims that on Saturday, September 7, nine days before the murder, he and Sprinkle went to the girl's house on Penfield Avenue, one block west of Hill Street.

"We got together the day he raped her because Billy come looking for me to hang out," Perruquet says. "After Billy come by, we go to this girl's house and she came out. We all went walking into that area by Hill Street, where the old farm was. Billy and her got to kissing, and I don't know, I really can't call it rape. I mean, he kind of forced himself on her, so yeah, it was rape, but she didn't fight back that much. Billy told me to go be the lookout. She said, 'No, don't go!' I took a short walk, and I can hear her put up a little struggle. I came back, then he got up and asked me if I wanted a turn. I was a virgin, and I would have never admitted that to Billy, so I said, 'No.' I'd never forced anybody to do any-thing—oh, maybe force a person to drink back then, but nothing sexually, so I didn't do it."

When I contacted the alleged victim, who wishes to remain anonymous, she admitted to "running" with Sprinkle but says she was not raped by him.

"The only time he tried anything was at his house," she says. "He tried to have sex with me, and I wanted no part of it. He tried undoing my blouse, and I kept telling him, 'Stop it!' Then he stuck his hand up the back of my shirt and tried to undo my bra. He pushed me down on the couch, and I just kicked him out of the way, slapped him in the face, and ran."

Despite the girl's denial, Perruquet stands by his account of the rape, and says he and Sprinkle returned to her house the next week.

"She didn't call the police, so me and Billy came back a few days later. I knocked on her door. She asked if Billy was with me. I said, 'No.' She never believed me, so Billy said to me, 'Go to the back.' I tried again. She looked out to see if Billy was with me, then let me in. She talked for a few minutes, but she was still fearful of Billy. He knocks on the door, and she sees him and calls me a liar and tells me to leave. Before that, I told her I was sorry that I didn't say anything when Billy raped her—that I was sorry for not standing up to him, but you know, at fourteen I idolized Billy and did everything he wanted, even if it went against how I felt. I was not guilty of any sex act with her or with David Stukel, but being there and not stopping what I knew was wrong makes me guilty, too."

Martin Rudman, who prosecuted Perruquet and Sprinkle, believes Perruquet's confession to be an accurate account of the crime, stressing that it is common for convicted felons to deny sexual assaults after they've confessed and been convicted.

"Everybody has their own set of values that they can live with and that they can't live with," Rudman says. "It's one thing to say, 'I killed somebody.' But a lot of people can't bring themselves to admit that they committed a deviate sexual act by force on somebody, because if they look in the mirror and say that, they're sort of slime. And if you're in the penitentiary, you're not low class if you're in for murder, but if you're in there for a sex crime, you ain't exactly the elite. So you've got to factor all this in when people are not admitting things."

Because of Perruquet's confession and Sprinkle's boasting, evidence wasn't necessary for convictions. And in February 1980, at the onset of the decade in which DNA would drastically change the face of forensics, every shred of evidence that was collected in the David Stukel murder case was destroyed to make room for new cases. All that's left is the case's paperwork tucked away in a file at the Illinois State Police's Forensic Science Laboratory, across the street from the historic former Joliet Correctional Center.

Poring over the inventory of evidence is tantamount to returning to the crime scene. The report includes a transistor radio; a blood-soaked algebra book; a bloodstained, partial concrete block; a Marlboro cigarette butt; a metal bar; a literature book with pages torn out; trousers of the victim; three pairs of underwear; and the taped statements of the co-defendants.

There is additional information listed under the heading: "David R. Stukel Microscopic and Serological Examination," which lists evidence, by number, followed by corresponding test results, the last of which reads:

There is seminal stain on item No. 20, but grouping tests are inconclusive.

Item number twenty is a pair of jockey-type shorts belonging to James Perruquet. When I present this information to the inmate, some of the pinkish hue disappears from his cheeks.

"I don't never remember them taking my underwear," Perruquet says. "I had blood spots on my shoes and the bottom of my pants, and I remember them taking those. But this is something I never knew about. That was one of the details I didn't remember."

Joseph Wichmann, the Illinois State Police Forensic Lab director, explains what the former lab analyst meant by grouping tests were inconclusive.

"By grouping, he means to determine the blood group. In other words, whether it was A, AB, whatever. He wasn't able to do that. They can't even tell the blood group of the person who left the semen; they can't get even the most elementary information out of it. Nowadays, the first thing we would look for is semen. If we found semen, we would do DNA on it. We'd have the potential of identifying the donor of the semen."

Asked if any forensic conclusions could be made from the semen found on Perruquet's underwear, Wichmann says, "You couldn't make any determinations from this. We try to be totally objective. An obvious assumption to some people would be, 'Well, it's in his underwear, and he's the person who did the attack.' You'd think it was his, but I wouldn't make that assumption."

Even if the semen did belong to Perruquet, determining how long it had been on his underwear would have been impossible, according to Wichmann.

"Once it's dried, there's no way to tell how old it is."

Former detective Dennis Jaskoviak believes that Perruquet's admission that both defendants sexually assaulted the victim is accurate. But he also agrees with Wichmann that the semen stain is non-evidence.

"Until you could match it up with something, I don't think it would mean anything other than there was a semen stain on somebody's underwear," Jaskoviak says.

On the morning of September 16, 1968, the second week of the school year, James and Fern Perruquet were home alone. Hazel Perruquet was having her appendix removed; Earnie Sr. was at work; Earnie Jr. and Stella were living with their spouses; Joe was in juvenile jail; and younger children Ila, Larry, and Donnie were staying with relatives while Hazel was in the hospital.

James was sleeping in a second-story bedroom at the front of the house when he heard a knock at the door. He rubbed his eyes, looked out the open, unscreened window, and saw his girlfriend, Doll Sprinkle.

James and Fern rushed to get ready for school—at 10:30 a.m.

With nearby Washington School out of commission because of the December fire, its students were being bussed five miles northeast to Gompers. To accommodate the doubled enrollment, Gompers instituted a split schedule—its students starting at 7 a.m., and Washington's at noon.

"Doll rode her bike to our bus stop 'cause she wanted to go to school with me," Perruquet says. "We felt we was lovers. We used to sneak out to the quarry and make out. Sometimes I would sneak to the tracks behind her house, and we would hold one another. She wrote me at Sheridan. When I ended up at Menard, we wrote for a while, and time just got the best of us."

James, in eighth grade, and Doll and Fern, in seventh, crossed the street in front of the Perruquet home a couple of minutes before the bus arrived.

"We all got on the bus and went to the back seats as always," Perruquet says. "We all sat in one seat together, Fern, Doll, and me. We was all clowning around as we picked up other kids. It was a nice, sunny day, and I really never wanted to be in school. But once at the school, we all went shooting for the school doors. I got to my locker, but I had to wait because I had an upper locker and the people below me was taking their time. Being short, I had to wait for them to move so I could step on the lip of their locker to get to mine. Once I got my books, I headed for my homeroom class. We all took a seat and when the bell rang the teacher had to go to the office to get something. While she was gone, some of the kids got up and was looking out the window, when one of the girls, a black girl named Jackie, hollered, 'James, there's Billy!' At first I said, 'I don't care,' and I just waved her off. Billy walked into the school door, and Jackie stuck her head out and goes, 'Hi, Billy. Here's James.'"

When James and Billy, who had walked out of class at Hufford on the West Side, made eye contact, James jumped up from his seat.

"I asked him, 'What's up, Billy?' He tells me he was going to talk to the principal about coming to Gompers," Perruquet says.

With the homeroom teacher not around to control the students, Perruquet and Sprinkle walked out of the classroom and into the deserted hallway.

"I says, 'Come on, Billy. We'll go in there and talk to Mr. Moss together.' Well, Mr. Moss didn't have time for us, so Billy was talking about how he was tired of everything and having to go to school; he talked about an uncle that lived in Kentucky, that he was thinking about running away, and I said, 'Yeah, let's go,' and we went out one of the doors and got his bike and left. You know, I never wanted to leave homeroom that day. We had a young homeroom teacher, and she was the best-looking teacher in the school."

Although Perruquet says that discussing details of the murder is a road he would rather not travel, he agrees to provide the specifics regarding the case's escalation of violence, and he reveals—for the first time—what he says was the motive for taking David Stukel's life.

"We got carried away," Perruquet says. "We took something farther than it should have been took. It was no planned thing. It was no thrill-seeker thing. It started out as robbing him, tearing up all his stuff, but it turned into a sexual assault and murder. The poor kid come down the road, and we took advantage of him.

"After the sexual deal, we were hitting him different times, different ways. He'd fall down, we'd drag him back up. We used him as a punching bag. At one point, I asked David, 'Do you know either of us?' and he said, 'I know Billy' or 'I know about Billy.' And Billy told him, 'You don't know me!' In a scared voice, David said, 'Yes I do.'

"Inside me, it was like I got shot. 'We're done for!' That's exactly what I told Billy, 'We're going to prison, man.' I do believe that if David would of said he never knew Billy, I feel he would of been let go. But we had to clean up this mess. It was talked about right then and there, and we never talked about killing nobody before. The kid didn't say nothin' like he wasn't gonna tell what happened. I got scared and I know at that point it was our intent to kill him, to shut him up, to keep from going to juvenile. See, my brother Joe, he had already been in juvenile, and we didn't want to go there. We knew we was in trouble. People seen us. We had been drinking, getting high, showing off.

"I think more or less I was coming off my high, and I knew we was in more and more trouble. And I pulled out the knife we'd stolen and tried to stab him with it and it bent. And Billy took it and bent it back and tried to stab him with it, but it bent again. Billy tried fixing it, and it broke. Billy seemed pissed off and lay David out with a roundhouse punch.

"Billy seen them iron bars. Some were half under the junk, but there were two I found—two that were rusty but OK. Billy grabbed David by the neck and pulled him from the ground to his knees and took one of the bars and said, 'Batter up!' and hit him right in the face. We got him up, and I took my turn at it. We started hitting him, taking turns seeing who can make him fly further. Each time he went down, we picked him up and made him go through it again.

"After a few hits with the bars, Billy said, 'That ain't going to do it' and told me to look for something heavy enough to drop on his head. All I could lift was a half-block. Being a little guy, my hands was small and I didn't want to look bad in front of Billy. I found half a block, and we both hit him hard with it several times. I picked it up about stomach-high and dropped it on him, and Billy said, 'No! It's not going to do anything like that. You got to pick it up over your head like this,' and he let it go, showing me how. I did as he did, and I missed him totally. We was smoking, and we flipped our cigs on him and walked out."

31

In the Blood

In the early stages of researching Billy Rose Sprinkle's life, it became part of my weekly routine to call directory assistance, request telephone numbers for parties with the last name of Brooks in the Nashville area, dial a number, then hang up without reaching his former common-law wife, Tammy.

In May 2003, I took one more shot in the dark of area code 615, and a young woman answered the phone:

"Hello."

Hi, I'm calling for Tammy Brooks.

"I'm sorry, there's not a Tammy Brooks that lives here. Who are you?"

I'm a writer. I'm trying to reach Tammy.

"Well, she doesn't live here, but I can try to get a message to her."

Oh, you know her?

"Yeah, but I don't know where she's living. Are you old friends?"

I'm doing research for a book, and I have talked to members of her ex-husband's family.

"Are you talking about Brando Brooks?"

No.

"Well, who is her ex-husband?"

Billy Sprinkle.

"Bill Sprinkle! That's my father! That's my father!" screamed seventeen-year-old Amanda Rose Sprinkle. "We've been trying to find him! We were thinking about hiring an investigator. He's about to be a grandfather! I'm having a boy and want him to see his grandson!"

Amanda Rose Sprinkle longs to have a relationship with a father who's been little more than a faded snapshot on her bedroom mirror.

"I haven't seen him since I was seven. I haven't talked to him since I was twelve," says Amanda as if she has recited those painful words a thousand times.

Amanda has not been shy about asking her mother questions about her father, and she has retained every shred of information she's been able to attain.

"My mom left him when I was six weeks old," Amanda says. "When my mom met Billy, she had just had my brother, and she had been married to a guy named Brando, who died. You know, my mother does live here, but we've been getting some weird calls here lately."

Amanda may be nine months pregnant and four months shy of her eighteenth birthday, but when she talks about reconnecting with her father, she sounds like an eight-year-old on Christmas Eve.

"For years, I've been wanting to find information about that side of my family," Amanda says. "I like to know why things are the way they are, and I don't know that part of my family. I went to see him in prison when I was four years old. I didn't really know too much about him. My mom had finally taken me to see him because when I was little, as soon as I was learning how to talk I was asking questions about 'My Daddy.' I wanted to know where 'My Daddy' was. I went to visit him and played around with some little toys, and we ate there with him. I knew that he loved me—I remember feeling that."

In December 1990, when Billy Rose Sprinkle was released from prison for the second time, he settled in the Springfield area with wife Sharon.

"My mom hunted him down," Amanda says. "And he got upset because the state of Tennessee was actually hunting him down, too, trying to sue him for child support because we had been on food stamps, and the state was trying to get their money back from him."

In the early 1990s, despite her father's reluctance to pay child support and the bitterness it created between her parents, young Amanda hoped that she would someday have a relationship with her dad.

"He actually came to the house one day. He had kept saying for the longest time that he was gonna see me, and we didn't really think he was gonna show up. But my dad woke me up one morning when I was seven, and he spent the weekend with me."

Amanda hasn't seen her father since, but she has fond memories of that visit.

"He bought my brother a bike, and he bought me a little three-story doll house for my Barbies. He had a really nice blue, glittery truck. And Sharon, his wife, was with him. We went riding around in the truck, and they stayed in a motel. We went out to eat at Krystals! And he took me to the park, and we spent time together. And he spent time getting to know my mom's boyfriend. And my dad spent a lot of time over there with us, and he was helping out mom's boyfriend with the yard, and I just went about playing with my friends, and it felt right, him being there. I don't think I'd ever been happier than that time."

Although Tammy is skeptical of Billy becoming a fixture in Amanda's life, she is happy that a reunion is possible.

"Amanda wrote him a letter a couple of years ago, mailed it to his last known address that we had for him in Springfield, and she never got a response, so she didn't know if he didn't get the letter or if he just didn't want anything to do with her," Tammy says. "I tried to comfort her. I said, 'I don't believe that he doesn't want anything to do with you.' I don't want to say he's not capable of being a functioning citizen, but I don't think he knows how."

Tammy emphasizes that she never bad-mouthed Billy when Amanda was a child.

"I didn't want her to grow up wondering if what I said was true or not and resenting me for it, so I tried to not say anything bad about him. I didn't tell her until she got a little bit older."

Amanda speaks candidly about conversations she's had with her mother that cast a negative light on her father.

"Billy used to beat her," Amanda says. "And just a couple weeks ago she told me that while she was pregnant, a week before she had me, they had gotten into an argument, and he had thrown her down into a ditch. She was trying to help ease me through some of the worry I was going through because I had a hard fall and felt the baby slam into the bottom of my stomach."

Asked if her mother talked to her about Billy's substance abuse, Amanda responds, "She told me Billy worshiped the ground she walked on when he was sober. But when he was drunk, he became the most vicious, vindictive man she'd ever laid eyes on."

Billy and Tammy passed down their physical features and rebellious natures to Amanda.

"I actually have Billy's blue eyes," Amanda says. "And when I get mad, my mom, she tells me I remind her a lot of Billy—she tells me I get that fire in my eyes."

When Billy would get that look, it usually meant that Tammy would get a beating, and throughout the 1990s, even though Tammy was far removed from Billy's world, abuse remained in her life.

"I lived with a man for ten years that scared me worse than Billy ever did," Tammy says.

Tammy found comfort in alcohol, and while she was numbing her pain, the state of Tennessee took custody of her children—first her son, eight days after his seventeenth birthday, then Amanda, just before her thirteenth birthday. Her son stayed in state custody for less than a year; Amanda for fifteen months. When Amanda returned home, her mother had her alcohol problem in check, but Amanda did as poorly in high school as her father did in junior high.

"I was staying stoned all the time, and I slept through my classes," Amanda says. "I didn't care. School was social hour. When I got pregnant, I was supposed to be a senior, but I only had one credit."

In high school, Amanda fell into a deep depression and considered suicide.

"I don't know why I was so depressed, but I decided that I was tired of everything, and I didn't feel like anyone would notice."

Amanda Rose was born exactly seventeen years after Billy Rose was arrested for murder. She entered the world on September 17, 1985, at Silver Cross Hospital, the same East Side facility where David Stukel's body was taken the night of the murder.

Asked if she is aware of the significance of September 17, 1968, Amanda replies, "Yeah, I know."

Asked what she has heard about the murder, Amanda relates the version of the crime that has been passed down from father to mother to daughter.

"They walked in on a boy raping his sister. They cut off his penis, stuffed a pipe in his ass, broke both his arms, busted out his knees."

Amanda pauses, then asks, "How exactly was this guy murdered?"

They beat him with iron bars, smashed his head with a concrete block. Billy's sister was not raped. The victim's penis was not cut off.

"With the reason I was given, I could understand it," Amanda says. "I would have no blame for him. I felt bad that a guy was killed in the process, but if you rape someone, you deserve punishment. But now, though, I guess no one really knows what the truth is. If you take someone's innocence from them, you deserve to be punished. I'm not saying that you deserve death, but you deserve a punishment, and in Billy's eyes that may have been what he deserved. But if I was to think there was any other reason as to why he killed this boy other than because he raped his sister, I would look badly upon him. I would never hate Billy, but at the same time a part of me is kinda like edgy about everything. I am really trying to look toward the future, not think about the past."

On the afternoon that Amanda learned that her father is incarcerated at the Big Muddy Correctional Center, she composed a letter to him:

DAD:

Hi, I found you and I'm writing you. I just hope that you'll respond. I hope I can form and develop some roots with you. I need to know where I came from. There is one thing you should know first off. Any day now, you will be a grand-father of a beautiful baby boy! His name is Devon Raymond and was due May 14th. He's being stubborn and doesn't want to come out. His Dad's name is James Tipton and he just turned 20. We're no longer together but we are good friends and he plans on being very much a part of Devon's life. James is a great guy with a big heart. He just still has a lot of growing up to do, as do I. He treats me good and is there when I need him. We are trying to work on things and hopefully get back together, so have no worries, he is a good man.

Now, as you know, I'm 17, but I just got my G.E.D. and plan on going to college to study for my associate's degree in Criminal Justice. I'm doing my best to pre-pare to be a mom and I can only pray that I will prove to do my job well. It's just scary as hell. I'm just so young and this new responsibility is terrifying, but mom has really been there for me. She's been so understanding and comforting. She is both my mom and my best friend. I'd be lost without her. There is so much to say, but we can get it all said and done through more contact, so hopefully you will write back. I want to know you. I want to know you love me. And I want you to know your grandson, so please write back.

Love Always,

Amanda Rose Sprinkle

Three days after writing the letter to her father, Amanda Rose Sprinkle gave birth to eight-pound, six-ounce Devon. And with her newborn baby waking in her arms, she had an awakening.

"I found Billy, and I'm just waiting to see where that step leads. I don't know if it's a can of worms I'm ready to open. I don't know if I want them in my life. I want some questions answered about my past. I want to hear his side and decide from there on whether or not I want to keep him in my life. I figure I've done this well without him, so I'm sure that I could survive without him."

Amanda talks as if she's fine with not having a relationship with her father, but when he responded to her letter, she did a turnabout.

"He sent me a letter, and he was absolutely thrilled to hear from me! I've contacted several family members that he gave me access to, and one of his sisters, Doll [Georgina], just started balling on the phone!"

Amanda had a long conversation with Doll but opted not to ask her if she was raped the day of the murder.

"I thought about it, but I figured it was best if I don't because that was before my time," Amanda says. "When I called her and told her who I was, she screamed, 'Oh, my God! You're my niece!' I asked her, 'Did you even know that I existed?' and she said, 'No!'"

Asked to describe the mood of her father's letter, Amanda doesn't restrain her joy.

"He's absolutely thrilled that he's going to be a grandfather!" says Amanda, whose enthusiasm soon turned to resentment.

"The first sentence in his letter was: 'Thank God! Thank God! Thank God! I finally heard from you!' When I wrote him back, I told him, 'It's great you're happy to hear from me, but how can you be thanking God that you heard from me when you knew where we were all this time?'"

Amanda was also hurt that her father never mentioned her to Doll.

"Why didn't she know I existed? Why not tell her about me? I'm his only child!"

Amanda can't let go of her father's poor record when it comes to her.

"Him not being there, that was something I've gone through life really upset about. Mom has always told me, 'No matter what he's doing, even if he's not contacting you, Amanda, he loves you.' I know he loves me, and I've known in my heart that he loves me. But it is my brain that's questioned his love, because if you love someone, how can you not contact them? Especially your own child!"

Amanda Rose is no shrinking violet. She challenged her dad to commit to their relationship for the first time in his life.

"I wrote and told him, 'I'm willing to give you this one last chance.' I told him, 'If he needs people to stand by him and help him, I'm willing to help him stay sober' because if he doesn't stay sober, he's not going to have me in his life. I'm not having that around my child. I'm not going to have my child get attached to someone, then have them screw it up. I am taking it slow, but I plan on seeing him."

Amanda was surprised when Billy wasn't offended that she berated him. Mimicking his mock authoritative response, she recited a portion of Billy's second letter: "Now see here, young woman, I'm quite impressed with your forthrightness, honesty and concerns. I've not now nor will I make any promise or commitment that I won't keep. I will keep in contact. If I were to get out tomorrow, I would be on the phone to you tomorrow letting you know I am out and how I am going to want very much for you to come to our house, call, visit, anything, anytime."

Despite Billy's promises, Amanda isn't convinced that she will have a relationship with him.

"I think a lot of what he says is just bullshit because I've caught him in several lies, like saying he went back in on a DUI. If he keeps lying to me, I'm cutting him off."

Amanda was particularly offended by a request he made early on in their letter-writing.

"He asked me to write the parole board for him, and I mean, 'No!' He says, 'You can just tell them you finally found me and plan to be actively involved in my life.' I'm not going to write the board! I told him I thought it was funny that the third letter I receive from him he's going to ask me to write the parole board when he hasn't even been in my life? I'm not going be his pawn to get out of prison!"

Amanda continues to waver over pursuing a relationship with her father.

"One minute I'm totally hyped up, ready to see him, and the next I'm just sketchy. I know that if he's not out of prison, I'm not taking Devon with me when I go see him. I just really don't know if I want Billy in my life."

32

Lasting Impressions

Connie Sprinkle lives with a constant reminder of Billy Rose Sprinkle's last day of freedom.

"I can't raise my right arm higher than halfway," Connie says of the rotator cuff injury she sustained in the tug of war with her husband in July 2001. Connie's arm movement may be limited, but she has a full range of emotions regarding whether to stick with Sprinkle.

"I know I can't take the beatings—him thinking more of the booze than he does me," Connie says. "I'm too old to be getting beatings. Well, I shouldn't be getting beatings anyway. I wrote and told him, 'You get out, I'll take you back, but if I smell booze, you won't even see me go because I will get out of this house and you will be gone when I come back.' I want him back, but I'm scared to have him back. My mind's saying one thing, my heart's saying a different thing. I deeply do love him. But if he drinks, we'll be divorced so fast he won't even see it coming."

Sprinkle said all the right things to Connie leading up to his September 2003 parole hearing.

"He says, 'When I get out I don't want no one around. I want the phone taken off the hook. I'm not calling nobody, not even my daughter, until at least two or three days afterwards. She's my daughter but you're my wife, and my wife comes first.' And that shocked me because I've never been first with anybody."

Sprinkle got creative in an attempt to ensure that he would be welcomed home by Connie if released.

"He said, 'I told you I'd never put a woman's name on my body? Well, I put a woman's name on my body and it's yours,'" says Connie, referring to Billy having had her name tattooed onto the rose on his left shoulder. "I think he needs a second chance because maybe he's changed."

On weekends, the racket in the visitors' room at the Big Muddy Correctional Center is mind-numbing, but Connie Sprinkle doesn't mind the incessant chatter of inmates reconnecting with loved ones.

"Everybody's yakking, but I never heard another person—all I heard was Billy," says Connie of her first visit to Big Muddy since deputies took her husband away in a wheelchair two years earlier because he was too drunk to walk.

"I didn't pay attention to nobody else," Connie says. "Billy was happy to see me, and I was happy to see him. I talked so much that my voice started to disappear. When you first go in, you can grab 'em and give 'em a big old smackaroo, and a passionate one at that. Then you sit down, but you can't kiss no more until you get ready to leave. But I can hold hands with Billy all the time I'm there. When you get up to leave, you walk over by the door, and then you can kiss 'em again."

Connie says they were so excited about seeing each other, and so wrapped up in each other, that they hardly ate.

"There's a bunch of vending machines, but I couldn't eat and he couldn't eat. We were both too nervous. My legs were shaking and wouldn't stop shaking the whole time I was there. He said all he wanted to do was stare at me."

The visits are as much a tonic for Connie's lonely heart as they are a boost to her husband's frame of mind.

"I'm still lonely, but by going down and seeing him, it's done wonders for me," Connie says. "It helps me to be stronger. I was getting pretty weak. I was tempted to go out, you know, but by seeing him, it puts some hope in me. It just makes me feel so good."

Connie believes that a transformation has taken place—that Billy is a changed man.

"When we sit down and talk, he sits there and he cries. He cries right there in front of everybody. He's just a different person when he doesn't drink—absolutely different. That's why I believe when he does get out he's gonna really work hard at it. He seems to be a lot stronger, and he knows if he drinks again he's gonna lose me for good. I'd told him that in letters, but now I've told him that in person."

Prior to Billy Rose Sprinkle's second parole interview since returning to prison, PRB member Milton Maxwell discovers that the inmate had spent time in segregation for staff assault and sexual misconduct. During the interview, Sprinkle contradicts statements he made ten months earlier to PRB member Barbara Hubbard, such as it was Perruquet, not he, who knew the victim. He also adds an outlandish twist—that Perruquet and David Stukel were glue-sniffing buddies. And equally bizarre, Sprinkle claims that his case has been heard by the U.S. Supreme Court seven times:

You were in segregation for sexual misconduct?

"Staff assault and sexual misconduct. They dropped it to insolence. I was painting the door frame. And Miss Owens comes through, and I picked up my paint rag and either my paint rag or my paint brush or handle hit her on the leg."

Why do you feel, after you've been given so many chances by the board, that you would violate?

"I didn't know how to deal with ... I started drinking. I've been on the substance program in here for twenty months. From September 2001 to May of 2003."

What kind of alcohol do you drink?

"Beer."

The person who was murdered, did you know him?

"No, no sir."

What were the circumstances?

"James Perruquet tried to sell the guy a radio. And it ended up in a fight."

Why did the fight start?

"He didn't want to buy the radio. And he got into it with my buddy. I didn't know at the time, but he knew my co-defendant—they had gotten high together. And push comes to shoving, and I shoved him, and me and him had a fight."

And what was the victim struck with?

"When he died, he was ... he killed him with a concrete block is what I heard."

Were you there?

"I was not there when it happened."

Where were you?

"On the street."

So Perruquet was the one that did the killing?

"Uh-huh. I have requested a DNA test so I could prove that I didn't do this sexual thing either."

What did Perruquet do with this concrete block?

"He beat him with it."

Did you observe the dead body?

"When I went to get James, I seen the body."

Your parole plans are to reside with your wife.

"Yes. And there's an inpatient and outpatient substance-abuse program in Springfield—the Triangle Center."

When you were out before, what kind of job did you have?

"Landscaping and roofing."

What kind of job will you get this time?

"Landscaping. Employment has never been a problem."

It is your statement to the board that even though you were convicted and sentenced that you had no part in causing the death of that individual?

"No, I never did it. I pleaded guilty to it. I was fourteen years old. I've been to the United States Supreme Court seven times, the Illinois Supreme Court five or six times."

You pled guilty.

"Yes."

But you deny actually killing the person?

"Yes."

OK, if you're granted parole, do you think this time will be different from the others?

"I know it will. I've lost everything except my wife and my home. I went through so much therapy in the alcohol program down here. I've just changed. For the first time in my life, I actually read my Bible every morning. I've got hepatitis C, which is a death sentence. Instead of doing like I did on parole before, negative things, I've got something real positive to look forward to. My downfall was that I started drinking. I'm not a thief, I'm not a murderer, I'm not a violent person. I'm just a hard-working fool."

Anything else you want to say?

"There's so much running through my head. I want to go home," says Sprinkle as he begins to cry. "I've got every reason in the world not to come back. I'm not a convict. I can be trusted. I definitely can be trusted. The only thing I had to do was get over the drinking."

The evening after being interviewed by the PRB's Maxwell, Sprinkle calls Connie, expresses confidence that he will be paroled, and asks her to attend the PRB session in Springfield, three miles from her home.

"I told him I am going to go," Connie says. "I'm going to tell them at work that I'll be a little late."

Ten days later, at 7:50 a.m., Connie walks into the eight-by-twenty waiting room of the PRB headquarters and forces a smile.

"I've just got a feeling it's going to be bad news," she says.

As Connie settles into her seat and prepares to listen to the discussion on the speaker resting on the end table, PRB Chairman Craig Findley opens the waiting-room door and invites us into the conference room. Connie and I sit in chairs in the near corner, five feet away from the massive faux-wooden table where Findley is joined by Maxwell, Barbara Hubbard, Susan Carol Finley, Arvin Boddie, Robert Dunne, Norman Sula, James Donahue, Mark Warnsing, and Eric Althoff.

Maxwell opens the session by stating that alcohol was a major factor in Sprinkle not being able to comply with his parole conditions.

"He did receive some alcohol treatment in Springfield, but I do not believe he completed that program," Maxwell says. "Regarding institutional adjustment since returning, he received a major disciplinary report involving sexual misconduct."

It is as if Connie Sprinkle has received a blow to the face when the words "sexual misconduct" register. Her jaw drops and her brown eyes widen.

"Mr. Sprinkle has been paroled on two separate occasions; each time Mr. Sprinkle has seen fit to violate the trust and confidence that the board placed in him," Maxwell says.

"Based upon his institutional adjustment, his failure to comply with the rules and conditions of parole, I find that I cannot make any favorable recommendation for the parole release of Billy Rose Sprinkle. It is therefore my motion that parole should be denied."

"I agree," James Donahue says without hesitation. "This young man is not only a man who committed a very egregious crime, he's a recidivist offender, a threat to the community. He says alcohol was a problem while he was committing crimes. He has not seen fit to even rehabilitate himself by completing alcohol counseling. He continues to get tickets, a serious ticket in this case."

Robert Dunne asks Maxwell for insight into the 1968 murder. "Was there any discussion with him of the committing offense back in 1968? Does he make any statements that he might have been a follower or that the other guy did all the physical harm? Does he make any excuses?

"Yes, there are excuses," Maxwell says. "Sprinkle tried to put the blame on his co-defendant. But there were other individuals whom Sprinkle stated what part he had in this murder. It is clear to me that he participated equally in the murder."

A motion to go into closed session passes.

Connie and I are escorted out of the room, across the hallway, and into an office. Connie, with tears welling in her eyes, whispers, "Sexual misconduct? I can't take any more of this. I'm getting a divorce."

Connie, sure that her husband will be denied parole, leaves the office, staggers down the hallway, into the waiting area, and out the front door.

Five minutes later, I return to the conference room, at which time Maxwell restates his grounds for recommending that Sprinkle's parole be denied.

"He cannot abide by the reasonable rules of parole release and his institutional adjustment in terms of the sexual misconduct. He has been paroled twice and has not seen fit to follow the regulations as set forth by this board. I would say for the record that the board in 1981 made a serious mistake."

Sprinkle's parole consideration is unanimously denied.

As I am preparing to leave, gathering my thoughts, notes, and tape recorder, Chairman Findley announces, "There's another motion on this case. Mr. Boddie has the floor."

"Thank you, Mr. Chairman," Arvin Boddie says. "I've listened very carefully to the information that was presented in regard to this case and in particular the more recent history since 1999 where we've had a series of violations of parole that resulted in action by the board. And then most recently misconduct in the institution of a very serious nature. All things considered, I don't think that it would be prudent to act favorably on parole in this case in the next three years. I move that we continue further consideration on this matter and parole for this inmate for three years."

James Donahue concurs: "This man was involved in the horrible beating death. He was involved in a stabbing that resulted in a serious injury in 1976. The murder in '68, the stabbing in '76 while in prison, and then he threatened to kill his wife; this guy is a recidivist offender. He's a habitual criminal. I think he's a threat to the community. Without a doubt, he should not be out on the streets and threatening society."

The board votes unanimously not to hear Sprinkle for three years.

Two days after Billy Rose Sprinkle is denied by the PRB, daughter Amanda learns that her father won't be heard by the board for three years.

"I didn't expect him to get through because this is his third time in prison," says Amanda, shaken by the news. "It hurts because I don't want the first time I see him after all these years to be in prison. I don't want my son in that environment. But I look at it as this is the man who helped create me, who is the grandfather of my child. I'll see him if for no other reason than that—he deserves to meet his grandson."

Still, Amanda wonders if becoming reacquainted with her ailing father would be opening herself up to more heartbreak.

"It's already hard for me to not really have my dad in my life, and I have a feeling with Billy's hepatitis C that he's not going to be around long. He sent me a new picture, and I just don't think he'll last, especially with being in the penitentiary, locked away from the world. I doubt that he's gonna get out when he comes up for parole again. I don't want to visit him in prison, but I've gone this long without him in my life. I do feel bad because I may not see him before he passes. But that's something that I think I could live with, and I don't mean that in a bad way, but I've gone this long without seeing him, without him in my life."

Although Billy has a tattoo on his chest with the name Amanda scrawled across a banner streaming from Pegasus' mouth, he has not been a permanent presence in her life.

"Connie once made a statement that Billy was a good dad," Amanda says. "And I almost started laughing. This is the man who created me, and I understand that. But I'll be damned if he raised me. He's a good man at heart, but a good dad? No! He has never been a good dad. If he was a good dad, he would have been a part of my life. He would have at least helped support me, if nothing else. He was not there! He did not help! He did not contribute anything but pain to me growing up. He filled me with lies, telling me that he was going to come see me, and I would sit and wait for him to show up, and only one time did he ever show up."

Amanda turns her attention to the murder.

"Hopefully, Billy has made amends with God. He owes the victim's family an apology, even if the boy did rape my aunt. Billy took the law into his hands, and if this guy didn't rape my aunt and he murdered him for some petty reason, he deserves to stay where he is."

When informed—again—that Billy has not mentioned the rape of his sister in letters to the PRB or in parole interviews, she says, "I haven't asked Doll about it. If there was a rape, I can understand wanting to murder someone."

Amanda pauses, then asks for copies of the court documents.

"I want to understand, and I know this is something I'm going to have to do on my own because I will pretty much never get a straight answer from Billy."

When Amanda and Tammy Brooks receive the case facts, they are repulsed by what they read.

"Amanda had a very emotional day," Tammy says. "The court docket is what got to her. She threw it all down and said it turned her stomach. She was so upset that she said she was going to legally change her name. But the next day Amanda was reading more of it and said she was past the shock. She said she did want to see him and that she wanted to ask him: 'Why?' She wanted him to help her understand, 'Why did this happen?' I told her, 'You know what, nobody knows exactly what happened except for James and Billy. You can ask him why. You can try to get him to explain it to you, but you can't get in somebody's head and know the truth.'"

Tammy is disgusted by the case details, but she is more in shock over what isn't included in the documents.

"Dolly's name was never mentioned. There wasn't anything about her."

Two days after absorbing the case information, Amanda is still open to a relationship with her father, but she remains in denial over his motive for targeting David Stukel.

"The murder was pathetic! I don't agree with any of it, even if the boy had raped my aunt, but I'm not going to cut him out of my life. I had to get over the impact of reading about it. It happened almost twenty years before I was born! I had to think about that and remember that people change. The only thing the murder has to do with me is that I'm the daughter of the man who did it and at the time he was a boy."

When Billy Rose Sprinkle calls home to learn his parole fate, he is unaware of the PRB's ruling earlier in the day, and Connie does not know about the three-year continuance. She only has to say "hello" for her husband to realize that he won't be walking out of prison.

"The way I answered, Billy didn't even have to ask—he says, 'I didn't get out, did I?'" Connie says. "I said, 'Billy, I'm sorry, it will be another year.' There was a long quiet. I says to Billy, 'It got bad in there.' It shocked me, especially the sexual misconduct. I said, 'When they said sexual misconduct, my mouth opened because the piece of paper you sent home didn't say nothing about sexual misconduct.' I told him, 'You lied to me!' He says, 'I didn't lie.' And I said, 'They said sexual misconduct up there.'"

When told that after she left, the PRB voted to not hear Billy's case for three years, Connie has a meltdown.

"Oh for fucking sake!" she screams. "That's terrible! I'm going to have to get a divorce. I've been waiting more than two years. Three more years! I'd be almost sixty years old! He's going to call me in ten days, so when he calls I've got to tell him. I'd be throwing away more than five years of my life."

When Billy calls, Connie can't bring herself to tell him that she no longer wants him in her life, and for nearly a year she wavers over whether to end the relationship. Despite the pain inflicted upon her by her husband, Connie agonizes over the decision. But after much introspection, she realizes that she is better off without him. She files for divorce and donates his clothes to the Salvation Army.

"I tore up all of his letters—must have been three hundred of them—and it felt like I had something lifted off of me," Connie says. "I think I stuck with him because I felt sorry for him, but Billy's never did nothing for me except been a pain in the rear."

What is not said is more surprising than what is said at Sprinkle's 2003 PRB hearing. The downgrading of the inmate's sexual misconduct charge to insolence was not addressed, and his extensive substance-abuse therapy behind bars was not mentioned.

Seven days after Sprinkle was charged with sexual misconduct and assaulting a staff member, the DOC's Adjustment Committee issued a report in which he was found "not guilty" of assaulting a staff member, and the sexual misconduct charge was reduced to insolence. It appears that the initial disciplinary report, referring to a sexual misconduct, reached the PRB but the adjustment did not. The PRB was not aware of the reduction, even though Sprinkle spoke of it in his interview. And at the hearing, there was no mention of the inmate's 1,137 hours of alcohol-abuse treatment in prison, which he talked about during his interview. Instead, PRB members focused on his outpatient failures that occurred before he returned to prison in 2001.

Connie concedes that even if the alcohol-treatment hours had been mentioned and the sexual misconduct had been represented as insolence, Billy's history of drinking likely would have sealed his fate.

"They figure that he keeps coming back for drinking, so why not keep him there. The last time Billy went to jail, he said, 'I didn't even know I was in jail until I woke the next morning.' Every time they've let him out, it's more alcohol, so that's why they're keeping him in. Maybe this is for the best. He's not changed before, and I don't mind being alone. I don't need a man, especially that man. Let somebody else have him."

James Perruquet and Billy Rose Sprinkle, first incarcerated in 1968, are again in Illinois penitentiaries in their mid-fifties and well into the new millennium.

James Perruquet

With the facts surrounding Perruquet's stabbing of a man entering his home not pointing toward a premeditated act—the requisite for first-degree murder—the inmate has more than a glimmer of hope that his murder conviction will be overturned, negating his life sentence. Perruquet's defenders argue that in 1995 he acted in self-defense. They say that at worst he should have been convicted of second-degree murder, the four-to-twenty-year crime-of-passion option that wasn't available to Woodford County jurors. With the flawed jury instructions and questionable defense tactics, a clemency ruling in Perruquet's favor is not out of the question.

Sprinkle, meanwhile, may be just a parole violator, not a two-time convicted murderer, but he is judged by a different set of rules because he has not been discharged from parole stipulations for the '68 murder. The present board strongly believes a previous board made a monumental error in setting Sprinkle free in 1981. With Sprinkle's 1986 burglary conviction; his recidivism on the trio of alcohol-related parole violations from 1999 to 2001, the last of which included a death threat; and his refusal to accept responsibility for the sexual assault and murder of David Stukel, it is not surprising that he is still incarcerated. And he could remain behind bars until his mandatory release date of August 2017, when he would be 64.

Billy Rose Sprinkle

Since returning to the DOC in 2001, Sprinkle has been eligible for parole for seven years—nearly twice the time he was parole-eligible before being released on the murder charge. Granted, Sprinkle was not heard by the PRB in 2004 and 2005 because of the three-year continuance issued by the board in 2003, but in 2007, on his fourth try—the same appearance in which he was released in 1981—the board voted unanimously to deny his release. Based on the '07 vote and two previous unanimous denials, the PRB clearly believes Sprinkle has neither paid his debt nor is capable of functioning as a free man—including holding a job—no matter how many alcohol rehabilitation certificates fill his file.

"Billy's family life growing up was horrible," says one of Sprinkle's former parole agents who asked not to be identified. "And if that's all you know, and then you're basically raised in a prison, how do you break that cycle? You get out, you can't deal with the stresses of life and maybe there's a chemical part of him that can't say no. It's an illness, an illness that's killing him. I couldn't get him to stop drinking. He had become a threat to himself. There were health issues, and he'd have to ride a bicycle because he didn't have a license, so he was drinking and riding a bicycle. He'd already gotten knocked off his bicycle once. He didn't have any money to pay for doctor visits, and he couldn't hold a job."

Lorraine Sprinkle contends that her brother's inability to stay employed wasn't entirely the result of his alcoholism.

"Every time he'd get a job he had to lie about his past," Lorraine says. "He'd tell them he's never been in the joint, and sure enough they'd find out and they'd fire him. If he'd tell them the truth, they would never hire him. He's a convicted murderer, but he deserves a chance too. With his record, Billy's never gonna be able to become what he wants to—a regular person. What kind of life has he got on the outside. He had no life. He was convicted in 1968 and they won't let it die."

Since the age of fourteen, James Perruquet has spent thirty-four years in prison—six out. He, too, finds it difficult to function as a free man and obviously is no slouch in the recidivism department, having been sentenced to prison five times compared with Billy Rose Sprinkle's three trips.

Since fourteen, Sprinkle has been incarcerated for twenty-five years and a free man for fifteen.

While Perruquet may be overweight and rarely exercises, he is in surprisingly good health.

The gaunt-looking Sprinkle may be a weight-room junkie, but his hepatitis C is taking a noticeable toll on him, so much so that Lorraine believes the sensory channels she shares with her brother will soon be severed. But with her deteriorating lungs and his barely functioning liver, she's not sure which end of the conduit will be disengaged first.

"I've not had contact with Billy since he got locked up this time," Lorraine says. "Billy's like my soul, but I told him if he ever went back, it's over. God, he'll probably—I don't even want to say the word. I was looking for something in my daughter's room, and I found a picture of Billy that she had printed out, and he didn't look well at all."

In 2008, 40 years after the murder of David Stukel, James Perruquet's executive clemency appeal will be heard by PRB and Billy Rose Sprinkle will go before the board for the fifth time since returning to prison. The scenario might be difficult to comprehend, but Perruquet, sentenced to life in prison for a second murder, could be a free man before parole violator Sprinkle. And it is Sprinkle, with tattoos of prison walls and tombstones on his chest, who likely will be buried along with the truth in a penitentiary plot.

33

"We've Been Blessed"

Nancy, Debbie and David Stukel in September 1968.

On a picture-perfect, seventy-three degree Sunday morning in 1968, after taking his family to Mass at St. Mary Magdalene, Ray Stukel snapped a photo of children Debbie, David, and Nancy in front of their home.

The photograph would be the final portrait of his three children.

"It was taken the day before David was killed," says Marilyn.

"September 15, 1968 ... I just had the photos enlarged," Marilyn says. "I gave one to each of the girls."

"Look at how tall Debbie is," says Ray, peering at the photo in which Debbie towers over David. "Five foot eight!"

"She was the tallest girl in her eighth-grade class," Marilyn says.

"Taller than a lot of the boys," Ray says.

A couple of hours after the photo was taken, on the last Sunday of David's life, the Stukel children's cousins, Mike and Susie Meurer and their parents, George and Barbara, came to visit the Stukels.

"It was a beautiful day, and we had such a good time playing and riding bikes into the night," Nancy says.

"I remember David riding his bike down the hill with Mike Meurer, who was six years younger, on the back of the bike," Debbie says. "And David was telling Mike, 'The brakes are gone! The brakes are gone!' And Mike came in the house saying, 'I was so scared!'"

Five days later, instead of blowing out the candles on his eighth birthday cake, Mike Meurer watched through tears as the casket of cousin David Stukel was lowered into the ground at Mt. Olivet Cemetery.

Mike was especially fond of David, who didn't allow their age difference to stand in the way of their friendship.

"David was great," Mike says. "When I'd go over there, he'd always include me in with the neighborhood kids. He put me under his wing. I followed him around and watched what he'd do, trying to be like him."

Mike was well aware of David's allegiance to East High.

"He was proud of the school," says Mike, who inherited the green-and-gold East High letterman's jacket David's parents bought for him just before the school year started.

"I still have the jacket. I wore it as a kid. It was important to me. It was a great gesture from my aunt and uncle when they passed that on to me. It kept David with me."

In the weeks and months following the murder, the Stukels spent many nights at George and Barbara Meurer's home ten miles east of Joliet.

"They would come out on Saturday nights," Barbara says. "Marilyn would knock on the door, stick her head in and say: 'Is it pizza time?'"

The Stukels did not come solely for the pizza.

"They needed to be with somebody," Barbara says. "The subject of David would come up, and we'd talk about how funny he was, like when David started playing records one night, and it was time to go home, and he didn't want to go home."

"He was dancing around the living room," George says. "He had his thumbs inside the front of his pants, and he was hopping up and down."

"It was hysterical," Barbara says. "And Ray's looking at his watch, 'C'mon, David, we've got to go home,' and David's not about to go home. He was having too much fun."

I had visited Ray and Marilyn Stukel's ranch-style home in New Lenox dozens of times. I would enter the modest foyer, pass through a short hallway and into the casual dining room, then spend a couple of seconds staring at an eye-teasing, dark-and-light-colored wooden object atop the corner china cabinet, trying to make out the word the Stukels could clearly see:

J-E-S-U-S

On a glorious June morning, with nine holes of golf on the horizon, I strain my eyes and finally see J-E-S-U-S in Ray and Marilyn's dining room. Then Ray and I get a glimpse of God's exquisite craftsmanship—a fawn and doe emerging from the woods as we turn into the parking lot of beautiful Woodruff Golf Course, the East Side sanctuary one and one-half miles east of Belmont Little League.

You can tell a lot about a person on a golf course. How they handle the inevitable highs and lows of a round is a good indicator of how they absorb life's trials and triumphs. Golf is never a good walk wasted for Ray Stukel. From his first drive to the drive home, his temperament is as smooth as his left-handed swing.

At the seventh tee, a picturesque, 155-yard par-3 over water, Ray relishes recapping the time Debbie and Nancy sent back-to-back shots skimming across the water, up an embankment, and onto the green. "They found the green that day, and I had a hard time getting there," says Ray with a hearty laugh.

On this day, with a gentle breeze in his face, Ray lofts a shot that lands softly on the green, and he pars the hole.

Two holes later, as we make our way up the ninth fairway, the doe and fawn reappear.

As we leave the wildlife and the golf course behind, Ray says, "What a beautiful day. I'm glad I'm alive."

We return to the Stukel home, and I see J-E-S-U-S again—this time without squinting.

Ray Stukel played his first round of golf at forty. "It was just a couple years before David was killed," Ray says. "I never had the chance to play golf with David. He was into other sports. I do think about what he would be doing now and what we would be doing together—probably playing golf. I would have enjoyed that. David and I would have had a good time. Now my grandson Kevin and I go golfing once in a while. He hits the ball so far I can't see it!"

The Stukel clan celebrating Christmas in 2003.

New generations of Stukel offspring are clearly the focal points of Ray and Marilyn's lives these days, especially with Nancy's two young children, Katie and Mikey, living next door.

"Our grandkids are our lives," Marilyn says. "And now great-grandkids—it's double the happiness. And it keeps you young, keeps you thinking young."

"Katie is artistic like me," boasts Ray, extending his arm in the direction of the petite, sandy-haired girl. "The other night she painted a snowman with a beautiful blue sky and snowflakes in the background."

Katie has inherited her grandfather's artistic proficiency and another trait as well: "She's stubborn like Dad," says Nancy of a father who has relaxed his rules somewhat, such as the one about limiting kids' exposure to television.

"When we were kids and we watched TV, it was the idiot box," Nancy says. "But now it's OK. And everything stops when one of his shows comes on. He won't miss his shows."

"It's my art shows," Ray says. "I'm learning!"

The manner in which Katie and Mikey interact takes Nancy back to her childhood, the one she says stopped at eleven when she lost her brother.

"I hung around with David just like Mikey follows Katie," Nancy says. "Katie knows that she's got an Uncle David, that she had an Uncle David. But she doesn't know any details, and she's never asked yet. What I'm going to say to her when she does ask, I don't know. I think it's a shame because my kids will never know him. My husband will never know him, my nephews will never know him."

"At family gatherings, we always think about David," Marilyn says.

"He's never out of our minds," Ray says.

"Everything going on with the family or has gone on with the family, it is always right there—him not being able to grow up and be a part of everything," Marilyn says. "Debbie got married, and he wasn't there. Then Debbie had her kids, and then Nancy got married and had her kids, and he wasn't a part of any of that. We think about David, especially with something that he would be a part of with the family because everything centers around our family."

Debbie says that for her it is impossible to put to rest the loss of her brother.

"That part of my life is never gone. You're always thinking, 'What would David be doing now? Would he be married?' He'd probably have kids. When it's Christmas, or any holiday, you think of that. It's, 'There would be more people; we would have had to put out more chairs; my kids probably would have had cousins their age.' If you think about that too much, it can make you crazy."

"The family has moved on, but it's still difficult knowing that you had a brother and he's not here," Nancy says. "I wouldn't change the time that I had with my brother for anything, but it's hard to think about him without thinking, 'Why isn't he here?' It's still hard not to think about how different things would be if he were here."

After losing David, Ray and Marilyn never lost sight of the world's beauty.

Ray and Marilyn Stukel at the unveiling of the David Raymond Stukel Memorial Computer Room at St. Mary Magdalene.

"Every year I'd get a Christmas card from David's eighth-grade teacher, Sister Virginia Marie, and I'd write back, and every year I'd make a point to tell her that I believe our lives are blessed, that we've had so much joy in our lives," Marilyn says. "But we had to work at it."

"I don't think I ever did stop seeing the beauty in the world," Ray says.

"We have so much to be thankful for."

Standing in his kitchen and engaging in conversation, Ray Stukel begins preparing grilled-cheese sandwiches.

"Ray's the official cook around here," Marilyn says.

"I like to eat, and I like to cook," Ray says. "I'm going to go pick some green onions. Would you watch the grilled-cheese sandwiches, Marilyn? They're already turned."

"Yes, go on," says Marilyn, waving her hand toward the sliding-glass door.

I distract Marilyn with a question about David's personality, and the sandwiches spend too much time on one side.

"I like 'em just like that, scorched on one side," I say.

"Well, you're gonna get 'em like that—you're family," replies Marilyn.

After countless conversations with Ray and Marilyn Stukel, I do feel like family. The Stukels had opened their homes, hearts, wounds, and photo albums to share their innermost thoughts about their lives with and without David. There were occasions when their courage was inspiring; on other days, witnessing their grief was overwhelming. Alternating between the Stukels and the families of their son's murderers was an unsettling balancing act—one day absorbing the Stukels' sadness, the next being immersed in the bleak worlds of the Sprinkles and Perruquets. But on this day in Ray and Marilyn's kitchen, nearly forty years after their son's murder, as we enjoy grilled-cheese sandwiches and garden-picked green onions, and watch Mikey wear more cheese than he eats, I am light-years from the dark side.

We eat, laugh and drink milk and juice from a set of glasses that David had given to his mom the year he died. Marilyn still has the complete set, eight glasses, decorated with colorful, overlapping oblong circles. She even has the original case they came in.

"Oh, I don't let the grandkids use these glasses," says Marilyn with a warm smile.

David Stukel's family wonders … Would David have gone to college? What would his life's vocation be? Who would he have married? How many children would he have? How many grandchildren?

"You wonder what he'd be like if he'd lived," Ray says.

"He was so kind-hearted that I think he would be doing something that would help people," Nancy says. "And I think he would still have a little bit of the devil in him."

"I used to go and watch David's baseball games because my parents always dragged my sister and me to all of his games," Debbie says. "Then when my boys played and I'd go to watch, I'd think about how David would really have enjoyed watching my boys play. And I'm sure he would have been watching his kids play, too."

David Stukel would have turned fifty in May 2004.

"You wonder what he'd look like," Marilyn says. "We don't talk a lot about his birthdays, but we acknowledge them."

On David's birthday each year, Ray and Marilyn visit his grave site at Mt. Olivet Cemetery.

"Last time we went, we put our flowers in, and there was a white artificial flower in the center," Marilyn says.

"Somebody puts an artificial flower there each year, and we don't know who it is," Rays says.

"Even Katie knows where David's gravestone is," Marilyn says. "The grandkids help us put flowers on his grave. Katie likes to go with us because we look at all the graves."

"I like to roll down the hill," Katie says with a giggle and a child's honesty.

After lunch, we enter the neatly arranged garage, and Ray puts his golf clubs away. I notice three bicycles from a long-gone era hanging from the ceiling. I am surprised to learn that the bikes are the ones Debbie, David, and Nancy rode as kids.

"Oh, yeah, Katie likes riding Nancy's old bike," Marilyn says.

The bike David rode the day before his murder is small and customized. Rust spots have formed on the butterfly handlebars and red fenders. The chain has more dust than grease. Well-worn tires display how much of an impression David made on the East High neighborhood.

"We didn't keep his bike for any special reason," Marilyn says. "We just kept all three bikes, but, boy, David loved that bike. In the summer, that's the first thing he'd do in the morning—jump on that bike and down the road he'd go, seeing who he could see. I didn't allow them on New Lenox Road because it wasn't wide enough for bikes and cars, but David would head over to Harlow Avenue, then cut through if he was going to Tommy Fenn's house."

No squinting is required to imagine David on a beautiful autumn day, sitting on the metallic-red banana seat of his red-white-and-blue Hawthorne, clutching the handlebars, with streamers flying from the grips and baseball cards clicking in the back-wheel spokes.

The bright, high-in-the-sky sun reflects off the STP sticker David had affixed to the back fender, which had been bent upward to accommodate wheelies.

David is gliding down Hill Street's gentle grade, past the old Fritz farm, and into the back entrance of East High. He's upright now, coasting, his right leg fully extended on the pedal as the breeze caresses his short, brown hair.

David Stukel is wearing his green-and-gold East High letterman's jacket and a smile from here to eternity.

He is—forever—fourteen.

978-0-595-43995-9
0-595-43995-0

Made in the USA
Lexington, KY
02 March 2014